Francis Jeffrey

Francis Jeffrey
Photograph courtesy of the National Galleries of Scotland.

Francis Jeffrey

Philip Flynn

NEWARK:
UNIVERSITY OF DELAWARE PRESS
LONDON: ASSOCIATED UNIVERSITY PRESSES

© 1978 by Associated University Presses, Inc.

Associated University Presses, Inc.
Canbury, New Jersey 08512

Associated University Presses
Magdalen House
136-148 Tooley Street
London SE1 2TT, England

Library of Congress Cataloging in Publication Data

Flynn, Philip.
   Francis Jeffrey.

   Bibliography: p.
   Includes index.
   1. Jeffrey, Francis Jeffrey, Lord, 1773-1850.
2. Critics — Scotland — Biography.   3. Judges — Scotland
— Biography.
PR4825.J2Z67   820'.9'007 [B]   76-27915
ISBN 0-87413-123-5

Printed in the United States of America

To Dotty,
Joslyn, Keating, and Philip

Contents

Preface   9

Acknowledgments   13

1 A Philosophical Education   17

2 Epistemology   47

3 The Moral Sentiments and Social Progress   69

4 Politics — The War   95

5 Politics — Reform   109

6 Aesthetics and Literary History   135

7 Poetry and Prose Fiction   151

Conclusion   177

Notes   181

Works Cited   204

Index   211

Preface

In the first three decades of the nineteenth century, Francis Jeffrey played a leading role in British letters. He was the editor and guiding spirit of the *Edinburgh Review*, the most powerful review of the age. "No man is better qualified for this situation," Hazlitt thought, "nor indeed so much so. He is certainly a person in advance of the age, and yet perfectly fitted both from knowledge and habits of mind to put a curb upon its rash and headlong spirit." Throughout his term as editor and critic, Jeffrey led a double life. He was a lawyer by profession, and he resigned from the *Review* to become Dean of the Scottish Faculty of Advocates. In later life he served in the House of Commons and became a Scottish law lord, Lord Jeffrey, on the bench of the Scottish Court of Session. When Jeffrey's reviews were republished in 1843, Macaulay claimed to know the best of them by heart. Reading them again, he was struck by the fertility and range of Jeffrey's mind. "And this is only as a writer. But he is not only a writer; he has been a great advocate, and is a great judge. Take him all in all, I think him more nearly an universal genius than any man of our time."

Periodical reviews are perishable stuff, and Jeffrey's talents as an advocate and judge were soon forgotten. "He was neither a pathetic writer nor a profound writer," Bagehot believed, "but he was a quick-eyed, bustling, black-haired, sagacious, agreeable man of the world. He had his day, and was entitled to his day; but a gentle oblivion must now cover his already subsiding reputation." Jeffrey's name survived as a curio of letters — the man who had written that Wordsworth's *Excursion* would never do. Leslie Stephen was amused: "Every critic has a sacred and inalienable right to blunder at times; but Jeffrey's blundering is amazingly systematic and comprehensive." Saintsbury was sympathetic but confused: "For

9

Jeffrey, in the most puzzling way, lies between the ancients and the moderns in matter of criticism, and we never quite know where to have him."

Saintsbury's instinct was sound. Jeffrey did belong to two worlds, the worlds divided by the French Revolution. His education was an eighteenth-century Scottish education, and he was schooled in a healthy, native critical tradition. Skeptical in temper, empirical in method, the young Scotsmen who began the *Edinburgh Review* were following the lead of Adam Smith and David Hume. But their essays are crowded with the men and ideas of Britain in the early nineteenth century. Jeffrey himself wrote or revised over two hundred essays for the *Edinburgh Review* — on politics, epistemology, sociology, ethics, and aesthetics. He was the man whom Bagehot described, a shrewd hand with a jury, a congenial veteran of clubs and dinner parties. He was also a perceptive and philosophic critic, a man whose work deserves a fresh appraisal.

There are problems of balance and of background that face any writer who attempts that appraisal. Jeffrey wrote at a time when political science, moral psychology, aesthetics, and epistemology had not yet fallen under specialists' control. He would have been surprised to learn that his later reputation would rest solely on our study of his writings on imaginative literature. Among readers in the early nineteenth century, Jeffrey's analyses of Dugald Stewart's argument for epistemology and of Cobbett's case for parliamentary reform were no less exercises in criticism than were his reviews of Wordsworth's poems. The circles in which Jeffrey moved defined *critic* in a comprehensive sense, and any study that pretends to do him justice must represent the range of his inquiry. Moreover, the circles in which Jeffrey moved were Scottish circles — the professional classes of Edinburgh, Glasgow, and Aberdeen — men who had inherited a common fund of philosophic prose. In ways both obvious and subtle, Jeffrey's thought was shaped by the literature of eighteenth-century Scotland. His essays on politics and epistemology were lessons learned from Hume and John Millar. His writings on aesthetics and on moral psychology take for granted our acquaintance with Hutcheson, Kames, and Adam Smith. The man was, in part, his milieu. A study of the critic must be, in part, a study of his critical inheritance.

Jeffrey did not give much thought to the question of his later reputation. If men could control such things, he might have chosen that gentle oblivion which Bagehot prescribed. But Jeffrey is still quoted and still damned by writers who know him only slightly. This book is an attempt to know him better — to find in his eclectic reviews a coherent criticism of life.

Acknowledgments

I am grateful to the Trustees of the National Library of Scotland for permission to quote from the Jeffrey correspondence, and to the staff of the Library of Political and Economic Science of the London School of Economics for their assistance with the Horner correspondence. A research grant and grant-in-aid from the University of Delaware have helped me in preparing this study. The Editors of *English Miscellany* and *Enlightenment Essays* have permitted the inclusion of material originally written for those periodicals.

Finally, I wish to thank John Clive, Byron Guyer, and other critics and historians who have studied Jeffrey's thought. In one way or another, I am indebted to them all.

Francis Jeffrey

A Philosophical Education

"Much may be made of a Scotchman, if he be
caught *young."*
  — Samuel Johnson, Boswell's Life *(1791)*

Among the books published at Edinburgh in 1768 was the
first volume of the *Encyclopaedia Britannica*. The subtitle
read, "A Dictionary of Arts & Sciences Compiled upon a
New Plan, in which the different Sciences & Arts are Digested
into Distinct Treatises or Systems. By a Society of Gentlemen
in Scotland." The new *Encyclopaedia* was a natural expression
of the spirit of the Scottish Enlightenment — that secular and
improving spirit which propelled an economically backward
and theologically obsessed people into the front rank of
European intellectual life. In part, Scotland shared that spirit
with England and the Continent. The rising empirical science
and corresponding reaction against religious enthusiasm that
liberalized eighteenth-century English and Continental
thought had a tempering effect upon Scottish minds. Scotland's cultural ties with France were strong, and men like
Hume and Adam Smith maintained personal as well as
intellectual contact with the encyclopaedists and philosophes.
But Scotland had been prepared to make a peculiar, native
contribution to the eighteenth-century Enlightenment by
those very religious struggles which, in earlier centuries, had
narrowed and embittered Scottish thought.

Out of the stormy exegetics of the Presbyterian Kirk,

out of the reforming scheme of local education proposed in
Knox's *First Book of Discipline* (1560), there had developed,
among all ranks of lowland Scotch society, a talent for
analysis and a tradition of democratic, practically oriented
education. By mid-eighteenth century, with religious
enthusiasm abated and the turmoil of Jacobite insurrection
behind them, the lowland Scots had turned their exegetical
talents to inductive study of the arts and sciences. Knox's
plan for an educational system that was open to all classes
and oriented toward the practical needs of the community
had been realized in the lowland grammar schools and
universities, although the realization sometimes assumed a
more secular shape than Knox would have allowed. The
Universities of Edinburgh and Glasgow were strong where
Oxford and Cambridge were weak — in medicine, in law, and
in their willingness to accept experimental science into the
curriculum or to apply inductive methods to traditional
disciplines. At the English universities education remained
a leisurely and largely upper-class affair, devoted to the
study of mathematics and classical language. North of the
Tweed the Scottish universities drew students of Presbyterian
seriousness and different economic status, and their "inde-
fatigable industry" seemed to one English visitor to "even
border on romance."[1] Sharing lodgings with students from
the Continent — or with English, Welsh, and Irish Noncon-
formists who had been barred from their own universities
for religious reasons — young Scots followed an undergraduate
curriculum that was both liberal in content and designed
to develop analytical, inductive minds for trade and the
professions. Meanwhile, within the university towns, the
worlds of pulpit, commerce, medical dispensary, lecture
room, and legal bar met through a network of private clubs
to discuss travel literature or the origin of language or the
circulation of blood.

These circumstances combined to provide Scotland with
a vigorous philosophical life. At its center, socially and
intellectually, stood David Hume. Hume was famous as a
moralist, as a historian, and as *le bon David*, the amiable
catalyst of discussion in clubs and societies throughout the

urban lowlands. Hume's attitude toward revealed religion was anathema to theological conservatives, and their influence denied him a university chair. But his epistemology raised even enlightened eyebrows, provoking in Aberdeen and Königsberg a reconsideration of what had been the premises of empirical epistemology since the time of Locke. By carrying Locke's epistemological premises to what he believed to be their logical conclusions, Hume undermined his contemporaries' basic assumptions concerning mind and matter. In reaction, Thomas Reid developed the epistemology of "Common Sense," an attempt to establish the validity of certain intuitive beliefs that are common to all men of ordinary intelligence and development. On an epistemological level, the story of Scottish philosophy in the latter eighteenth century can be read as the debate between Hume and Reid. It was a debate that touched, at one point or another, most of the Scottish philosophers of the age.

For the majority of those philosophers, however, that debate was of limited interest. Their curiosity concerning social institutions and moral conduct was too practical, their suspicion of metaphysical subtlety was too ingrained, to allow them to be intimidated by the specter of epistemological skepticism. Except for Hume, the leaders of the Scottish Enlightenment were practicing lawyers, clergymen, or university professors, and many of them held the chair of Moral Philosophy at Edinburgh, Glasgow, or Aberdeen. The range of Moral Philosophy was wide — including ethics, jurisprudence, political theory, history, and aesthetics — and the lectures of Francis Hutcheson, Adam Smith, Reid, Adam Ferguson, and Dugald Stewart were interdisciplined. Hutcheson, Professor of Moral Philosophy at Glasgow, lectured on ethics, jurisprudence, natural theology, and political economy. Smith, who held that chair after Hutcheson, established his reputation by lectures on rhetoric and belles lettres and by *The Theory of Moral Sentiments* (1759), before publishing the *Wealth of Nations* (1776). On Smith's retirement, Reid became Professor of Moral Philosophy at Glasgow, having previously lectured on logic and mathematics at King's College, Aberdeen. At Edinburgh, Ferguson lectured on Natural Philosophy, or physics, as well as on Moral Philosophy, and his *Essay on the History of Civil Society* (1767) was a pioneering work in comparative sociology. Ferguson was succeeded by Dugald Stewart, the last of that eighteenth-century academic line, whose interdisciplinary interests and moral eloquence sparked curiosity and "breathed the love of virtue into whole generations of pupils."[2] Within and without the universities, Hugh Blair, Lord Kames, Lord Monboddo, William Robertson, and John Millar thought and wrote with the same wide interests. There was a Baconian thirst for human knowledge in these men. They considered their studies to be part of a broad, communal study of the nature of man and society.

It was possible to maintain that communal spirit because the circles in which these men moved were tolerant and close-knit. The population of Edinburgh was 31,000 at mid-century, that of Glasgow and Aberdeen even less, and the professional classes of each of these cities were bound together by a network of clubs and societies.[3] Smith, Blair, and Hume served on the Committee for Belles Lettres and Criticism of the Select Society of Edinburgh, of which Monboddo, Robertson, and Kames were members. At Kames's suggestion, Smith delivered his lectures on rhetoric and belles lettres to the Philosophical Society of Edinburgh, to an audience that included Kames, Blair, and Hume. Those lectures led to Smith's appointment as Professor of Logic at Glasgow, where he initiated the Literary Society of Glasgow, an organization in which James Watt, the engineer-inventor, Joseph Black, the physician-chemist, Smith, Millar, and Reid discussed matters aesthetic, scientific, and historical. While still Professor of Logic at King's College, Reid had been a member of the Philosophical Society of Aberdeen, known locally among "the vulgar and uninitiated" as the "Wise Club,"[4] where George Campbell, Alexander Gerard, and James Beattie wrestled with the disturbing implications of Hume's epistemology. On Hugh Blair's advice, Reid sent the early sections of his *Inquiry into the Human Mind on the Principles of Common Sense* (1764) to Hume, that Hume's theoretical position might be fairly stated. Hume enjoyed the work despite its attack upon his own principles, and he sent back suggestions and encouragement. Campbell sent Hume the manuscript of his *Dissertation on Miracles* (1762), an answer to Hume's "Of Miracles" (1748), and he received a friendly reply.[5] "A little philosophical society here," Reid wrote Hume, ". . . is much indebted to you for its entertainment. Your company would, although we are all good Christians, be more acceptable than that of St. Athanasius; and since we cannot have you upon the bench, you are brought oftener than any other man to the bar, accused and defended with great zeal, but without bitterness. If you write no more in morals, politics, or metaphysics, I am afraid we shall be at a loss for subjects."[6]

The theoretical interests of these clubs and societies were usually subordinate or directly related to the practical improvement of Scottish life. The distinguishing character of the Scottish Enlightenment as an intellectual movement was its practical and democratic thrust, an insistence that theory be validated by the empirical realities of common experience. "For though, in matters of deep speculation, the multitude must be guided by philosophers," Reid warned, "yet, in things that are within the reach of every man's understanding, and upon which the whole conduct of human life turns, the philosopher must follow the multitude, or make himself perfectly ridiculous."[7] The Preface to the Philosophical Society's *Essays and Observations* noted that the physical and social sciences "are more promoted by the observation of facts, than by the most ingenious reasonings and disputations." The Preface then expressed the hope that "our collections will be a species of magazine, in which facts and observations, the sole means of true induction, will be deposited for the purposes of philosophy."[8] In the physical sciences, these societies collected "facts and observations" that had an immediate bearing on the local economy. Kames, who Monboddo feared could write "a great deal faster than I am able to read," presented "Observations upon . . . Shallow Ploughing" and essays "On the Laws of Motion" and "Of Evaporation" to the Philosophical Society. The editors of *Essays and Observations* accepted an essay on "The

Method of Securing Houses from the Effects of Lightning"
from a colonial, Benjamin Franklin. The Edinburgh Society
for Encouraging Arts, Sciences, Manufactures, and Agriculture
offered awards for "the best piece of printed linen or cotton
cloth," for "the best printed and most correct book," for
"good worsted stockings," and for "the best tun of Whiskey,"
the last competition to be judged in a manner which the
Society, in its wisdom, deemed fit. The debates in that
Society on "the best method of getting highways made and
repaired" led to an immediate improvement of Scottish roads.
And at Glasgow, where local merchants met in the Political
Economy Club to discuss commercial problems, Adam Smith
gathered data for the *Wealth of Nations*.[9]

Through this combination of private friendship and
professional association, there had developed an intellectual
community that the resolutely cosmopolitan Hume could describe as the "most distinguished for Literature in Europe."[10]
By *Literature* Hume meant critical and expository prose,
because it was in these forms, rather than in poetry or the
novel, that Enlightened Scotland found its voice: the Histories,
Essays, and Inquiries of Robertson, Ferguson, Kames, Smith,
and Hume; Henry Mackenzie's *Mirror* (1779-80) and *Lounger*
(1785-87), Edinburgh imitations of the *Spectator* and *Tatler*;
the first and short-lived *Edinburgh Review* (1755-56); the
"Distinct Treatises" of the *Encyclopaedia Britannica*. Their
concentration upon prose was a consequence of their ambition
to develop an inductive "science of man."[11] The stylistic
virtues that they honored most were clarity, propriety,
and the "classical" elegance of Addison and Swift. It was
probably a conscious striving after clarity, or "perspicuity,"
that made life at the literary societies so rewarding. The
members of those societies, drawn from various trades and
professions, expected papers on the principles of evaporation
or epistemology to be, first of all, intelligible. *The Wealth
of Nations*, Kames's *Elements of Criticism* (1762), and
Ferguson's *Essay on the History of Civil Society* are enviably
readable today because they had their geneses in papers read
before audiences of practical and diverse interests.

The concern with propriety and elegance, however, was a

function of Scotland's lingering sense of cultural disadvantage. The 1707 Act of Union had brought home to educated Scots the necessity of speaking and writing in a style acceptable to "South Britain." They had attacked the problem in a characteristic fashion, forming The Rankenian and other clubs to Anglicize the Scottish tongue — a dialect which, Smollett lamented later in the century, "certainly gives a clownish air even to sentiments of the greatest dignity and decorum."[12] From its beginnings this eighteenth-century study of proper English took a belle-lettristic cast. The "new method" developed for teaching English in Scottish schools involved readings from the *Spectator, Guardian,* and *Tatler,* and the study of grammar based upon those models.[13] Literary societies not only heard with interest the preliminary drafts of Gerard's *Essay on Taste* (1759) and Campbell's *Philosophy of Rhetoric* (1776); the members criticized all papers on grounds of style as well as content. William Smellie, the principal editor of the *Encyclopaedia Britannica,* believed that the members of the Newtonian Society of Edinburgh had prepared him for his task as much by their criticisms of his writing style as by their broad intellectual interests.[14] When, in the summer of 1761, Thomas Sheridan delivered lectures on "Eloquence and the English Tongue" at St. Paul's Chapel, Edinburgh, the *Scots Magazine* reported that the lectures were attended "by more than 300 gentlemen, the most eminent in this country for their rank and abilities."[15] A contemporary recalled that Sheridan's audiences "were charmed with his instructive criticisms, and still more with the select readings from the English classics which followed every lecture."[16]

This enthusiasm of the educated class for rhetoric and belles lettres was paralleled by the gradual displacement of Latin by English as the language of the Scottish lecture room. John Stevenson, the influential Professor of Logic at Edinburgh and a veteran of the Rankenian Club, illustrated the principles of logic for several generations of students by readings in Dryden, Addison, and Pope. Stevenson's synthesis of logic, rhetoric, and belles lettres shaped Kames's *Elements of Criticism,* Blair's *Lectures on Rhetoric and Belles Lettres*

(1783), the lectures on rhetoric and belles lettres that Adam Smith delivered to the Philosophical Society of Edinburgh, and the Glasgow College Lectures of Jeffrey's mentor, George Jardine. The Scottish Enlightenment found its characteristic voice in critical and expository prose because those forms gave expression to a cultural preoccupation of the age — a desire to pursue the inductive science of man in an English style conspicuous for elegance, propriety, and clarity. Without those stylistic graces, warned the Belles Lettres Society of Edinburgh, "the Abstruse Philosopher or Systematic Devine [sic] will in vain endeavor to communicate their Knowledge. Besides great Penetration, Elegance and Propriety are now requisite."[17]

Francis Jeffrey was born in Edinburgh in 1773.[18] A few months before his birth the great North Bridge had been completed over drained North Loch. The medieval wynds and closes and the dizzy tenements of the Old Town that Hume had known were now connected with the still abuilding classical proportions of a New Town, "the Athens of the North." By the time that Jeffrey came of age in the last decade of the century, the important work of Hume's generation was done. But their habit of inductive and interdisciplinary study, their gregarious and practical activity, and their concentration upon prose style lived on in modern Athens. As the century closed, Edinburgh's reputation and influence were at their peak. The center of ecclesiastical and legal life in Scotland, the city could boast of a printing trade second only to London's and of a University second to none. Edinburgh had always been more open than other Scottish cities to English and Continental influence, and the arrival of émigrés from revolutionary France quickened thought and dinner parties throughout the Old and New towns. When war closed the Continent to English travelers, the beau monde substituted a visit to Edinburgh for the Grand Tour. "Over all this," Lord Cockburn reminisced, "there was diffused the influence of a greater number of persons attached to literature and science, some as their calling, and some for pleasure, than could be found, in proportion to the population, in any other city in the Empire. . . . Thus learning was improved by society, and society by learning."[19] The Reverend Sydney Smith, soon to suggest the idea of a second *Edinburgh Review*, arrived in 1798 as tutor to Michael Hicks Beach. He was impressed: "I like this place extremely & cannot help thinking that for a literary man, by which term I mean a man who is fond of Letters, it is the most eligible situation in the Island. It unites good Libraries liberally manag'd, learned men without any other System than that of pursuing truth — very good general Society — large healthy virgins with mild pleasing countenances & white swelling breasts — shores wash'd by the Sea — the romantic grandeur of antient & the beautiful regularity of modern buildings — and boundless floods of Oxygen."[20]

Jeffrey's family had a respectable status in the social order of the Old Town. His father was a Clerk in the Court of Session, and members of both sides of the family had been bred to the church or the law. His formal education began at the age of eight, when he was sent to the High School of Edinburgh. Designed for students who were destined for the universities, the high schools provided an intensive study of Latin grammar and a superficial study of the rudiments of Greek. For most of the eighteenth century the Edinburgh High School was the most distinguished of its kind, drawing sons from the gentry outside Edinburgh and from commercial and professional families within.[21] When Jeffrey came as a student, the school was enjoying its brightest days, under the long, enlightened rectorship of Dr. Alexander Adam. Adam was an educational reformer in the Scottish mold, an established scholar in geography and history, the author of textbooks used throughout Scotland and abroad. Formally and informally, he enriched his High School's intellectual life through his own wide interests. Jeffrey was not yet a voracious reader, but he found in the school library subjects that would shape his thinking — travel literature, Hume's *History of England* (1754-62), and Conyers Middleton's *Life of Cicero* (1741).

Apparently, education at the High School had limitations.[22] The classrooms were large, and classroom drill was often tedious. But Adam took a personal and consistent hand in enlarging the minds of his best students. He did not toil alone, in a cultural vacuum. The traffic of Edinburgh streets was itself an excitement to young men of literary and philosophic interests. On any day an idler in the Lawnmarket might see Mackenzie and Robertson or Dugald Stewart pass by in conversation. Throughout his life Jeffrey remembered a wintry day when, still a student at the High School, he stood staring at a handsome man who had passed him in the High Street. "Aye, laddie! Ye may weel look at that man!" said someone in the doorway behind him. "That's Robert Burns."[23]

Henry Brougham, Walter Scott, and Henry Cockburn were all students under Adam, and they went on to the city's University. But Jeffrey was destined for other scenes. His father was a man of fierce Tory principles, "a desperate . . . aristocrat" in politics,[24] and the pied piper of Edinburgh University, Dugald Stewart, was famous for his liberal views. Probably to avoid that attraction, the younger Jeffrey was sent to Glasgow University and Oxford. He matriculated at Glasgow in 1787, at the age of fourteen, coming promptly beneath the spell of Glasgow's Professor of Logic and Rhetoric, George Jardine.[25] Jardine's name is relatively unknown today. He published only one book, late in life, the *Outlines of Philosophical Education* (1818), a description of the curriculum that he followed during forty years of undergraduate teaching. But his "First Class of Philosophy" was Scottish education at its best — rigorous, liberalizing, designed to develop independent analysis and an awareness of the critical methods relevant to different areas of thought and composition. Jardine's influence on his students was profound. "I heard him talked of in a particular style of commendation," John Lockhart wrote, "one day in a large company of the Edinburgh literati, among whom it appeared there was a great number of his former disciples. . . . They represented him as a person who, by the singular felicity of his *tact* in watching and encouraging the developments of youthful minds, had done more good to a whole host of individuals, and gifted individuals too, than their utmost gratitude could ever adequately repay."[26]

Jardine conducted his "First Class of Philosophy" on lines first established at Edinburgh University by Stevenson and then at Glasgow by Adam Smith. Smith had been appointed the Professor of Logic and Rhetoric in 1751 on short notice. Without time or inclination to prepare a traditional logic curriculum in Latin, he delivered the lectures on rhetoric and belles lettres that he had recently read before the Philosophical Society of Edinburgh. Jardine continued the practice of lecturing in English, combining Smith's study of rhetoric and belles lettres with elements of the traditional curriculum in logic. His intention, as he explained it in the *Outlines*, was "the formation of those intellectual habits of thinking, judging, reasoning, and communication, upon which the farther prosecution of Science, and the business of active life, almost entirely depend."[27] With that end in view, he led his students through "the elements of the science of mind, with an analysis of the different intellectual powers, in the order of their connexion and dependence – the theory of language, as illustrative of human thought, – the principles of taste and criticism, – and the means of improving the powers of communication by speech and writing, as exhibited in the best models of ancient and modern composition."[28] This was not the empty rhetoric of modern liberal arts curricula. Jardine's classes on "the science of mind" included readings from and classroom analyses of Aristotle, Aquinas, Bacon, Locke, Hume, and Reid, with a special emphasis on Bacon's pivotal position in British philosophy. Students were asked to study the developing vocabularies of younger brothers and sisters and the powers of college servants to express abstractions, to better understand "the theory of language, as illustrative of human thought." On "the principles of taste" Jardine was admirably open-minded, recognizing that the active eighteenth-century debate on that subject proved "too clearly that the Philosophy of Taste has not yet attained to Perfection."[29] He was more concerned that his students should know the basic documents of that

debate, so his class of fourteen- and fifteen-year-olds read
Horace, Quintilian, Boileau, Addison, Burke, Hutcheson,
and Hume.

What kept tender minds to the hard tasks at hand were
Jardine's charm as a teacher and the almost daily requirement
of written themes, the requirement that gained his course a
reputation as "the intellectual grindstone of the college." [30]
For Jeffrey, who would spend his adult life analyzing legal
briefs and writing critical essays for the Edinburgh Review,
the "First Class of Philosophy" was the most liberal and
practical of educations. Early in the term students were
required to give a written account of the distinguishing
analytical methods of Bacon, Locke, Reid, or Hume.
Following the model of their own or Jardine's choice, they
then analyzed the arguments of a Ciceronian oration or
Spectator paper. In their critical essays on imaginative
literature they were taught to consider "the Object, or
Purpose, of the Author — the Quality of the Materials which
he brings forward to accomplish his End — and the Skill
which he displays in their Arrangement; together with the
Propriety, and Eloquence, of the Language in which they
are Embodied." [31] As the term progressed Jardine assigned
original essays on subjects like "the Benevolent Affections,"
"the Immortality of the Soul," and "the law of Primo-
geniture," [32] and he chose ten or twelve of his best students,
whom he dubbed "Examinators," to criticize the essays of
the rest of the class. The essays, with criticisms, were then
read aloud. Jeffrey was among the chosen. On one occasion
he was assigned an essay written by Robert Haldane, later
Principal of the College of St. Mary's, St. Andrews. "My
exercise fell into the hands of Jeffrey," Haldane recalled,
"and sorely do I repent that I did not preserve the essay,
with his remarks upon it. For though they were unmercifully
severe, they gave early promise of that critical acumen which
was afterward fully developed in the pages of the Edinburgh
Review. In returning my essay to me, the good professor,
willing to save my feelings, read some of the remarks at the
beginning of the criticism, but the remainder he read in a
suppressed tone of voice, muttering something as if he

thought it too severe." What Jeffrey may have lacked in discretion, he made up in hard work and talent. As Haldane graciously admitted, he was "the ablest student of the class."[33]

Jeffrey's intellectual debt to Jardine was more general than specific. Epistemologically, Jardine admired the Common Sense philosophy of his friend and university colleague Thomas Reid. His theories of human nature were teleological and influenced by Christian eschatology. Jeffrey's thinking took a different turn. But Jardine's course did shape Jeffrey's habits of mind and work. It introduced him in systematic fashion to the Western traditions of moral, epistemological, and aesthetic inquiry, drilled him in analysis, taught him the right questions to ask when studying the methodology of a physical scientist, political economist, or aesthetician. It encouraged him "to take pleasure in the activity of his own mind"[34] and to discipline his intellectual life by the regular exercise of analytical essays. Jardine's classroom was a school for critics. Years later, when Jeffrey became Rector of Glasgow College, he singled out Jardine in his inaugural address: ". . . the individual of whom I must be allowed to say *here*, what I have never omitted to say in every other place, that it is to him, and his most judicious instructions, that I owe my taste for letters, and any . . . literary distinction I may since have been enabled to attain."[35]

Jeffrey remained at Glasgow for two years, attending classes in Moral Philosophy and Greek. Perhaps upon his father's orders, almost certainly against his own inclinations, he did not enroll in the class of Glasgow's celebrated Professor of Civil Law, John Millar. But Jeffrey's later writings show the influence of Millar's *Observations Concerning the Distinction of Ranks in Society* (1771) and *Historical View of the English Government* (1787), an influence apparently first felt while still at Glasgow or shortly after.[36] It would have been difficult to avoid that influence, because Millar's reputation and personality pervaded the town and University.[37] It was to hear his lectures that the English Whig aristocracy matriculated at Glasgow, and his influence on the Continent gave the University an eminence in legal studies equal to that of

Edinburgh's in medicine. Millar had extended the scope of the course in Civil Law to include a broad sociological study of human laws, customs, and institutions. Using histories and travel literature, he concerned himself and his students with questions on the relationship of nomadic, agrarian, and commercial economies to the ethics and social structures of different communities. He lectured on the significance of property to "the Distinction of Ranks" and on the complex political and psychological factors that lead to the establishment and continuance of institutional authority. Millar's approach to these subjects was liberal, Whig, and, within limits, iconoclastic. Like Hume, whose friendship and writings he valued, he recognized the essential social value of institutional tradition and rule under law. But he believed that institutions must not be obstructed by tradition or "superstition" in their natural evolution to fit the changing character of society. He taught his students to judge laws, customs, and institutions on the basis of "utility" — their potential for encouraging the full development of those individual and collective talents found at different stages in a community's evolution. His political allegiance to the Whigs was of a piece with this philosophy. In his *Historical View of the English Government*, a book that developed what is now known as "the Whig interpretation of history," he described the reign of the Stuarts as a return to absolutism, an attempt to shroud the business of government in ignorance and superstition. He saw the Glorious Revolution as a critical moment in English political history, and he believed the Whigs to be the party of rational politics, utility, and progress.[38]

It is difficult to determine how or when Jeffrey first encountered Millar's thought, but the course in Civil Law did draw many of the English and Scottish Whigs who would form Jeffrey's circle in later years. During the 1780s and 90s Millar's listeners included Thomas Campbell, the poet; William Lamb, the second Viscount Melbourne; Thomas Muir, whose trial for sedition left a permanent impression on Jeffrey's mind; and James Moncreiff and George Cranstoun, both to become prominent Whig lawyers and allies of the *Edinburgh Review*. Millar's impact on his students was the greater because he did not confine himself to the high road of political and sociological theory. Through his lectures and through the evening entertainments that he held for his students, Millar was an active reformer. He campaigned for abolition of the slave trade, for prison reform, for constitutional control of government expenditure, and for improved education of the British lower classes. Those causes the *Edinburgh Review* would shortly adopt as its own. In the mid-nineteenth century an Edinburgh Reviewer, assessing the utilitarian and iconoclastic influence of Millar's thought, allowed "that the bold lines of thought on which the 'Edinburgh Review' was afterwards constructed, were first laid down by his masterly hand."[39] For Alexander "Jupiter" Carlyle, no friend to Millar or bold reviewers, the "democratic principles and that sceptical philosophy which young noblemen and gentlemen of legislative rank carried into the world with them from his law-class" were cause for lamentation.[40] When Jeffrey's Whig sympathies became apparent shortly after he left Glasgow, his father realized that his plans might gang agley and blamed himself for having allowed "the mere vicinity of Millar's influence" to corrupt his son.[41]

Jeffrey left Glasgow in May 1789, and for the next two years he lived at home in Edinburgh. He attended courses in Scotch and Civil Law at the University, but most of his energy was channeled into a self-imposed regimen of reading and essay writing. Jardine had warned his students that "Vigour of Intellect, an Active Imagination, and a Correct Judgment can be acquired in no other way than by a constant and regular exertion of them,"[42] and Jeffrey took his former teacher at his word. Undistracted by companions and bored by the law, he read his way through Locke, Dryden, Pope, Johnson, James Beattie, Voltaire, Fénelon, Racine, Rousseau, Buffon, and Montesquieu. He followed independently the procedure of the "First Class of Philosophy," writing critical appraisals of the authors he had read, original essays on a wide range of topics, and then "unmercifully severe" criticisms of his own compositions. Although his models were Addison, Steele, Johnson, and Mackenzie, "the principal persons who have exhibited their abilities in periodical and short essays,"[43] he did not yet think of his exercises as vocational. He wrote criticisms, essays, and self-criticisms because he was concerned with the development of his own judgment:

> The human mind, at least mine, which is all I have to do with, is such a chaotic confused business, such a jumble and hurry of ideas, that it is absolutely impossible to follow the train and extent of our ideas upon any one topic, without more exertion than the conception of them required. To remedy this, and to fix the bounds of our knowledge and belief on any subject, there is no way but to write down, deliberately and patiently, the notions which first naturally present themselves on that point; or if we refuse any, taking care it be such as have assumed a place in our minds merely from the influence of education or prejudice, and not those which the hand of reason has planted, and which has [sic]been nurtured by the habit of reflection. [44]

Among the subjects on which Jeffrey wrote in the two years after leaving Glasgow were several that would concern him in the pages of the *Edinburgh Review* — "The Use of Philosophy," "On a State of Nature," "On Slavery," "On Human Happiness," "On Ancient and Modern Learning." He spelled these efforts with attempts at poetry and exhortative prose, composing mock speeches to read before the House of Commons against the slave trade and for the constitutional control of government expenditure, two of Millar's favorite causes. At some point in this period he took up the *De Rerum Natura* with delight. Reading it, he wrote "An Epitome of Lucretius" and a criticism of his own "Epitome":

> Having heard the philosophy of Lucretius much under-valued, and partly ridiculed, by personages whose condem-nation I have been accustomed to regard as an infallible token of merit in the object of it, I resolved as usual to employ my own judgment, either to reverse or confirm their award. A bare perusal I at first thought would be sufficient for this purpose; but so uniformly was I trans-ported and carried away by the charms of the poetry, and the inimitable strength of the expressions, that I generally

forgot the subject on which they were displayed — and in the enthusiasm of admiration, lost that cool impartiality which alone can produce a correct judgment. It was necessary, then, to divest the philosophy — the reason — of this poem of that blaze of light, which, by dazzling the senses, prevented them from judging truly. . . . My judgment, I hope, for some years, will not at least be decaying — and while that is not the case, I should wish it always to form its daily opinion from a daily exertion. The authority of our own opinion, though perhaps the least dangerous of any, still participates in those inconveniences which all species of authority create, and while a man's powers are unimpaired, it were a lucky thing if he could every day forget the sentiments of the former, that they might receive the correction or confirmation of a second judgment.[45]

This was strong stuff, too good to last. In September of 1791 Jeffrey was sent to Queen's College, Oxford, and the soul within the Scotsman almost died.

"It is painful to have to say that Jeffrey hated Oxford," wrote Saintsbury, "because there are few instances on record in which such hatred does not show the hater to have been a very bad man indeed."[46] But Saintsbury, an Edinburgh man himself, found extenuating circumstances in Jeffrey's case. To begin with, Jeffrey was desperately lonely. Their mother's early death and father's gloomy disposition had drawn the four Jeffrey children very close together, and letters sent home from Oxford show that Jeffrey missed his family sorely. The separation might not have weighed so heavily if his course work and companions had been more attractive. But the curriculum of Queen's seemed dull when compared with memories of Jardine's Glasgow, and the English undergraduates were sunk in fashionable ennui:

But these blank parties! oh! the quintessence of insipidity. The conversation dying from lip to lip — every countenance lengthening and obscuring in the shade of mutual lassitude — the stifled yawn contending with the affected smile upon every cheek, and the languor and stupidity of the party gathering and thickening every instant by the mutual

contagion of embarrassment and disgust. For when you
enter into a set of this kind, you are robbed of your
electricity in an instant, and by a very rapid process are
cooled down to the state of the surrounding bodies. In
the name of heaven, what do such beings conceive to be
the order and use of society? To them it is no source of
enjoyment; and there cannot be a more complete abuse of
time, wine, and fruit.[47]

He did not give over essay-writing completely. His Oxford
papers include a dialogue on beauty and an essay on "The
Philosophy of Happiness," both of which show the influence
of the associationist psychology that informs his later work.
But loneliness and melancholy nourished "a visionary and
romantic temper of mind," and the poetic fit was upon him.
While it lasted it warred uncomfortably with "that cool
impartiality which alone can produce a correct judgment."
"I feel I shall never be a great man unless it be as a poet," he
wrote his sister. "Notwithstanding all this, my poetry does
not improve; I think it is growing worse every week. If I
could find it in my heart to abandon it, I believe I should be
the better for it."[48] Jeffrey never succumbed to Oxford's
bell-rung charms and eventually convinced his father to give
up the experiment. He escaped Queen's with relief after ten
months.
    In the decade that followed, until the inauguration of
the *Edinburgh Review*, Jeffrey's prospects were uncertain.
He returned half-heartedly to the law, resumed studies
at Edinburgh University, and was called to the Scottish
bar in 1794. But law still held no innate interest for him,
and he watched himself sliding into genteel poverty. His
physical appearance was striking — slender, quite small
of stature, with thick, wiry black hair, and eyes that could
be lively or soulful. But his manner and conversation did
not always please on first encounter. "I do not promise
that you will, on meeting, find him greatly calculated to
please in conversation," wrote the Edinburgh bluestocking,
Mrs. Anne Grant of Laggan, to a young lady who desired his
acquaintance. "The fertility of his mind, the rapidity of his
expression, and the fire of his countenance, altogether give

an air of ungraceful impetuosity to his conversation. . . . He is lavish of thought, and gives a guinea where a sixpence might do as well; but then he has no change, and pays all in gold."[49]

Throughout this period he considered other occupations: literary hackwork in London, civil service in India, or a chair in Oriental Studies at some university, the last two projected with the enthusiasm of a travel-book addict. He felt a particular attraction toward medicine, and followed a course of lectures on chemistry with the short-lived intention of taking a medical degree. With time on his hands he attended Dugald Stewart's lectures on political economy, wrote abstracts of the *Wealth of Nations* and *Novum Organum*, studied Spanish so that he might read Cervantes and Lope de Vega, and churned out translations from the Greek "with a fine poetical fury."[50] He was also reading "democratical books" with "great zeal and satisfaction,"[51] developing a pragmatic, liberal temper that distrusted both doctrinaire egalitarians and autocratic Tories. But the frantic, conservative reaction that gripped official minds in Scotland made dissent a most dangerous game. "Pray, Bob, are you a democrat? or what?" he wrote to Robert Morehead, a Scottish friend at Balliol. "You need not be afraid of my exposing you."[52] In 1793 he watched with disgust the sedition trial of Thomas Muir and other members of the Edinburgh Society of the Friends of the People, where "Hanging Judge" Braxfield proclaimed that "the British Constitution is the best that ever was since the creation of the world and it is not possible to make it better."[53] In the same year, the most repressive in recent Scottish history, he described to his brother in America "the destructive violence of both parties — a violence which, even in its triumph, can never be productive of peace; since opinion is endeared by contradiction — since force is insufficient to convince — and since affection is rivited to those principles in whose cause we have suffered."[54]

Politics, political economy, or Greek poetry, it was all grist for his private essay mill. By 1798 his models had changed, but his purpose was set. "I should like . . . to be the rival of Smith and Hume, and there are some moments, (after I have

been extravagantly praised, especially by those to whose
censure I am more familiar,) when I fancy it possible that I
shall one day arrive at such a distinction."[55] The praise or
censure that made a difference was that of the members of
the Speculative Society, whose ranks Jeffrey had joined early
in the decade. "The Spec" had been established in 1764
by students at Edinburgh University for "improvement in
Literary Composition and Public Speaking." With its own
meeting-hall and library on the College grounds, it had
evolved into the most famous of Edinburgh literary clubs.
When Jeffrey joined in 1792, shortly after his Oxford mis-
adventure, the older members included Dugald Stewart;
William Smellie, editor of the *Encyclopaedia Britannica*;
James Mackintosh, whose pro-revolution *Vindiciae Gallicae*
(1791) had just appeared; and Harry Erskine, leader of
the Scottish Whigs and Dean of the Faculty of Advocates.
On his first night in attendance Jeffrey was struck by an
essay on ancient ballads read by a young man whose head
was wrapped in a huge woolen nightcap. It was Walter
Scott, suffering from a toothache, and Jeffrey asked for an
introduction. The next evening he called on Scott at home
and found him in a small den on the sunk floor of his father's
house in George Square, surrounded by antiquarian books,
Scots and Roman coins, a Claymore and Lochaber axe, and a
print of Prince Charlie. Scott showed his amused visitor these
beginnings of the library-museum of Abbotsford, and the two
then retired to a tavern for supper and conversation.[56]

Although they remained friends, Scott and Jeffrey would
come to be the leading representatives of two different
Scottish casts of mind. At the Speculative, Jeffrey found
more sympathetic company in Brougham, Francis Horner,
John Allen, Charles Kinnaird, and Henry Petty-Fitzmaurice.
These were young lawyers, professors, or students at the
University, who still had their way to make in the world, and
who shared Jeffrey's liberal politics and taste for the utilitarian
analysis of traditional attitudes and institutions. Jeffrey read
five papers before the Society, each of which he adapted
from the essays, epitomes, and abstracts he had been writing
since Jardine's class at Glasgow: "On Nobility" — "a defence

of inequality of rank, and a discussion of the principles on which it ought to rest"; "On the Effects Derived to Europe from the Discovery of America"; "On the Authenticity of Ossian's Poems"; "On Metrical Harmony"; "On the Character of Commercial Nations."[57] Whatever subject was proposed for debate, Jeffrey appeared to have something already down on paper in his desk. Brougham, not naturally inclined to toot other men's horns, remembered that Jeffrey "bore a most distinguished part" at the Speculative, "and its members never can forget the brilliant display so often made in that seminary, of his singular readiness in debate, the subtlety of his reasoning, and the extraordinary liveliness of his fancy."[58] To avoid the political violence of the times, the members passed a resolution shortly after Muir's trial "that the Society at the present juncture should be cautious in admitting as subjects of discussion or debate, the political topics of the day."[59] The rule was more honored in the breach, and a showdown of sorts occurred in 1799 when older Tory members resigned in protest against the liberal attitudes of Jeffrey and his set. Cockburn first noticed Jeffrey in this crisis. Looking back, he cited the Society as an important influence in the development of Jeffrey's mind. "It is easy to suppose what sort of an evening it was to Jeffrey when he had to struggle in debate with Lansdowne [Petty-Fitzmaurice], Brougham, Kinnaird, and Horner, who, with other worthy competitors, were all in the Society at the same time. It has scarcely ever fallen to my lot to hear three better speeches than three I heard in that place, — one on National Character by Jeffrey, one on the Immortality of the Soul by Horner, and one on the Power of Russia by Brougham."[60]

But brilliant speeches at "the Spec" did not pay the bills. At the turn of the century, Jeffrey was still a struggling member of the Faculty of Advocates. He spent his days with other briefless lawyers in the outer precincts of Parliament House, the seat of Scottish law, a venerable and gloomy pile, essentially unchanged since the early sixteenth century, that shared with St. Giles' Cathedral a close off the High Street. Lockhart described the conversation of this group in the days that preceded and immediately followed the founding of the *Edinburgh Review*: "The best table-talk of Edinburgh was, and probably still is, in a very great measure made up of brilliant disquisition — such as might be transferred without alteration to a professor's note-book, or the pages of a critical Review — and of sharp word-catchings, ingenious thrusting and parrying of dialectics, and all the quips and quibblets of bar pleading."[61] It was in this company, "the chief community of loungers and talkers in Edinburgh,"[62] that Scott won the nickname of "Duns Scotus." In the grip of his romantic memory they became "a very happy mixture of good breeding and liberal information, with a disposition to lively rattle, pun, and jest" — "lively young men, in the heyday of youth and good spirits, playing the part which is common to the higher classes of the law at Edinburgh, and which nearly resembles that of the young Templars in the days of Steele and Addison."[63] In *Heart of Midlothian* (1818) Scott recalled the days when advocates of Jeffrey's generation lounged about the Outer House, their coats crammed with "old play bills, letters requesting a meeting of the faculty, rules of the Speculative Society, syllabus of lectures — all the miscellaneous contents of a young advocate's pocket, which contains everything but briefs and bank-notes."[64]

For lawyers of liberal persuasion, all this rattle, pun, and jest was gallows' humor. Advancement at the Scottish bar was traditionally slow, but the temporary Tory monopoly of Edinburgh legal life denied young Whig lawyers any hope of active practice. They congregated in proud banishment at the north end of the Outer House, nursing their wounds and waiting for the main chance. "One is quite buried here, among a great crowd of men of decent abilities and moderate expectation," wrote Jeffrey to his brother, "and it is almost necessary that some great man, or some great accident, should pull you out of it, before you can come into any kind of desirable notice."[65] For Jeffrey, the accident was Sydney Smith. Smith had not been long in Edinburgh when he joined the Academy of Physics, where Jeffrey, Horner, Brougham, and Thomas Brown were deep in "the investigation of nature, the laws by which her phenomena are regulated, and the history of opinions concerning these laws."[66] Smith quickly recognized the special talents of this group, and at some point in the winter of 1801-02 he suggested to Jeffrey and Horner over tea the idea of starting a critical review.[67] That suggestion led to meetings at Jeffrey's flat in Buccleuch Place, where Brougham, Brown, and other kindred spirits from the Speculative were sounded on the scheme. Apparently, Jeffrey was the least sanguine among them, but Smith and Brougham were not to be denied. Would not Smith act as editor? Was there not Brown for metaphysical subjects, Horner for political economy, Thomas Thomson for legal and antiquarian matters, Brougham for mathematics and colonial administration, and John Allen for medical subjects?[68] Was there not Jeffrey himself, *"facile princeps* in all kinds of literature," *"de omni scribili,"* who had already read everything and written critical essays upon it?[69] "All of this was irresistible," at least to Brougham.[70] Jeffrey still had doubts about their chances for success, but subjects were selected at a series of secret meetings, and Jeffrey assumed with Smith the burden of editorial chores. During one of these meetings, Cockburn records, a wild storm raged outside their windows, "and I have heard him [Jeffrey] say that they had some merriment at the greater storm they were about to raise."[71] There remained the problem of a motto for the new review. Smith suggested *Tenui musam meditamur avena* — "We cultivate literature upon a little oatmeal" — but that was rejected as "too near the truth to be admitted."[72] They chose instead a no-less-revealing motto from the Roman writer Publius (Publilius) Syrus — *Judex damnatur cum nocens absolvitur* — "The judge is condemned when the guilty is acquitted." An enterprising Edinburgh publisher, Archibald Constable, agreed to take them on. Throughout the spring and summer of 1802 the young judges sat in session.

The first number appeared in October 1802, with an Advertisement that stated that the editors, yet anonymous, would sometimes be guided in their choice of subjects "by the tendencies of public opinion." The opening article was Jeffrey's review of Jean Mounier's *De l'influence attribuée aux philosophes . . . sur la révolution de France* (1801), a subject on which British public opinion was sharply divided. Mounier, once the President of the French National Assembly, had written to absolve French philosophers of blame for the French Revolution.[73] That question was not an academic one in 1802, because conservative British opinion repeatedly cited the unhappy French experience as a warning against and condemnation of those British thinkers who had subjected government to public and utilitarian scrutiny. For Jeffrey's circle, the issue was essential. The intellectual tradition in which they had been schooled — the Enlightenment tradition of philosophical analysis and public education — was under indictment. If Montesquieu and Turgot were to be involved in the guilt of Robespierre and the Jacobins, then John Millar and Dugald Stewart were dangerous to public order. Jeffrey studied Mounier's case for the defense. To James Mackintosh, who had recently suffered through a painful reassessment of his early revolutionary enthusiasm, Jeffrey's opening review seemed "a chef d'oeuvre" of temperance and candor.[74] For later readers, it can stand as a paradigm of his best reviewing — the review as a judicial hearing.

He begins by stating Mounier's qualifications as a writer on the origins of the French Revolution, remarking that Mounier "was not only a witness, but an actor, in those scenes, of the origin of which he is treating." Then, early in the criticism, Jeffrey states the caveat that appears in his student essays and throughout his adult writings — the fallibility of individual opinion:

> With all these claims to our attention, M. Mounier cannot, however, expect that his authority should be taken for decisive upon so vast and complicated a question. In an affair of this nature, it is not enough to have had a good opportunity for observation. Where so many interests are concerned, and so many motives put in action, a man cannot always give an account of every thing he sees, or even of every thing he has contributed to do. His associates may have acted upon principles very different from his; and he may have been the dupe of his opponents, even while he was most zealous in his resistance. It will be remembered, too, that M. Mounier, after co-operating

in a revolution that was to consummate the felicity of his country, was obliged to leave it to the mercy of an unprincipled faction; and it may perhaps be conjectured, that he who was disappointed in the issue of these trans- actions, has also been mistaken as to their cause. M. Mounier, finally, is a man of letters, and is entitled to feel for philosophers some of the partialities of a brother. In denying that they had any share in the French Revolution, he vindicates them from a charge that sounds heavy in the ears of mankind; and he judges wisely, that it is safer to plead not guilty to the fact, than to the intention.

Through paraphrase Jeffrey describes the elements in French public life that Mounier had advanced as explanations of the outbreak of revolution: the stormy convocation of the Estates-General, the crisis in French finance, the vacillations of Ministers and Crown. He paraphrases without comment, and Mounier's arguments are given strong statement. It is only at their conclusion that he raises an objection:

This account is certainly entitled to the praise of great clearness and simplicity, and cannot be denied to have a foundation in truth; but it appears to us to be deficient in profundity and extent, and to leave the revolution, in a great measure, to be accounted for, after all these causes have been enumerated and recognized. . . . The circumstances enumerated by M. Mounier, seem to us to be only the occasions, and immediate symptoms of disorder, and not the efficient and ultimate causes. To produce the effects that we have witnessed, there must have been a revolutionary spirit fermenting in the minds of the people, which took advantage of those occurrences, and converted them into engines for its own diffusion and increase. M. Mounier, in short, has given us rather an history of the revolution, than an account of its causes; he has stated events as depending upon one another, which actually proceeded from one common principle; and thought he was explaining the origin of a disorder, when he was only investigating the circumstances that had determined its eruption to one particular member. . . . He has stated, as the first causes of the revolution, circumstances that really proved it to be begun; and has gone no farther back than to the earliest of its apparent effects.

Jeffrey then proceeds to reexamine Mounier's arguments, observing that "it is in many cases . . . a matter of great difficulty to distinguish between the predisposing and the occasional causes of a complicated political event, or to determine in how far those circumstances that have *facilitated* its production, were really indispensable to its existence." He points out that, of those elements in French public life which Mounier had cited to explain the events of 1789-90, all were, by Mounier's own admission, present in France a century before:

> But if events might have happened in 1690, without endangering the Monarchy, that were found sufficient to subvert it in 1790, it is natural to inquire, from what this difference has proceeded? All parties, it is believed, will agree in the answer — It proceeded from the change that had taken place in the condition and sentiments of the people; from the progress of commercial opulence; from the diffusion of information, and the prevalence of political discussion. Now, it seems difficult to deny, that the philosophers were instrumental in bringing about this change; that they had attracted the public attention to the abuses of government, and spread very widely among the people the sentiment of their grievances and their rights.

The writings of French philosophers, however, were not the only influence upon the sentiments and condition of the French people. "The constant example, and increasing intimacy with England — the contagion caught in America — and, above all, the advances that had been made in opulence and information, by those classes of the people to whom the exemptions and pretensions of the privileged orders were most obnoxious — all co-operated to produce a spirit of discontent and innovation, and to increase their dislike and impatience of the defects and abuses of their government." To charge French philosophers with primary guilt for the revolution was, therefore, even more unjust a judgment than that of those who, like Mounier, would deny their influence entirely:

> We are persuaded . . . that the writings of those popular philosophers who have contended for political freedom, had some share in bringing about the revolution in France; how great, or how inconsiderable a share, we are not qualified to determine, and hold it indeed impossible to ascertain. There are no *data* from which we can estimate the relative force of such an influence; nor does language afford us any terms that are fitted to express its proportions. We must be satisfied with holding that it existed, and that those who deny its operation altogether, are almost as much mistaken as those who make it account for everything.

On the fundamental issue, the relationship of free inquiry to social authority, Jeffrey makes a distinction to which "M. Mounier, throughout his book, has attended too little." Among the French philosophers of the eighteenth century there were men, like Montesquieu, who confined themselves to "sober reasoning and practical observations." There were also men, like Rousseau and Condorcet, who "intruded upon the public with every species of extravagance and absurdity":

> That there were defects and abuses, and some of these very gross too, in the old system of government in France, we presume will scarcely be denied; that it was lawful to wish for their removal, will probably be as readily admitted; and that the peaceful influence of philosophy, while confined to this object, was laudably and properly exerted, seems to follow as a necessary conclusion. . . . Every step that is taken towards the destruction of prejudice, is attended with the danger of an opposite excess: But it is no less clearly our duty to advance against prejudices; and they deserve the highest praise, who unite the greatest steadiness with the greatest precaution.[75]

A few months before the *Review* made its debut, Jeffrey

wrote pessimistically about its chances. "Perhaps we have omitted the tide that was in our favour. We are bound for a year to the booksellers, and shall drag through that, I suppose, for our own indemnification."[76] But Jeffrey was wrong, the tide was right, and their first number announced a new age in the history of British periodicals. The initial printing was an edition of 750 copies, and a second edition was called for in a month. By the close of 1803 some 2,150 copies of the first number had been sold in Edinburgh, and single copies often passed through many hands.[77] Printings of subsequent numbers were enlarged to meet the unexpected demand, and Thomas Longman, who knew a good thing when he saw it, acquired publication rights for the London trade. By 1809 there were 9,000 copies being printed quarterly. Walter Scott observed, with misgivings, that "no genteel family *can* pretend to be without it."[78]

The *Review* had an electrical effect upon educated readers, a success beyond its founders' wildest dreams, because it was something truly new under the British sun. The contributors to latter-eighteenth-century reviews had been mainly minions of the booksellers, who financed those reviews to tout the books they wished to sell. In the early 1800s the elders of the English and Scottish bars still looked with contempt upon advocates who sold their souls for Grub Street shillings, and real or would-be gentlemen condescended to reviewing only under direst financial necessity. But the *Edinburgh Review* was established on a different plan. Constable agreed not to dictate subjects or in any way interfere with the independence of reviewers. The books chosen for review were often only pretexts for long expository essays on the principles of political economy, epistemology, or aesthetics. The contributions were anonymous, and contributors were handsomely paid at a rate of £10 per sheet, a rate that Jeffrey accurately believed to be "without precedent."[79] Because every reviewer, regardless of his social or financial status, was required to accept payment, those who reviewed out of need could do so without loss of caste. When pressed to accept a permanent position as editor, Jeffrey still worried that a formal connection might hurt his chances for success at the bar. But he was now a family man, having made a love match in 1801 with a young woman of no fortune, and the annual salary of £300 that Constable and Longman were offering was "a monstrous bribe to a man in my situation."[80] Horner sympathized with Jeffrey's professional scruples, but he hoped that, "if the Review continues to maintain that character, with which it set out, for independence and candour, the [?] editor of it must hold a highly respectable position in literature; such as was formerly filled by LeClerc, and by Bayle."[81] Jeffrey accepted the position in 1803. "If we had searched all Europe," Brougham thought, "a better man, *in every respect*, could not have been found."[82] Under Jeffrey's diligent and tactful editorial hand, the review dreamed up over Edinburgh tea enlisted many of the best minds and pens in Britain: Hazlitt, Malthus, Wilberforce, Thomas Arnold, Leigh Hunt, Viscount Melbourne, James Mill, Henry Hallam, Moore, Campbell, Macaulay, and Carlyle.

In the mid-nineteenth century, the *Quarterly Review* described its old Edinburgh rival as "a child of the Speculative,"[83] a shrewd hit but incomplete as genealogy. Young Whigs from the Speculative did figure prominently in the founding of the *Edinburgh Review*, and subjects discussed at the Society's meetings reappeared in the essay-reviews of Jeffrey, Brougham, and Horner. But the Speculative itself was a descendant of the literary clubs of Smith, Kames, and Hume. The catholic interests and analytical skills of its members were the fruits of Jardine's, Millar's, and Dugald Stewart's instruction. Both the Speculative and the *Edinburgh Review* were, in fact, late children of the eighteenth-century European and Scottish Enlightenment. Jeffrey's ambition "to be the rival of Smith and Hume," Horner's hope that he might rival Bayle and Le Clerc, were statements of patrimony. In an atmosphere of Jacobin extremism and Tory reaction, Jeffrey and his friends kept alive that spirit of analytical philosophy which Adam Smith had prescribed as "the great antidote to the poison of enthusiasm and superstition."[84] From the time of his undergraduate concern with "judging truly," Jeffrey tried to cultivate the practicality and undogmatic skepticism that he had found in Cicero and Hume. The spirit of the *Edinburgh Review* was that which Peter Gay has defined as the spirit of Enlightenment philosophy — "the organized habit of criticism" — "its favorite instrument . . . analysis, its essential atmosphere freedom, its goal reality."[85]

But for a man like Jeffrey, who had studied his Hume, what was reality?

Epistemology

The wise in every age conclude
What Pyrrho taught and Hume renewed,
That dogmatists are fools.
> — A verse by Thomas Blacklock,
> quoted in David Hume's letter to
> John Clephane, 20 April 1756

I cannot see what there is to prevent me from accepting what seems to be probable, and rejecting what does not. Such an approach avoids the presumption of dogmatism, and keeps clear of irrationality, which is the negation of all accurate thinking.

> — *Cicero,* On Duties

"And as the science of man is the only solid foundation for the other sciences," Hume wrote in the Introduction to his *Treatise of Human Nature* (1739-40), "so the only solid foundation we can give to this science itself must be laid on experience and observation." Thus spake British empiricism. Hume followed the lead of Locke and Berkeley in applying the empirical method in his study of the workings of the human mind. As an epistemologist Hume was a rigorous empiricist, consistently refusing to speculate beyond the boundaries of experience and observation, believing that "to explain the ultimate causes of our mental actions is impossible." And the very rigor and consistency of his

empiricism led him to conclusions that would have disturbed
Locke and Berkeley, conclusions that questioned not only
the metaphysical assumptions of the physical sciences but
also the theoretical validity of inductive reasoning.[1]

The relationship of Hume's epistemology and psychology
to those of Locke and Berkeley is an interesting chapter
in philosophical history. Like many eighteenth-century
philosophers in France and Britain, Hume revered Locke as
the man who had rescued philosophy from the grip of
seventeenth-century Continental rationalism. He believed, as
did Locke, that knowledge begins with the immediate data of
sense experience, and he employed with some modifications
Locke's argument that the human mind does not know
external objects directly. The mind has direct knowledge
only of its own "perceptions." But Locke had been wary of
the skeptical implications of his epistemology, and it had
remained for Berkeley to develop those implications more
fully.[2] In doing so, Berkeley had rejected Locke's theory that
an unknowable, material "substance" is the ontological
substratum of qualities perceived, substituting in its place his
own theory of immaterial substance — a perceiving "mind"
or "spirit" or "soul." Hume followed Berkeley in the skeptical
direction, arguing that man has no proof that his perceptions
are caused by independently existing objects: "The mind
has never any thing present to it but the perceptions, and
cannot possibly reach any experience of their connexion with
objects. The supposition of such a connexion is, therefore,
without any foundation in reasoning."[3] He then turned
Berkeley's analysis of Locke's theory of material substance
upon Berkeley's own theory of immaterial substance, concluding that "the question concerning the substance of the
soul is absolutely unintelligible."[4]

On the related psychological question of personal identity,
Hume declared that introspection had revealed no idea of a
self independent of present or remembered perceptions:

> For my part, when I enter most intimately into what I
> call *myself*, I always stumble on some particular perception
> or other, of heat or cold, light or shade, love or hatred,

pain or pleasure. I never can catch *myself* at any time without a perception, and never can observe any thing but the perception. . . . If any one upon serious and unprejudic'd reflexion, thinks he has a different notion of *himself*, I must confess I can reason no longer with him. All I can allow him is, that he may be in the right as well as I, and that we are essentially different in this particular. He may, perhaps, perceive something simple and continu'd, which he calls *himself*; tho' I am certain there is no such principle in me.

That men have the notion of a simple and continuing substratum of identity could not be denied, but Hume attributed this notion to the associative activity of the memory and imagination, which not only produce the conviction of the continued existence of external bodies, but also create an illusion of continuing personal identity by combining remembrance of perception from the past with that of the present. In the spirit of cool tolerance that fascinated Boswell and infuriated Johnson, Hume reduced the *self* to "a bundle or collection of different perceptions." For those who wished to believe in the survival of personality after death, the inference was disturbing.[5]

Just as disturbing — to those contemporaries who read and understood it — was Hume's discussion of the idea of causation. That idea, he argued, is not derived from any common quality observed in the objects or forces we call causes, because we cannot discover any quality common to them all. The idea of causation must arise, therefore, from some observed relationship between what we call the cause and the effect, relationships of contiguity and succession. We repeatedly observe a relationship between fire and heat, and we come to expect their necessary connection in the future. But the idea of *necessary* connection cannot be justified by repeated connections of fire and heat in the past. We have no intuitive knowledge of the essences of fire and heat — given Hume's empiricist and phenomenalist attitude, we have no intuitive knowledge at all — and our past experiences of their connection justifies only the probability of their connection in the future. Our assumption "that the course of nature continues always uniformly the same" is based on neither logical certainty nor demonstration. What, then, is the source of men's idea of *necessary* connection, the basis of causal inference? Hume found the source of that idea in the same associative activity that gives us a notion of personal identity: "For after we have observ'd the resemblance [of contiguity and/or succession] in a sufficient number of instances, we immediately feel a determination of the mind to pass from one object to its usual attendant. . . . [The idea of] Necessity, then, is the effect of this observation, and is nothing but an internal impression of the mind, or a determination to carry our thoughts from one object to another." Hume thus reduced the idea of necessary connection and the causal inference, upon and through which so much inductive reasoning is based and proceeds, to a propensity of the mind to pass associatively from one phenomenon to another with which it has been related in the past. True to his empirical method, he refused to speculate teleologically on that common human propensity or "determination." He was aware that his analysis of the idea of causation threatened theological proofs from evidence of design, but he dropped the subject at what he believed to be the limits of "experience and observation," content to allow epistemologists or theologians or physical scientists to pick up the pieces as they might.[6]

Among contemporaries who had either not read or not understood him, Hume's reputed opinions were cause for ridicule or boggled wonder. The majority of educated Scots tempered their national genius for speculation with a healthy suspicion of metaphysical subtlety. In matters of practical importance, and the practical concerns of Scottish life were foremost in their speculations, they considered the experiential common sense of their milieu to be the surest guide. Hume's *Treatise,* by his own admission, "fell *dead-born from the press.*"[7] Despite his growing fame as a moralist and a historian, his epistemological writings made their way very slowly. In *The Philosopher's Opera,* a contemporary farce by the advocate John Maclaurin, Satan returns to

Edinburgh to inquire how his cause is faring. He is informed that Hume is his leading spokesman and listens to Hume's arguments on the ideas of causal relationship and personal identity. But Satan, like the rest of Hume's audience, is bewildered: "'Faith, I don't know well what to think of him. Are you sure he is true blue on our side? I confess, I have some suspicion, that he is a shrewd fellow, endeavouring to convert men to Christianity, by writing nonsense against it.'"[8]

In Aberdeen, however, the *Treatise* had awakened Thomas Reid from his dogmatic slumber. "Your system appears to me not only coherent in all its parts," he wrote to Hume, "but likewise justly deduced from principles commonly received among philosophers; principles which I never thought of calling in question until the conclusions you draw from them in the Treatise of Human Nature made me suspect them." The principle most to be questioned, Reid believed, was Locke's theory of knowledge, a theory that Berkeley and Hume had developed to consistent but absurd conclusions. "Bishop Berkeley, proceeding upon this foundation, demonstrated very easily that there is no material world. . . . But the Bishop, as became his order, was unwilling to give up the world of spirits. . . . Mr. Hume shows no such partiality in favour of the world of spirits. He adopts the theory of ideas in its full extent; and, in consequence, shows that there is neither matter nor mind in the universe; nothing but impressions and ideas." Those conclusions, Reid feared, were fast making "philosophy . . . contemptible to every man of common understanding."[9]

In his *Inquiry into the Human Mind on the Principles of Common Sense* and later *Essays*, Reid attempted to reconcile contemporary philosophy with contemporary common sense, arguing for the validity of certain "natural judgments" and "common principles" shared by all men of ordinary intelligence and development. According to Locke's theory, or according to Reid's interpretation of it, "the first operation of the mind about its ideas, is simple apprehension; that is, the bare conception of a thing without any belief about it; and . . . after we have got simple apprehensions, by comparing them together, we perceive agreements or disagreements between them; and . . . this perception of the agreement or disagreement of ideas, is all that we call belief, judgment, or knowledge." But Reid believed that the basic act of perception involves a natural judgment on or belief in the existence of the thing perceived: ". . . every operation of the senses, in its very nature, implies judgment or belief, as well as simple apprehension. . . . When I perceive a tree before me, my faculty of seeing gives me not only a notion or simple apprehension of the tree, but a belief of its existence, and of its figure, distance, and magnitude; and this judgment or belief is not got by comparing ideas, it is included in the very nature of the perception." Such beliefs or judgments are intuitive, "part of that furniture which Nature hath given to the human understanding," and no man, save those beguiled by skeptical philosophers, ever thought of questioning their validity.[10]

No less basic to human reasoning, Reid argued, are our intuitive beliefs that "those things did really happen which I distinctly remember," that "whatever begins to exist, must have a cause which produced it," and that "in the phenomena of nature, what is to be, will probably be like to what has been in similar circumstances."[11] Reid did not hesitate to offer a teleological explanation of these natural judgments: "They are the inspiration of the Almighty, no less than our notions or simple apprehensions. . . . They are a part of our constitution; and all the discoveries of our reason are grounded upon them. They make up what is called *the common sense of mankind*; and what is manifestly contrary to any of those first principles, is what we call *absurd*."[12] Reid was not proposing that all philosophical questions be decided by majority opinion. He believed that philosophy must "strike sail" to common experience and opinion only "in things that are within the reach of every man's understanding, and upon which the whole conduct of human life turns."[13] Nonetheless, Reid's appeal to "the common sense of mankind" in these basic matters was an expression of faith in the *consensus gentium,* a faith that Arthur Lovejoy has cited as one of the premises of Enlightenment philosophy, "widely accepted as too self-evident to need, as a whole, formal exposition or defense."[14] In reaction to Hume's analysis of that *consensus,* Reid and his disciples attemped such a formal exposition. But the Scottish philosophy of Common Sense only reinforced that reliance upon the common epistemological and ontological assumptions of mankind which already served as a practical philosophy for Maclaurin's Satan and for most Scottish men of letters.

And for Hume. His opponents often missed the point, but Hume was in his own way a champion of common sense. He did not deny that causal relations or the objects of our perceptions do exist. Nor did he deny that "the course of nature continues always uniformly the same." Hume asked only if empirical reason can validate our "natural beliefs" on these subjects. He concluded that reason can not, but such a conclusion does not of itself invalidate these natural beliefs. It shows only that, in many of its basic epistemological and ontological assumptions, mankind is guided not by reason but by psychological custom. Although he thought that teleological explanations of such assumptions could not be supported by "experience and observation," Hume recognized that these assumptions or natural beliefs are part of the basic common sense of mankind. And he believed, as strongly as did Reid, that all men, including skeptical philosophers, must act and make decisions in daily life on the basis of these assumptions. Considering the limited role that reason really plays in basic conduct and belief, this is how it must be. The skeptic in his study may entertain doubts concerning these assumptions. But happily, "since reason is incapable of dispelling these clouds, nature herself suffices to that purpose. . . . I dine, I play a game of back-gammon, I converse, and am merry with my friends; and when after three or four hours' amusement, I wou'd return to these speculations, they appear so cold and strain'd and ridiculous, that I cannot find in my heart to enter into them any farther. Here then I find myself absolutely and necessarily determin'd to live, and talk, and act like other people in the common affairs of life." That all men must live as if their natural beliefs are valid does not of itself refute skeptical objections. But Hume believed that "a true sceptic will be diffident of his philosophical doubts, as well as of his philosophical conviction." He thought that a "mitigated scepticism," a skepticism that admits both the limitations of the reason and the practical demands of human life, is useful as a check against dogmatism. But that "excessive scepticism" which sinks man "in a total lethargy" he dismissed on the practical and characteristically Scottish grounds that "no durable good can ever result from it." A wise man will live according to those natural beliefs which, although unverified by reason, are basic to human activity, beliefs which constitute the basic common sense of his kind. Speculation is, after all, only speculation. "Be a philosopher; but, amidst all your philosophy, be still a man."[15]

Common sense, then, was Scotland's *genius loci*. Like other divinities, however, it showed a different face to different devotees. To those men of letters who did not aspire to the formal hieratic functions of epistemological and ontological analysis, the common sense was the unexamined epistemological and ontological assumptions of mankind. To Thomas Reid, the common sense included mankind's intuitive beliefs concerning causation, personal identity, the accuracy of distinct memory, the existence of the objects of perception, and the uniform operations of physical nature — intuitions which, upon examination, proved to be "the inspiration of the Almighty." To David Hume, who declined to speculate on the methods of the Almighty, the common sense on these matters appeared to be vulnerable to the skeptic's objections. Such are the ambiguities of human reason. But human nature, he observed, is always stronger than skeptical objections. Once outside his study, he was as ready as was Reid or his cook or his coachman to proceed according to the practical dictates of common sense.

"The human mind, at least mine, . . . is such a chaotic confused business, such a jumble and hurry of ideas," Jeffrey lamented during student days. In his early essays he was attempting "to fix the bounds of our knowledge and belief," trying to clear his undergraduate mind of ideas that "have assumed a place . . . merely from the influence of education or prejudice," to make a place for "those which the hand of reason has planted." It was tough going, and in the process he realized how much "indolence, enthusiasm, or authority" confuses human reasoning.[16] He assumed the public role of critic during dogmatic times, when a host of prophets, reformers, and reactionaries elbowed one another for attention, hawking schemes for the reformation or conservation of European religion, politics, and poetry. To Horner he was "my dear Pyrrhonist,"[17] a man whose awareness of the fallibility of individual reason led him to oppose dogmatism wherever he encountered it — in the "revolutionary cant" of Jacobin philosophers, in the utilitarian panacea of Bentham, or in the aesthetic absolutes of Wordsworth's 1800 "Preface."[18] Jeffrey thought that the best corrective to dogmatism or willful eccentricity of thought was exposure to strong minds of different persuasions, a lesson he had learned through the "igenious thrusting and parrying of dialectics" at Parliament House and through discussions at the Speculative Society and Academy of Physics. "I think it has been your misfortune not to have mixed sufficiently with intelligent men of various opinions, and open and intrepid minds," he wrote to young Thomas Carlyle, who was brooding in oracular isolation at Craigenputtock. "Learn to respect and esteem men who are your equals in intellect and honesty, tho' they dissent entirely from your creed in taste and philosophy, and temper your bigotry as far as to think it *possible* that people may differ from you in all your fundamentals, without being in a *damnable* error."[19]

Few modern critics would be bold enough to commit themselves publicly on the variety of subjects that Jeffrey discussed. He was bold enough, partly because he had read widely at a time when learning was only beginning to become specialized, partly because his formal and informal education had prepared him to criticize the methodology of writers on a broad range of topics. On the basic epistemological issues, his opinions had been shaped through his analysis of the epistemological activity of the eighteenth century, and his position was in some ways close to Hume's. Like Hume, Jeffrey was concerned with the empirically verifiable content of metaphysical language: "This is a sure test of sheer nonsense, and moreover an infinite resource for the explication of obscure truth, if there by any such thing."[20] He was suspicious of anything that smacked of "mysticism," be it the Quaker doctrine of Inner Light or the "misty metaphysics" of Goethe's *Wilhelm Meister's Apprenticeship*.[21] He found British materialists equally obscure. Analyzing David Hartley's and Joseph Priestley's writings, he decided that Hartley's physiological interpretation of the workings of the mind belonged to the realm of what Dugald Stewart called "metaphysical romances" — those theories "which it is difficult to confute, because it is impossible to comprehend them." "That sensation may follow motion in the brain, or may even be produced by it, is conceivable at least, and may be affirmed with perfect precision and consistency; but that the motion is itself sensation, and that the proper and complete definition of thought and feeling is, that they are certain vibrations in the brain, is a doctrine, we think, that can only be wondered at, and that must be comprehended before it be answered."[22]

Jeffrey believed that a sound epistemology is one that confines itself to the description and classification of the phenomena of common consciousness, "those primary functions of the mind, which are possessed in common by men of *all* vocations and *all* conditions." All men have experiential knowledge of the operations of those functions, and epistemologists can describe the laws by which they appear to be governed. But "we only know the existence of mind by the exercise of its functions," so the question of "the essence of the thinking principle" remains a matter "of mere conjecture and uncertainty," and the teleology of mental life is "a domain, into which our limited faculties do not . . . permit us to enter." He admitted that Hume's analysis of the idea of causation had revealed "some very gross inaccuracies in the opinions and reasonings which were formerly prevalent on that subject." Like Hume, he believed that the common sense concerning the existence of the objects of perception can not be validated through analytical reason. And, like Hume, he believed that skepticism on these questions is only closet play, that philosophers must carry on in accordance with the common sense. "With regard to perception, indeed, and some of the other primary functions of mind," he wrote in an early *Edinburgh Review*, " ... the profoundest reasonings lead us back to the creed and the ignorance of the vulgar." It is healthy to recognize our limitations in these epistemological matters, because that recognition discourages the dogmatist. But philosophy has real concerns short of these ultimate questions. "As this speculative scepticism neither renders us independent of the ordinary modes of investigation, nor assists us materially in the use of them, it is inexpedient to dwell long upon it in the course of our philosophical inquiries, and much more adviseable to proceed upon the supposition that the real condition of things is conformable to our natural apprehensions."[23]

In the *Edinburgh Review*, Jeffrey defined his own episte-mological position through a series of critical responses to the arguments of other authors. The epistemologists to whom he gave most attention were members of the school of Common Sense, whose thought he had encountered in Jardine's class at Glasgow and among the students of Dugald Stewart at the Speculative Society. Reviewing the *Academical Questions* (1805) of the scholar-diplomat William Drummond, he analyzed the debate between Reid and Berkeleian idealists on men's belief in the existence of the objects of perception. Jeffrey acknowledged that Reid had demonstrated the inadequacies of Locke's representational theory of ideas — "that hypothesis which represents the immediate objects of the mind in perception, as certain *images* or *pictures* of external objects." But exposing the inadequacies of that hypothesis was one thing; proving that the objects of our perception must exist was another. At the heart of the debate was Reid's theory of *perception*, "that affection of the mind which consists in an apprehension and belief in the existence of external objects." The idealists did not deny that the human mind has such an affection. They denied only that the existence of such an affection proves per se the existence of external objects. "Upon this subject," Jeffrey wrote, "we entertain an opinion which will not give satisfaction, we are afraid, to either of the contending parties. We think that the existence of external objects is not *necessarily* implied in the phenomena of perception; but we think that there is no complete proof of their nonexistence, and that philosophy, instead of being benefited, would be subjected to needless embarrassments by the assumption of the ideal theory."[24]

The existence of matter is not necessarily implied in the existence of that natural affection which Reid designated as *perception*, because it is always possible to account for that affection through the idealist's hypotheses: " . . . we might have been so framed as to receive all the impressions which we now ascribe to the agency of external objects, from the mechanism of our own minds, or the particular volition of the Deity. The phenomena of dreaming, and of some species of madness, seem to afford experimental proofs of the possibility we have now stated, and demonstrate, in our apprehension, that perception . . . does not necessarily imply the independent reality of its objects." Nor was it accurate for Reid to claim that we have the same evidence for the existence of external objects that we have for the existence of our own sensations. Our belief in the former derives from our consciousness of the latter: the evidence for the existence of external objects is of a derivative and secondary character. We cannot doubt the existence of our sensations, but we can doubt without logical contradiction that their source is a material world that exists independently of those sensations.[25]

On the other hand, if our perception-beliefs in the existence of a material world do not of themselves prove that such a world exists, it does not *necessarily* follow that a material world does not exist. In other words, it does not necessarily follow "that every thing is not, which may possibly be conceived not to be." Reid's arguments do not logically compel us to believe in an external world, but it is still possible to suppose "that such a thing as matter may exist, and that an omnipotent being might make us capable of discovering its qualities." And that supposition, unlike the reasonings of the skeptics who oppose it, gives pragmatic respect to the common sense of mankind. "The instinctive and insurmountable belief that we have of its [matter's] existence, certainly is not to be surrendered, merely because it is possible to suppose it erroneous, or difficult to comprehend how a material and an immaterial substance can act upon each other. The evidence of this universal and irresistible belief is not to be altogether disregarded; and, unless it can be shown that it leads to contradictions and absurdities, the utmost length that philosophy can warrantably go, is to conclude that it may be delusive; but that it may also be true."[26]

And what had philosophy to gain by accepting the idealist's "rigorous maxim, of giving no faith to any thing short of direct and immediate consciousness"? If, following this maxim, we refuse to believe in the existence of matter, we must by the same rule reject the evidence of memory. The logical conclusion is a solipsism that "reduces the whole universe to the mind of the individual reasoner, and leaves no existence in nature but one mind, with its complement of [immediate] sensations and ideas." It is true, Jeffrey admitted, "that we are *absolutely sure* of nothing but what we feel at the present moment; and that it is possible to distinguish between the evidence we have for the existence of the present impression, and the evidence of any other existence." The evidence of the first kind is undeniable. We may entertain doubts about the rest without logical contradiction.

But the distinction, we apprehend, is in itself of as little use in philosophy, as in ordinary life; and the absolute and positive denial of all existence, except that of our immediate sensation, altogether rash and unwarranted. The objects of our perception and of our recollection, certainly *may* exist, although we cannot demonstrate that they *must*; and when, in spite of all our abstractions, we find that we must come back, and not only reason with our fellow creatures as separate existences, but engage daily in speculations about the qualities and properties of matter, it must appear, at least, an unprofitable refinement which would lead us to dwell on the possibility of their nonexistence. There is no sceptic, probably, who would be bold enough to maintain, that this single doctrine of the nonexistence of any thing but our present impressions, would constitute a just system of logic and moral philosophy; and if, after flourishing with it as an unfruitful paradox at the outset, we are obliged to recur to the ordinary course of observation and conjecture as to the nature of our faculties, it may be doubted whether any real benefit has been derived from its promulgation, or whether the hypothesis can be received into any sober system of philosophy.[27]

Jeffrey was not kicking stones to refute Berkeley. He objected to Reid's use of "the old joke, of the sceptical philosophers running their noses against posts, tumbling into kennels, and being sent to a madhouse." A skeptic, he pointed out, may take steps to preserve life and limb without involving himself in logical contradiction: "The sceptic, . . . who has been taught by experience that certain perceptions are connected with unpleasant sensations, will avoid the occasions of them as carefully as those who look upon the objects of their perceptions as external realities. Notions and sensations he cannot deny to exist; and this limited faith will regulate his conduct exactly in the same manner as the more extensive creed of his antagonists." He believed, contra Reid, that mankind's "instinctive and insurmountable belief" in the existence of external objects is not conclusive proof that such objects exist, and he admitted the theoretical validity of distinctions between the evidence of immediate consciousness and the evidence of distinct memory. Perhaps if there had been no Hume, Jeffrey would have spent more time in demonstrating how the common sense is vulnerable to skeptical objections. But Hume had already done the thing, only to conclude that a total skepticism is practically impossible and speculatively sterile. Jeffrey agreed. A wise man will be content with uncertainty in the question of the existence or nonexistence of matter and in the question of the accuracy of distinct memory. A wise man will admit that the common sense on these matters in unverifiable, and then practically proceed "upon the supposition that the real condition of things is conformable to our natural apprehensions."[28]

Judged by those standards, James Beattie was not a wise man. Beattie's *Essay on the Nature and Immutability of Truth, in Opposition to Sophistry and Scepticism* (1770) was an angry response to the "Rise and Progress of modern Scepticism,"[29] which Beattie traced with rising rhetorical fury through Descartes, Malebranche, Locke, Berkeley, and Hume. Beattie was a friend and disciple of Reid, and the *Essay* took theoretical shape in the discussions of the Philosophical Society of Aberdeen. But the personal bitterness of Beattie's attacks upon Hume distressed even Hume's philosophical opponents, and the *Essay* was never so popular in Scottish circles as it was in London, where Beattie was "caressed, and invited, and treated, and liked, and flattered" by George III, Samuel Johnson, and assorted champions of orthodoxy.[30] Jeffrey recalled the history of the book's mixed reception when reviewing *An Account of the Life and Writings of James Beattie* (1806). He wondered, or pretended to wonder, why the *Essay* was written with such fanatic zeal: "Every one has not the capacity of writing philosophically; but every one may at least be temperate and candid; and Dr. Beattie's book is still more remarkable for being abusive and acrimonious, than for its defects in argument or originality. There are no subjects, however, in the wide field of human speculation, upon which vehemence appears more groundless and unaccountable, than the greater part of those which have served Dr. Beattie for topics of declamation or invective."[31]

Prominent among those subjects was the debate between "the sceptics" and the school of Common Sense on matter and memory. Jeffrey thought that both questions are without practical or moral consequence, looming large only in the philosopher's closet. The conduct of men is not affected by the opinions they may hold on the existence or nonexistence of matter. Even those skeptics who would deny the existence of a material world leave us our sensations and perceptions, and both skeptics and their opponents guide their conduct by these same sensations and perceptions. "The whole dispute is about the *cause* or *origin* of our perceptions; which the one party ascribes to the action of external bodies, and the other to the inward development of some mental energy. It is a question of pure curiosity; it never can be decided; and as its decision is perfectly indifferent and immaterial to any practical purpose, so, it might have been expected that the discussion should be conducted without virulence and abuse." In questioning the basis and validity of faith in distinct memory, the skeptics argue only that we do not have the same kind of evidence for the past existence of remembered sensation that we have for the existence of immediate sensation. "We think this undeniably true; and so we believe did Dr. Beattie. He thought it also very useless; and we agree with him; but he thought it very wicked, and very despicably silly; and there we cannot agree with him at all. It is a very pretty and ingenious puzzle, — affords a very useful mortification to human reason, — and leads us to that state of philosophical wonder and perplexity in which we feel our own helplessness, and in which we *ought* to feel the impropriety of all dogmatism or arrogance in reasoning upon such subjects."[32]

Jeffrey had Beattie at a disadvantage. The latter's tone was arrogant and dogmatic, but the sections in the *Essay* on these specific epistemological subjects were, as Jeffrey knew, part of Beattie's general attack upon "the speculative metaphysics of the moderns."[33] Those metaphysics included Hume's arguments on the ideas of causality and personal identity and on the moral sentiments, arguments that Beattie believed to have theological and moral implications for eighteenth-century Christians. His rhetoric was furious because he believed that contemporary skepticism of all kinds did have a practical effect upon men's conduct, serving "to harden and stupify the heart, bewilder the understanding, sour the temper, and habituate the mind to irresolution, captiousness, and falsehood."[34] So it might appear to a man like Beattie, who was committed to the "Immutability" of ethical, theological, and eschatological "Truth." But Jeffrey never lusted after "Truth" in those areas, and he was wary of the mentality of men who did. His own ethical theory, very close to

Hume's, was not threatened by the moral subjectivism that infuriated Beattie. He did not speculate publicly in theology or eschatology, partly because he believed that those subjects lie outside the legitimate empirical domain. Therefore, he could contemplate with cool detachment the rise and progress of skeptical attacks upon faith in memory and belief in matter. It was, after all, only a speculative game:

> all men have a practical and irresistible belief both in the existence of matter, and in the accuracy of memory; and . . . no sceptical writer ever meant or expected to destroy this practical belief in other persons. All that they aimed at, was to show their own ingenuity, and the narrow limits of the human understanding, − to point out a curious distinction between the evidence of immediate consciousness, and that of perception or memory, − and to show that there was a kind of logical or argumentative *possibility*, that the objects of the latter faculties might have no existence. . . . To this extent, we are clearly of opinion that the sceptics are right; and though the value of the discovery certainly is as small as possible, we are just as well satisfied that its consequences are perfectly harmless. Their reasonings are about as ingenious and as innocent as some of those which have been employed to establish certain strange paradoxes as to the nature of motion, or the infinite divisibility of matter. The argument is perfectly logical and unanswerable; and yet no man in his senses can admit the conclusion.[35]

Games are good things in their way. But had philosophy made significant advance through the debate between the school of Common Sense and its skeptical opponents? Were the majority of thinking men very much the wiser? Jeffrey thought not, and he doubted "that the condition of mankind is likely to derive any great benefit from the cultivation of this interesting but abstracted study." Although he believed that epistemology should be carried on empirically, carried on with strict reference to "those primary functions of the mind, which are possessed in common by men of *all* vocations and *all* conditions," his analysis of the epistemological activity of the eighteenth century had convinced him that empirical

the subject of proper experiment, where the substances are actually in our power, and the judgment and artifice of the inquirer can be effectually employed to arrange and combine them in such a way as to disclose their most hidden properties and relations. The other class of phenomena are those that occur in substances that are placed altogether beyond our reach, the order and succession of which we are generally unable to controul, and as to which we can do little more than collect and record the laws by which they appear to be governed. These substances are not the subject of *experiment*, but of *observation*; and the knowledge we may obtain, by carefully watching their variations, is of a kind that does not directly increase the power which we might otherwise have had over them. It seems evident, however, that it is principally in the former of these departments, or the strict *experimental philosophy*, that those splendid improvements have been made, which have erected so vast a trophy to the prospective genius of Bacon. . . . It will scarcely be denied, either, that it is almost exclusively to this department of experiment that Lord Bacon has directed the attention of his followers. His fundamental maxim is, that knowledge is power; and the great problem which he constantly aims at resolving is, in what manner the nature of any substance or quality may, by experiment, be so detected and ascertained as to enable us to manage it at our pleasure. The greater part of the *novum organum* accordingly is taken up with rules and examples for contriving and conducting experiments; and the chief advantage which he seems to have expected from the progress of these inquiries, appears to have centered in the enlargement of man's dominion over the material universe which he inhabits. To the mere observor, therefore, his laws of philosophising, except where they are prohibitory laws, have but little application; and to such an inquirer, the rewards of his philosophy scarcely appear to have been promised.[41]

Jeffrey thought that this distinction between experiment and observation was worth marking to clarify the role of epistemology in contemporary intellectual life. The epistemologist is "the mere observor." The processes of perception, memory, and imagination are the subjects of observation. "We feel, and perceive, and remember, without any purpose or contrivance of ours, and have evidently no power over the mechanism by which those functions are performed. We may observe and distinguish those operations of mind, indeed, with more or less attention or exactness; but we cannot subject them to experiment, or alter their nature by any process of investigation. . . . The province of philosophy in this department, therefore, is the province of observation only; and in this department the greater part of that code of laws which Bacon has provided for the regulation of experimental induction is plainly without authority." If this were true, then epistemologists had been misled in claiming for "their favourite studies" a role parallel to that of the physical sciences:

> In the proper experimental philosophy, every acquisition of knowledge is an increase of power; because the knowledge is necessarily derived from some intentional disposition of materials which we may always command in the same manner. In the philosophy of observation, it is merely a gratification of our curiosity. . . . No metaphysician expects by analysis to discover a new power, or to excite a new sensation in the mind, as a chemist discovers a new earth or a new metal; nor can he hope, by any process of synthesis, to exhibit a mental combination different from any that nature has produced in the minds of other persons. . . . In metaphysics, certainly, knowledge is not power; and instead of producing new phenomena to elucidate the old, by well-contrived and well-conducted experiments, the most diligent inquirer can do no more than register and arrange the appearances, which he can neither account for nor controul.[42]

Jeffrey sent an advanced copy of his review of the *Account* to Horner, who was then reading law in London. Horner objected to some of Jeffrey's remarks, fearing that they might give needless pain to Stewart, "who is sensitive to an extreme, & whom I love and venerate so much that I would save him from a moment's pain at a considerably greater expense to my own blunt nerves."[43] Jeffrey's reply was conciliatory but consistent: "I cannot help thinking that there is some value in my view of the limitation of metaphysical discoveries, and I will take any wager you please, that when we are both eighty, you will be very much of my opinion."[44] There was value in Jeffrey's view. In defining the methods of epistemology and the physical sciences, he identified a confusion that was frequent in Enlightment philosophy before Kant. In his conviction of "the limitation of metaphysical discoveries," as in his refusal to seriously consider speculation that does not affect "the conduct of men" or "the ordinary modes of investigation," he suggests the positivist and pragmatist lines on which empirical philosophy would evolve later in the century. There is also, in his definition of the proper function of the metaphysician, an anticipation of the twentieth-century philosophical concern with linguistic analysis: ". . . we cannot help thinking that the labours of the metaphysician, instead of being assimilated to those of the chemist or experimental philosopher, might, with less impropriety, be compared to those of the grammarian who arranges into technical order the words of a language which is spoken familiarly by all his readers."[45] There was sharp analysis but no extraordinary prescience at work here. Hume's phenomenalist attitude and strict attention to the empirical content of metaphysical language influenced the development of positivism, pragmatism, and linguistic analysis. It is not surprising that elements of those schools appear in Jeffrey's writings, considering the lessons he had learned from Hume.

Jeffrey's criticism of eighteenth- and early ninetheenth-century epistemology was the work of a modern scientific mind, in the sense that he refused to speculate publicly on final causes. It was also the work of a Scottish mind, in the sense that he combined a conviction of the radical limitations of human reason with that concern for practical workaday life which characterized the Scottish intellectual community. But man, or a philosophical Scotsman, does not live by epistemology alone. There were other questions to consider, among them the elements of human happiness.

[3]

The Moral Sentiments and Social Progress

Since the revival of learning, no controversy has been more keenly agitated, especially among British philosphers, than that about the principles of action in the human constitution.

They have determined, to the satisfaction of the learned, the forces by which the planets and comets traverse the boundless regions of space; but have not been able to determine, with any degree of unanimity, the forces which every man is conscious of in himself, and by which his conduct is directed.

— *Thomas Reid*, Essays on the Active
Powers of the Human Mind *(1788)*

"How little does happiness depend upon ourselves!" Jeffrey wrote while a prisoner at Oxford. "Moralists may preach as they please, but neither temperance, nor fortitude, nor justice, nor charity, nor conscious genius, nor fair prospects, have power to make anybody happy for two days together. For the little power they have they are indebted to their novelty. In short, all our enjoyment here seems to depend upon a certain energy and vigour of mind, which depend upon — we know not what."[1] At the time, his philosophical acumen was touched with a bad case of undergraduate gloom, but the question of human happiness, individual and social, had interested him since his days at Glasgow. And the "Moralists" whose formulas he questioned, at Oxford and after, included those Scottish moralists and sociologists of the eighteenth century who had aspired communally to establish a "science of man" that would parallel the achievement of Newton in physical science.

The Scots who played a prominent part in that attempt — Hutcheson, Ferguson, Hume, Kames, Smith, Reid, and Millar — were never unanimous in the conclusions they reached. They were unanimous in their agreement on the method through which the attempt should be made — the inductive method, based upon experience and observation, a method free of the a priori reasoning that had beguiled European philosophy at the time of Descartes. For their methodology they looked to Newton and Bacon, and they derived specific inspiration from the example of Locke's study of mind and morals. The title page of Hume's *Treatise* reads "A Treatise of Human Nature: Being An attempt to introduce the experimental Method of Reasoning into Moral Subjects." By "the experimental Method" Hume and his contemporaries meant observation, and their starting point was introspection. Every man is conscious of his own ideas, passions, and sentiments, and broad observation convinces us of the existence of those same ideas, passions, and sentiments in others. "We must therefore," wrote Hutcheson, "search accurately into the constitution of our nature, to see what sort of creatures we are."[2] In developing their ethical theories and standards of moral conduct, they politely declined the guidance of divine writ and appealed to experiential evidence — to what cumulative human experience had proved to be good. At the same time, most of them tried very hard to show that man's subjective moral feelings operate according to the designs of a benevolent Creator.

An inquiry that involved minds and personalities as disparate as those of Hume, Ferguson, and Reid was never in danger of dull uniformity. Apart from a common dedication to inductive method, the Scottish thinkers differed in varying degrees on many specific issues. There were, however, certain attitudes and assumptions that the majority of them shared.[3]

In their reaction against Cartesian rationalism, they came to regard the "passions," "sentiments," and "feelings" as the motivating forces in human conduct. "Since reason alone can never produce any action, or give rise to volition," argued Hume, "I infer, that the same faculty is as incapable of preventing volition, or of disputing the preference with any passion or emotion. . . . Nothing can oppose or retard the impulse of passion, but a contrary impulse."[4] And if, as human experience has shown, reason is sometimes a plaything of the passions, it is also evident that all men are not equally endowed to develop or appreciate a moral system based upon abstract reason. "Unhappy would it be for Mankind," Hutcheson remarked, "if a Sense of Virtue was of as narrow an Extent, as a Capacity for such Metaphysicks."[5] But all men are endowed with certain basic sentiments, feelings, and passions, and these impulses universally and effectively determine human conduct. The study of human nature must begin, therefore, with these nonrational aspects of personality, and an adequate moral standard or standard of normative conduct must be developed from an understanding of them.

The Scottish thinkers shared with their century the belief in a common human nature and in the predictability of human behavior. Amidst the variety of human conduct, they discerned basic emotions and attitudes that determine human conduct in all historical periods and geographical climes. "It is universally acknowledged," noted Hume, "that there is a great uniformity among the actions of all men, in all nations and ages, and that human nature remains the same in its principles and operations. The same motives always produce the same actions: The same events follow from the same causes. Ambition, avarice, self-love, vanity, friendship, generosity, public spirit; these passions, mixed in varying degrees, and distributed through society, have been, from the beginning of the world, and still are, the source of all the actions and enterprizes, which have ever been observed among mankind."[6] It seemed to follow, then, that a basic uniformity could be observed in studying the histories of different societies. "There is . . . in man," Millar wrote, "a disposition and capacity for improving his condition, by the exertion of which, he is carried on from one degree of advancement to another; and the similarity of his wants, as well as of the faculties by which those wants are supplied, has every where produced a remarkable uniformity in the several steps of his progression."[7] Millar and Ferguson were sensitive to the apparent disparity in human conduct, and they attempted to explain behavioral patterns in terms of the stages of economic development and degrees of social organization found among different culture groups. But in the records of antiquity or in the strange conduct reported in the travel literature of their day, they traced common human impulses — as those impulses were shaped in their expression by the peculiar cultures of Greece, North America, or the Sandwich Islands.

In truth, man could be studied satisfactorily only in terms of his social culture. The Scottish thinkers were convinced that man is by nature a social animal and that his very humanity is dependent to some extent upon social intercourse. "Send him to the desert alone," wrote Ferguson, "he is a plant torn from its roots: the form indeed may remain, but every faculty droops and withers."[8] "It is not more evident that birds were made for flying, and fishes for swimming," Reid argued, "than that man, endowed with a natural desire of power, of esteem, and of knowledge, is made, not for the savage and solitary state, but for living in society."[9] There is nothing artificial or contrived in our gregariousness and sympathy: men function naturally in company with other men, and their moral code is shaped in part by their cumulative experience as social animals. Thus these Scots opposed both the Hobbesian and Rousseauist conceptions of a "state of nature" and any general indictment of contemporary European society as an artificial arrangement. "If we are asked therefore, Where the state of nature is to be found?" Ferguson advised, "we may answer, It is here; and it matters not whether we are understood to speak in the island of Great Britain, at the Cape of Good Hope, or the Straits of Magellan. While this active being is in the train of employing his talents, and of operating on the subjects around him, all situations are equally natural. . . . If the palace be unnatural, the cottage is so no less; and the highest refinements of political and moral apprehension, are not more artificial in their kind, than the first operations of sentiment and reason." [10]

In their century's debate between the party of Shaftesbury and the party of Hobbes and Mandeville, the Scottish moralists followed Shaftesbury in affirming man's social nature and capacity for benevolence. Hutcheson, Hume, and Kames played variations on Shaftesbury's idea of man's "moral sense," while Smith traced moral sentiments to the operation of our sympathetic imaginations. [11] But all agreed that man is by nature a social animal and that the basis of moral conduct lies in that essential gregariousness. Man desires his own happiness and seeks naturally for harmonious relationships with others. The degree to which he is benevolent depends upon the scope of his social sympathies, and the scope of those sympathies depends in turn upon the stage of cultural progress achieved by the society into which he is born. In an enlightened society, a society of sufficient experiential moral wisdom, men realize that self-love and benevolence are not contradictory but complementary. In such a society — in eighteenth-century Edinburgh, for example — man's sympathy or moral sense or desire for harmony finds sanction and generous expression. With Hutcheson, Smith, Reid, and Kames, this argument took ultimately a teleological turn: the interaction of self- and social love is part of the design of a benevolent Creator. At this turn Hume parted company. He was as convinced as were his fellows that man is a social animal, and he recognized that power of sympathy by which we participate in the pain and pleasure of others. But the moral feelings were to Hume a naturalistic phenomenon governed by the psychological laws of association. As in epistemology, he declined teleological speculation — "We must stop somewhere in our examination of causes" [12] — and his moral philosophy was the most naturalistic of his group.

The majority of these writers judged the general movement of European history to be progressive. While they attempted

to appreciate the achievements of different societies in
different stages of cultural development, they tended to
consider the diffusion of property and wealth, and the
subsequent increase in civil liberty, as the ultimate indices
of social progress. They were often sophisticated in their
treatment of past and alien cultures, but they were also
aware of the advantages of life in eighteenth-century Britain.
The advancement of civil liberty and enlightened self-interest,
Smith argued, is connected with the opportunity for pursuit
of private gain. In the history of modern Europe the Scottish
moralists and sociologists traced the evolution of a small-scale
capitalist economy, the slow but irresistible advance of civil
liberty, and the gradual awakening of a broad and enlightened
social sympathy. Except for Hume, they believed it to be
part of a general progress ordained by a benevolent Creator.
And they called it good.[13]

Jeffrey's own ideas on the moral sentiments, like his ideas
in epistemology, were shaped by his study of the theories of
eighteenth-century Scottish philosophy. In epistemology he
entertained the most skeptical elements of that philosophy.
In moral psychology he accepted the most subjective. To
begin, he believed that men are motivated entirely by the
desire to enjoy pleasure and avoid pain: "There must be a
motive to excite volition, as certainly as an impulse to begin
motion; and a motive neither does nor can mean any thing but
an apprehension of good to be attained, or evil or uneasiness
to be avoided." "The only difference between the sensualist
and the ascetic is, that the former pursues an immediate, and
the other a remote happiness; or, that the one pursues an
intellectual, and the other a bodily gratification." The degree
of pleasure or pain involved in any attitude of mind or course
of conduct "is ascertained by feeling, and not determined
by reason or reflection." Our feelings of moral approbation
and disapproval are functions of these "instinctive and
involuntary" evaluations, and our ideas of good and evil

develop associatively through the repetition of pleasurable or painful experiences.[14]

In citing the feelings as the basic element in moral psychology, Jeffrey was following the lead of his Scottish predecessors. But he was closest to Hume, whose ethical theory, "when rightly understood," he considered to be "both salutary and true."[15] Hume's psychology was "true" in that Hume had acknowledged that a rigorous empiricism may lead to subjectivist confusion in moral psychology, just as it leads to subjectivist confusion in epistemology.[16] The diverse pleasures that men do feel are sometimes not those which philosophers believe they should feel. Human pleasures — and the feelings of approbation to which those pleasures give rise — cannot all be reduced to man's supposed apprehension of propriety or moral harmony or general utility, however reassuring such reductions may be to philosophers who wish to use empirical psychology to illustrate the workings of Divine Goodness. Jeffrey thought that man's psychological variety was a hard but salutary fact that could not be blinked. If men are motivated by desire for pleasure and aversion to pain, it is evident that the pleasures men feel are complex and varied. There is no universal agreement on the summum bonum, nor can we expect that even the most enlightened society will atain such agreement. "All questions of this kind turn upon a comparison of the opposite advantages and disadvantages of any particular course of conduct or habit of mind: But these are of very different magnitude and importance to different persons; and their decision, therefore, even if they all saw the whole consequences, or even the same set of consequences, must be irreconcilably diverse." Some men find pleasure in ease and obscurity; some seek danger and contention. Some find their greatest pleasure in intellectual activity, some in gratification of the senses. Walter Scott loved society, Wordsworth loved solitude, "and so on, through all the infinite variety of human tastes, temperaments, and habits." Granted, this infinite variety poses problems for philosophers. But the most pleasing philosophical hypotheses have to stand the test of human experience. "It has always appeared to us, indeed, that too much importance has been attached to *theories* of morals, and to speculations on the sources of approbation. Our feelings of approbation and disapprobation, and the moral distinctions which are raised upon them, are *facts* which no theory can alter, although it may fail to explain. While these facts remain, they must regulate the conduct, and affect the happiness of mankind, whether they are well or ill accounted for by the theories of philosophers."[17]

Jeffrey was not giving up ethics to Chaos and old Night. While he insisted on the essentially subjective nature of the moral sentiments, his practical instinct was too strong to allow him to settle for a thorough moral relativism. He developed a practical standard of ethics through a philosophical maneuver very similar to that by which he developed a practical episte- mological code. It may be that men's natural beliefs concerning the existence of external objects and the accuracy of distinct memory cannot be fully verified by empirical reason. But all men have these natural beliefs, and men must pragmatically be guided by them. "As this speculative scepticism neither renders us independent of the ordinary modes of investi- gation, nor assists us materially in the use of them," Jeffrey advised, a wise man will proceed "upon the supposition that the real condition of things is conformable to our natural apprehensions." So too, the degree of pleasure involved with any attitude or act will vary among different men, and there can be no universal agreement on what provides the greatest pleasure. But there are, Jeffrey argued, "common impressions of morality, the vulgar distinctions of right and wrong, virtue and vice." Those common impressions are a record of mankind's cumulative experience of pleasure and pain, its experiential moral widsom, and a wise man will judge his own attitude and conduct by the standard of that moral common sense. Jeffrey did not attempt a teleological explanation of the moral common sense, and his position here was consistent with his position in epistemology. He had ignored Reid's teleological explanation of men's natural beliefs in the existence of matter and in the accuracy of memory. Empirical epistemology is properly limited to an analysis of the primary functions of the mind and of the laws by which those functions appear to be governed. So too, in moral psychology he rejected as "presumptuous and inconclusive" teleological explanations of man's moral sentiments. We feel what we feel. Beyond the recognition of those feelings and of the laws by which they appear to be governed, empirical psychology can not take us. But prominent among the observable "facts" of man's psychological life are common impressions of morality, and those impressions are the surest guide that men possess.[18]

Because of his pragmatic approval of man's moral common sense, Jeffrey was cautious in his appraisal of contemporary attempts to reshape the moral consciousness of mankind. A case in point is his critique of Bentham's *Traités de législation* (1802).[19] Bentham had developed elaborate tables of pleasure-pain calculus to determine the quality of pleasure and pain that different actions produce. Personal moral sentiments, he argued, are variable and irrational, affording no fixed standard for individual conduct or social legislation. Jeffrey countered that Bentham's utilitarian calculus was open to the same objection because it equated the greatest happiness of the greatest number with the sensibility of the social reformer:

> How shall utility itself be recognized, but by a *feeling* similar to that which is stigmatized as capricious and unaccountable? How are pleasures and pains, and the degrees and relative magnitude of pleasures and pains to be distinguished, but by the feeling and experience of every individual? And what greater certainty can there be in the accuracy of such determinations, than in the results of other feelings no less general and distinguishable? If right and wrong be not precisely the same to every individual, neither are pleasure and pain; and if there be despotism and absurdity in imposing upon another, one's own impressions of wisdom and propriety, it cannot be just and reasonable to erect a standard of enjoyment, and a rule of conduct, upon the narrow basis of our own measure of sensibility. It is evident, therefore, that by assuming the principle of utility, we do not get rid of the risk of variable feeling.[20]

Jeffrey himself was utilitarian, in the broad eighteenth-century sense of that term. In the manner of Smith and Millar, he evaluated political institutions and social legislation according to their contribution to the common weal. While he recognized the diversity of moral sentiments, he agreed with Hume that there is a general human tendency to feel approbation for those actions and attitudes which better the lot of our fellow man.[21] Those feelings, through repeated experience, have produced many of "the common impressions of morality, the vulgar distinctions of right and wrong, virtue and vice." But Bentham would throw out the baby with the bath, rejecting the common impressions of morality along with eccentricities in moral sentiment. In the place of those common impressions, our experiential moral wisdom, he proposed to substitute a calculation of the "naked utility" of individual conduct and social legislation. "The moral feelings, of which Mr. Bentham would make so small account, are the feelings which observation teaches us to impute to all men; those in which, under every variety of circumstances, they are found pretty constantly to agree, and as to which their uniformity may be reasoned and reckoned upon with almost as much security as in the case of external perceptions." If utility means a preponderance of pleasure over pain, a wise utilitarian will study closely the cumulative human experience of those sensations, as that experience has been recorded in the common impressions of morality. "The established rules and impressions of morality . . . we consider as the grand recorded result of an infinite multitude of experiments upon human feeling under every variety of circumstances, and as affording by far the nearest approximation to a just standard of the good and the evil that human conduct is concerned with, which the nature of our faculties will allow."[22]

In short, the common impressions of morality are our best safeguard against the vagaries of existential feeling. "They are observations taken in the calm, by which we must be guided in the darkness and the terror of the tempest." By ignoring "that large average which is implied in the prevalence of moral impressions," in order to calculate the general utility in any given situation, a man can be led to commit the most

heinous acts in the name of mankind. The Jacobin extremities
of the French Revolution were evidence enough. Writing in
The Prelude of his own infatuation with the utilitarian
schemes of Godwin's *Enquiry Concerning Political Justice*
(1793), Wordsworth recalled the time when

> speculative schemes —
> That promised to abstract the hopes of Man
> Out of his feelings, to be fixed thenceforth
> For ever in a purer element —
> Found ready welcome. Tempting region *that*
> For Zeal to enter and refresh herself,
> Where passions had the privilege to work,
> And never hear the sound of their own names.
> (XI. 224-31)

Jeffrey believed that Bentham's pleasure-pain calculus was
only an elaborate mask of Bentham's own feelings, feelings
working under other names. And Bentham or Godwin or any
radical reformer might be expected to overlook or undervalue
important aspects of what constitutes the general utility:

> It is in aid of this oversight, of this omission, of this
> partiality, that we refer to the *general rules* of morality;
> rules, which have been suggested by a larger observation,
> and a longer experience, than any individual can dream of
> pretending to, and which have been accommodated by the
> joint action of our sympathies with delinquents and
> sufferers to the actual condition of human fortitude and
> infirmity. If they be founded on utility, it is on a utility
> that cannot always be discovered, and that can never be
> correctly estimated in deliberating upon a particular
> measure, or with a view to a specific course of conduct;
> it is on a utility that does not discover itself till it is
> accumulated, and only becomes apparent after a large
> collection of examples have [*sic*] been embodied in proof
> of it. Such summaries of utility, such records of uniform
> observation, we conceive to be the *general rules of morality*,
> by which, and by which alone, legislators or individuals
> can be safely directed in determining on the propriety of
> any course of conduct.[23]

But men ignore the common impressions of morality. Human nature is such that the majority of men will often, and the wisest men will sometimes, pursue an immediate and transient pleasure at the expense of what they themselves acknowledge to be a distant but more lasting good. So, while Jeffrey might pragmatically defend the general rules of morality, he could only laugh at confident predictions of the moral perfectibility of mankind. "Perfectibility" was an idea whose time had come with the French Revolution. It exercised a potent spell for Continental thinkers and British radicals in the last decade of the eighteenth century. But Jeffrey considered it a grand illusion, "founded on a radical ignorance of what it is that constitutes the real enjoyment of human nature, and upon the play of how many principles and opposite *stimuli* that happiness depends." Madame de Staël had argued the perfectibilitarian case in her *De la littérature considérée dans ses rapports avec les institutions sociales* (1800), basing her hope upon the general human advancement in intelligence and useful knowledge. Jeffrey admired de Staël's mind, but he noted "the extreme narrowness of the induction" through which she had developed her argument, an argument that failed to explain the stagnant condition of African and Chinese culture or the retrogressive movement of Egypt, India, and Persia. Within modern European culture, moreover, there was evidence of something in human nature that confounded Aquarian predictions:

Take the case, for example, of war, — by far the most prolific and extensive pest of the human race, whether we consider the sufferings it inflicts, or the happiness it prevents, — and see whether it is likely to be arrested by the progress of intelligence and civilization. . . . Men delight in war, in spite of the pains and miseries which it entails upon them and their fellows, because it exercises all the talents, and calls out all the energies of their nature — because it holds them out conspicuously as the objects of public sentiment and general sympathy — because it gratifies their pride of art, and gives them a lofty sentiment of their own power, worth, and courage, — but principally because it sets the game of existence upon a higher stake, and dispels, by its powerful interest, those feelings of *ennui* which steal upon every condition from which hazard and anxiety are excluded, and drive us into danger and suffering as a relief. While human nature continues to be distinguished by those attributes, we do not see any chance of war being superseded by the increase of wisdom and morality. We should be pretty well advanced in the career of perfectibility, if all the inhabitants of Europe were as intelligent, and upright, and considerate, as Sir John Moore, or Lord Nelson, or Lord Wellington, — but we should not have less war, we take it, with all its attendant miseries.[24]

Those feelings of ennui which drove some men to Napoleonic war drove other men to gaming houses, or to chasing foxes or servant girls. The remedy for the malaise is not in wealth. "The real and radical difficulty is to find some pursuit that will permanently interest." "It is a fact indeed rather perplexing and humiliating to the advocates of perfectibility, that as soon as a man is delivered from the necessity of subsisting himself, and providing for his family, he generally falls into a state of considerable unhappiness; and, if some fortunate anxiety, or necessity for exertion, does not come to his relief, is generally obliged to seek for a slight and precarious distraction in vicious and unsatisfactory pursuits." Men do not dissipate their lives for lack of moral instruction: " . . . moralists and divines have been occupied with little else for the best part of a century; and writers of all descriptions indeed, have charitably expended a good part of their own *ennui* in copious directions for the innocent and effectual reduction of that common enemy." The problem is human nature itself, man's "eagerness for strong emotion and engrossing occupation." A sadder but wiser humanity will continue to progress in experiential moral wisdom, and that wisdom is the soundest index of pleasure and pain that men possess. But so too will individual men continue to transgress that general wisdom in the process of growing sadder but wiser.[25]

Jeffrey himself lived by what he once called "a sort of epicurean fatalism."[26] He found his own greatest pleasure in friendship and family affection, in doing things for others. He was generous and often anonymous in financing bankrupt authors. Carlyle considered him to be "one of the most *loving* men alive; has a true kindness, not of blood and habit only, but of soul and spirit. He cannot *do* without being loved. He is in the highest degree social. . . . The great business of Man he — intellectually — considers as a worldling does: *To be happy*. I have heard him say: 'If Folly were the happiest, I would be a fool.' Yet his daily life belies this doctrine, and says: — 'Tho' Goodness were the most wretched, I would be good.'"[27] When Horner pressed him to write a book on ethics or aesthetics, Jeffrey begged off. The book would steal time that he might better spend with his family. It would stir up all the vanities of authorship, and civilization would survive without it.[28] As his legal career began to flourish, he appeared to his contemporaries to be an uncommonly busy man, spending days in court, evenings with his family, and the early hours of the morning with the *Edinburgh Review*. But he had an Epicurean sense of something ridiculous in his own and his Scottish friends' hectic careers. "Labour and exertion do infinitely less for our happiness and our virtue than you stern philosophers will allow yourselves to believe," he advised Horner, "and half the pains and suffering to which we are exposed arise from the mortification of this ridiculous self-importance which is implied in all your heroic toils. . . . I do think ambition a folly and a vice, except in a schoolboy."[29]

His fatalism began to appear in letters written in his early thirties, shortly after the death of his young wife in 1805. He was deeply shaken by the loss, and he buried himself in legal and editorial work with increasing doubts about the meaning of it all. In the summer of 1806, while he was visiting Horner in London, he came close to ending it all in a duel with Tom Moore. Moore had been incensed by Jeffrey's review of *Epistles, Odes, and Other Poems* (1806), poetry that Jeffrey had called "a public nuisance."[30] Jeffrey accepted Moore's challenge, and arrangements were made for a duel at Chalk Farm. But the fateful dawn found neither party very sanguine. "And then was it," Moore remembered, "that, for the first time, my excellent friend Jeffrey and I met face to face. . . . We, of course, had bowed to each other on meeting; but the first words I recollect to have passed between us was Jeffrey's saying, on our being left together, 'What a beautiful morning it is!' 'Yes,' I answered with a slight smile, 'a morning made for better purposes;' to which his only response was a sort of assenting sigh."[31] Luckily, their duel was interrupted at the last moment by the arrival of police. The duelists were carried off to Bow Street Station, where Jeffrey's pistol was found to be empty, and conversation turned to a literary topic while they awaited bail. "Jeffrey, I recollect, expatiated upon it with all his peculiar fluency and eloquence; and I can now most vividly recall him to my memory, as he lay upon his back on a form which stood beside the wall, pouring volubly forth his fluent but most oddly pronounced diction, and dressing the subject out in every variety of array that an ever rich and ready wardrobe of phraseology could supply."[32] There was some talk of crossing to the Continent to finish matters, but the social gifts of both men prevailed at a late breakfast, and apologies were made.[33] "I am glad to have gone through this scene," Jeffrey wrote to a Scottish friend, "both because it satisfied me that my nerves are good enough to enable me to act in conformity to my notions of propriety without any suffering, and because it also assures me that I am really as little in love with live, as I have been for some time in the habit of professing."[34]

Jeffrey made a second happy marriage, but his mature letters express an increasingly ironic attitude toward great men, great events, and great ideas. No Byronic confrontations with the cosmos, not much Sturm und Drang. "Having long ago set my standard of human felicity at a very moderate pitch, and persuaded myself that men are *considerably* lower than angels, I am not much given to discontent, and am sufficiently sensible that many things that appear and are irksome and vexatious, are necessary to help life along."[35] He went down to the House of Commons in 1831 as Lord Advocate of Scotland, to manage the Scottish side of the First Reform Bill. It was chaotic, time-consuming business, with "the respective *doctrinaires* . . . hooting, and hissing, and abusing us for not regenerating all things." "I often think seriously of cutting and running," he wrote to Cockburn, " . . . and the only thing that prevents me is the difficulty of deciding what to run to, and a sort of epicurean fatalism in my creed, which has long made me believe that as we must *do something*, and suffer something in this uncontrollable world, it is better to leave Providence to determine what it shall be, than to vex one's-self, and increase one's responsibility, by trying to alter it."[36] Although they differed on most fundamentals, Jeffrey recognized Carlyle's peculiar gifts, and the two had long converstions late into the night. "Alas, light, light, too light!" Carlyle lamented. "He will talk of nothing *earnestly*, tho' his look sometimes betrays an earnest feeling."[37] Carlyle was torn between the creature comforts of Jeffrey's fireside and the frustration of his editor's refusal to talk of transcendentals. Jeffrey was an "intellectual Ariel," a "Scotch Voltaire"![38] "You may talk as long as you like," Jeffrey advised him, "about . . . the necessity of having a right creed on your relations with the universe — but you will never persuade anybody that the regulation of life is such a mighty laborious business as you would make it or that it is not better to go lightly thro' it, with the first creed that comes to hand, than to spend the better part of it in an anxious verification of its articles."[39]

Did Christianity have a place in Jeffrey's own creed? Lockhart did not think so. When Jeffrey's letters were published Lockhart remarked, with malice aforethought, that the letters made no allusion to the doctrines or moral influence of Christianity.[40] "The whole set," he wrote of the *Review* circle, "were really most thorough infidels."[41] Not the whole set. While he might make sport of Evangelicals and Methodists, Sydney Smith's rational, eighteenth-century Anglicanism was sincere.[42] But Horner and Brougham had studied Hume's *Dialogues Concerning Natural Religion* (1779), and their private letters show their skepticism about the immortality of the soul and the theological argument from design.[43] They were discreet, lest "the cry of atheism & Jacobinism becomes very loud against us."[44] Horner, especially, was anxious to stay "in the safe and honest medium, upon these ticklish subjects": "I should be sorry to have betrayed any of the scepticism, which is my real sentiment, and still more to have the appearance of assuming the language of the dogmatists."[45] It was only after Brougham had moved to London and begun to court the political support of Evangelicals that he was brought to admit that there might be more to Christianity "than the Edinburgh wits dreamed of."[46] Horner took Brougham's quasi-conversion as proof of what the Edinburgh wits had always suspected — that Brougham would say anything to get votes. "We are infinitely amused with Brougham with the Saints here, the salt of the earth," Horner reported to Jeffrey; "he has been dining with Wilberforce, & keeping the night at Stephen's house where he had family worship to join in, morn & even. Would not you have given all your hopes of heaven, (not a great price on your part), for a sight of Brougham upon his knees?"[47]

For all this brittle and enlightened banter, it is difficult to pinpoint Jeffrey's own position. He described the doctrine of immortality as "this pleasing belief,"[48] and his occasional remarks in reviews and letters suggest a vague and genteel theism.[49] But he had reasons for discretion, perhaps even dissimulation. He was concerned that the *Review* should not incur the wrath of pious readers, and he was developing a brisk legal specialty in ecclesiastical cases. He recommended Paley's *Natural Theology* (1802) as the strongest statement of the theological argument from design that Britain had yet produced. But the argument from design held a special place in British thought. It was considered the rational foundation of all theism — in a sense, the rational foundation of moral life — and even skeptics like Hume who questioned its validity were reluctant to bring down social opprobrium by attacking it too openly. To do so was bad form, a provocation to religious reactionaries, and Adam Smith persuaded Hume to save the *Dialogues Concerning Natural Religion* for post-humous publication. Consequently, Jeffrey's comment at the close of his review of Paley's work is perhaps more revealing than Jeffrey wished it to be: "If we were inclined to point out any defects in a performance which has gratified us so much, both in its plan and its execution, we would observe, that the *metaphysical* objections of the atheistical philosophers are not perhaps sufficiently weighed and refuted: it is probable that this was thought less necessary in a work intended for general perusal; but as this treatise is announced as the completion of a general system in Ethics and Theology, we cannot help thinking that it ought not to have left any plausible objection unanswered."[50] Jeffrey apparently found the argument from design probable but not conclusive. In his own reasonings on ethical, aesthetic, and epistemological matters, neither the teleological corollaries of that argument nor the distinguishing doctrines of Christianity played a part. When he referred to Christianity or the Protestant Reformation, he confined himself to remarks on the humanistic value of the Christian ethic or on the Reformation's tendency to further civil liberties and independent reasoning.[51] If Jeffrey was paying lip service to his community's beliefs, he was following the example of Cicero and Hume. If he held a personal faith based on psychological evidence that Hume and the Edinburgh wits would not have admitted, he kept it to himself.

What he gave to others was pragmatic advice on "the ways and means of ordinary happiness," "the ethics of common life."[52] "No one could take a walk, or pass a day or an evening with him," Cockburn reminisced, "without having all his rational and generous tastes confirmed, and a steadier conviction than before of the dependence of happiness on kindness and duty."[53] Through luck and talent he won his way to the top of two professions. The law and the *Review* filled his days — saved him from ennui — but he did not think that fame brought contentment. He believed that the majority of men find what contentment life allows them only through the tolerant cultivation of friendship and family affection. But that contentment itself demands that men first discipline their personal ambitions. It requires the acceptance of all those duties and irritations which adult life brings. That was tame philosophy for an age whose style was set by Regency bucks, Byronic heroes, and Napoleonic generals. But Jeffrey preached the virtues of domestic affection and civic duty to "that great proportion of our readers which must necessarily belong to the middling or humbler classes of the community."[54] Although he knew that the possibilities for a full life were not limited to the proprieties of Presbyterian drawing rooms, Jeffrey had pragmatic respect for the middle class and its virtues. Raised above the animal subsistence of agricultural and industrial workers, the middle class had time for intellectual culture — time to read the *Edinburgh Review*. Shaped by the discipline of regular exertion, the middle class was spared the dissipation and ennui that cursed aristocratic life. Jeffrey wrote for that middle class, believing that the quality of British life would be increasingly determined by their life style and opinions.

"For my part," he confessed to Carlyle, "the more I see of philosophers and men of genius the more I am inclined to hold that the ordinary run of sensible, kind people, who fill the world, are after all the best specimens of humanity, and that the others are, like our cultivated flowers, but splendid monsters, and cases of showy disease."[55] He knew many of the geniuses and most of the philosophy of his age. But his long analytical career only deepened his youthful awareness of the fallibility of human reason and the elusiveness of human happiness. Writing five years after his retirement as editor, in his second year as Advocate General in the reformed House of Commons, he confided, "I think zeal for creeds more and more ludicrous — and that all discussion, which aims at much more than exercising our faculties, and exposing intolerance, is very tiresome and foolish." We must cultivate our gardens.

If his view of mankind's future was less than millennial, Jeffrey cast an equally cool eye on contemporary primitivism. A lifelong addict to travel literature, he understood the problem of evidence. "We seldom see foreign nations either fully or fairly; and scarcely ever consider what we do see without prejudice or partiality: novelty is sure either to magnify or diminish the objects with which it is associated;

and the spectator of strange manners is almost irresistibly tempted either to despise them for differing from his own, or to admire them as something incomparably superior."[57] But, by comparing the accounts of different writers of different prejudices, he concluded that neither man's imaginative power nor his benevolent impulses are strongest in primitive societies. "There is always something very interesting in an account of rude or remote nations of men," he wrote in reviewing a book on Korea. "But there is almost always something very painful too. . . . Cruelty, duplicity, sensuality — war without generosity — profligacy without elegance or decency — debasing and sanguinary superstitions — lawless tyrannies — continual insecurity of life and property — childish levity and caprice, or brutal apathy. — Such is the picture, we fear, of about three-fourths of our species."[58] He found it difficult to explain why modern European society had outstripped the older and more sophisticated societies of Asia. Granted, Europeans enjoyed greater civil liberty, religious tolerance, and security of life and property. It remained to be explained why Europeans had progressed in those areas while Asians continued in the grip of despotism and fanaticism. "We come then, though a little reluctantly, to the conclusion, that there is a natural and inherent difference in the character and temperament of the European and Asiatic races — consisting, perhaps, chiefly in a superior capacity of patient and persevering thought in the former — and displaying itself, for the most part, in a more sober and robust understanding, and a more reasonable, principled, and inflexible morality."[59]

He was not tempted to trade Edinburgh for Tahiti or Kowloon. When compared with the condition of three-fourths of our species, the European condition seemed enviable. But Jeffrey believed that the development of modern European society involved human loss as well as gain. He recognized in his own time the early effects of what twentieth-century critics have come to call "the knowledge explosion," and he doubted that "the human intellect will gain in point of dignity and energy":

So many easy and pleasant elementary books, — such tempting summaries, abstracts and tables, — such beautiful engravings, and ingenious charts and *coups-d'oeuil* of information, — so many museums, exhibitions and collections, meet us at every corner, — and so much amusing and provoking talk in every party, that a taste for miscellaneous and imperfect information is formed, almost before we are aware, and our time and curiosity irrevocably devoted to a sort of encyclopedical trifling.

In the mean time, the misfortune is, that there is no popular nor royal road to the profounder and more abstract truths of philosophy; and that these are apt, accordingly, to fall into discredit or neglect, at a period when it is labour enough for most men to keep themselves up to the level of that great tide of popular information, which has been rising, with such unexampled rapidity, for the last forty years.[60]

Thus the modern mind devotes more time to remembering and less time to independent reasoning and reflection. In the days of Bacon, Hooker, and Hume, "the business of reasoning" and "the business of collecting information" could still be combined.[61] Now few men have the time for patient analysis or the courage for novel hypotheses, and "the age of original genius, and of comprehensive and independent reasoning, seems to be over."[62] When men of general intelligence and curiosity are seldom tempted into authorship, "the inferior persons upon whom that task is consequently devolved, carry it on, for the most part, by means of that minute subdivision of labour which is the great secret of the mechanical arts, but can never be introduced into literature without depriving its higher branches of all force, dignity, or importance."[63]

That "minute subdivision of labour" in "the mechanical arts" was an economic matter, and Jeffrey was increasingly troubled by the economic conditions of early nineteenth-century Britain. Smith and Millar had not indulged in visions of mankind's moral perfectibility, but they had argued that modern European history showed signs of social and economic progress. They defined progress, and they explained the development of different societies, in terms of the nature and diffusion of property. The decline of the European feudal system and the rise of a European middle class was a process of improvement of landed property and of development of "manufactures." In turn, the economic emancipation of the middle class from feudal conditions brought an increase in civil liberties. These theories were the economic catechism of the young Scotsmen who began the *Edinburgh Review*. Horner, the best economist among them, thought the dissemination of Smith's ideas to be one of the more important tasks of the *Review*.[64] Brougham compared Smith with Newton in the course of recommending "the master principle of individual interest — the power which connects and maintains the whole system, as gravitation regulates the movements of the heavenly bodies."[65] In his early comments on economic matters, Jeffrey followed suit. He cited the relationship between the development of trade and manufactures and the evolution of a politically powerful and cultured middle class. He speculated on the potential benefits of an international confederacy of manufacturing nations, "ministering to each other's enjoyments by a free and liberal intercourse."[66]

But Jeffrey was to have second thoughts on the contemporary economic scene. To some extent he was influenced by Malthus, who became a contributor in 1808. Even more, he was disturbed by the growth of industrial monopolies and the outbreak of organized, retaliatory machine-breaking in the English Midlands. He had early admitted that "the comforts of a labourer in the lowest ranks of society . . . are scarcely superior, in most civilized societies, to the ordinary life of a savage." By 1813, a year of desperate Luddite activity and harsh government reprisals, he publicly recognized that the emancipation of the middle class had brought economic slavery to the lower:

> Increasing refinement and ingenuity lead naturally to the establishment of manufactures; and not only enable society to spare a great proportion of its agricultural labourers for this purpose, but actually encourage the

breeding of an additional population; to be maintained out of the profits of this new occupation. For a time too, this answers; and the artisan shares in the conveniences to which his labours have contributed to give birth: But it is in the very nature of the manufacturing system, to be liable to great fluctuation, occasional check, and possible destruction; and at all events, it has a tendency to produce a greater population than it can permanently support in comfort or prosperity.[67]

For the past forty years, he argued, the wage-rate had remained fixed at a level insufficient to support a laborer with a large family. In the same period the manufacturing population of England had increased at an alarming rate, in accordance with what seemed to be "the general law of our nature, that the population should be adopted to the highest, and not to the average rate of supply." It was in the interest of the "great capitalists" that the country be burdened with an excess labor force, so that wages might be maintained at the lowest rate. Thus, early in the century, there was fast developing the condition that Marx and Engels would describe in the *Communist Manifesto* (1848), that situation which Disraeli's *Sybil* (1845) would describe as "two nations":

The effect then which is produced on the lower orders of society, by that increase of industry and refinement, and that multiplication of conveniences which are commonly looked upon as the surest tests of increasing prosperity, is to convert the peasants into manufacturers, and the manufacturers into paupers; while the chance of their ever emerging from this condition becomes constantly less, the more complete and mature the system is which had originally produced it. When manufactures are long established, and thoroughly understood, it will always be found, that persons possessed of a large capital, can carry them on upon lower profits than persons of any other description; and the natural tendency of this system, therefore, is to throw the whole business into the hands of great capitalists; and thus not only to render it next to impossible for a common workman to advance himself into the condition of a master, but to drive from the competition the greater

part of those moderate dealers, by whose prosperity alone
the general happiness of the nation can be promoted. The
state of the operative manufacturers, therefore, seems
every day more hopelessly stationary; and that great body
of the people, it appears to us, is likely to grow into a
fixed and degraded *caste,* out of which no person can hope
to escape, who has once been enrolled among its members.[68]

Publicly, Jeffrey could still express the hope that, through
a system of working-class education, middle-class morality
might be taught to the masses — "habits of foresight and self
control, and rigid economy."[69] But cutting down on gin and
sex would not of itself lift many laborers into the economic
ranks of the middle class, and Jeffrey was privately pessimistic
about the shape of things to come. With the end of the
Napoleonic Wars, the country suffered from a crisis of over-
production and unemployment, what Malthus called a
"general glut." "Our present radical evil," Jeffrey wrote to
an American correspondent in 1819, "is the excess of our
productive power — the want of demand for our manufactures
and industry; or, in other words, the excess of our population.
. . . It may seem a strange paradox to mention, but I am
myself quite persuaded of its truth, that, in our artificial
society, the consequences of those great discoveries and
improvements which render human industry so much more
productive, and *should* therefore render all human comforts
so much more attainable, must be to plunge the greater part
of society into wretchedness."[70]

Jeffrey understood the horrors of the new industrial order,
but he could think of no humane remedy that would not
endanger the security of private property. And private
property was sacrosanct to his generation. Hume, Smith,
Stewart, and Millar had taught them that the security of
private property was the basis of the culture they enjoyed.
Jeffrey might introduce a toast to "Freedom of Labour" at
a public dinner celebrating the 1824 repeal of Combination
Laws against labor unions. But he followed the toast with a
speech that warned that Labor, in exercising its own rights,
"cannot be permitted to violate the rights of others."[71]

In 1830, in the midst of the intense public agitation that preceded the passing of the First Reform Bill, he confided to Carlyle the nineteenth-century fears and confusion of an eighteenth-century Scottish man of property:

> I wish I had time to explain to you the grounds of my horror of radicalism. It is nothing but the old feud against *property*. . . . But there is no remedy, but the utter destruction of the right of property altogether, and the establishment of a great co-operative system, which no sane man will seriously consider as practicable. Anything short of that — sumptuary laws, maximum of allowable accumulation, compulsory charity, agrarian reparations — obviously tend, not to make the poor better off, but to make *all poor*, of the very lowest description, and that by no long process — besides importing the entire destruction of all luxury, elegance, art, and mental cultivation, and in short reducing the whole race to the wretched condition of savages toiling and scrambling for mere animal subsistence. It is only by protecting and assuring the right of *property* that we have emerged from that condition, and are still kept out of it, and tho' its ultimate establishment produces many evils, and a most revolting spectacle of inequality, I do not see how you can touch it, without bringing in still greater evils.[72]

"The real battle that is soon to be fought," he wrote in 1831, "and the only one now worth providing for, is not between Whigs and Tories, Liberals and Illiberals, and such gentleman-like denominations, but between property and no property — swing and the law."[73]

In 1865 a brooding but apparently sane man would emerge from the reading room of the British Museum with the manuscript of *Das Kapital*, a work that announced the coming of the "great co-operative system" that Jeffrey thought "no sane man will seriously consider as practicable."[74] Britain would avoid widespread class warfare through emigration, reform bills, and the fortuitous diversion of two World Wars. In 1945 the country would take the first significant steps toward socialization. "Compulsory charity" is now enforced through income tax; "agrarian reparations" have become "farm subsidies" in the United States; and a "maximum of allowable accumulation" is now unthinkable only for those classical economists who still follow the dimming light of Adam Smith. Times have changed, and modern readers may have the vague feeling that these early-nineteenth-century socio-economic questions, phrased in unfamiliar terms, must somehow have been resolved in the intervening century and a half. The terminology has changed, but the questions have not been resolved. It is still a lively argument whether life in twentieth-century communist societies — in Russia, China, Cuba — refutes or confirms Jeffrey's fears. The struggle between giant corporations and giant labor unions may yet create a condition of inflation in which Jeffrey's "moderate dealers" must go completely under. If unemployment mounts in the modern "artificial" economies of the West, there may be further contests between Captain Swing and the law. The broad social and economic questions that troubled Jeffrey are still a trouble to most thinking men. Political Economy, Carlyle's "Dismal Science," has made great advances in the collection of data since Adam Smith's day. It has not yet solved our problems.

Politics — The War

One can almost forgive Englishmen who write like Scotch Reviewers, but there is no pardon for Scotch Reviewers who write like Frenchmen.
   — *Anon.*, The Talents Run Mad *(1816)*

At the turn of the century Jeffrey was a Whig, a member of the Opposition, an "out."[1] The Scotsmen who professed Whig sympathies at that time deserve to be judged by the standard that Dr. Johnson suggested for the appraisal of women preachers and performing dogs. It is irrelevant to ask how well the thing was done; the wonder is that it was done at all. By 1795 all significant Scottish opposition to the Pitt administration had been stifled. County electors and town councils were in government hands. There were no opposition newspapers or periodicals; the majority of Church livings belonged to large landowners or to the Crown. Banks operated on the basis of political sympathy, and cases argued by Whig lawyers were consistently defeated. "Thus," Cockburn remembered, "politically, Scotland was dead. It was not unlike a village at a great man's gate. Without a single free institution or habit, opposition was rebellion, submission probable success."[2]

The great man at whose gate the village lay was Cockburn's uncle, Henry Dundas, Viscount Melville, successively Home Secretary, Secretary of War, and Lord of the Admiralty in the Pitt administrations. Dundas ruled Scotland with a genial despotism. He was a native Scot "who knew the circumstances, and the wants, and the proper bait of every countryman worth being attended to,"[3] and he effectively controlled the avenues of advancement in Scottish legal, ecclesiastical, and political life. It was Dundas, in his capacity as Home Secretary, who had stifled the first sounds of popular discontent in the years immediately following the French Revolution. A society of Friends of the People had been formed in Edinburgh in 1792, in close alliance with the London Corresponding Society, and reform organizations from all parts of Scotland had sent representatives to an Edinburgh Convention of Delegates of Reform Societies. Their immediate aim was Scottish burgh reform and an extension of the electoral franchise. But Dundas initiated a series of State Trials for Sedition, the most sensational of which was the trial of Thomas Muir, who was sentenced on circumstantial evidence to fourteen years of penal servitude. Those trials — and the reports of Jacobin activity issued by Dundas's Committees of Secrecy — intimidated reformers and effected a conservative reaction among the influential segment of the Scottish population. Public meetings of Whigs or reformers of any stripe ceased in 1795, and an Opposition dinner was not held again in Scotland until 1811. "There were many," Cockburn wrote, "with whom horror of French principles, to the extent to which it was carried, was a party pretext. But there were also many with whom it was a sincere feeling, and who, in their fright, saw in every Whig a person who was already a republican, and not unwilling to become a regicide. In these circumstances, zeal upon the right side was at a high premium, while there was no virtue so hated as moderation."[4]

In an early unpublished essay, Jeffrey described his own political intelligence as "a mind of itself disposed to accommodation."[5] That moderate, pragmatic temper turned him against both the doctrinaire monarchism of his father and the doctrinaire democracy of Jacobin theorists. In undergraduate days, his father's politics had denied him the lectures of John Millar and Dugald Stewart. By 1793, however, he was politically his own man. He wrote an essay in that year, "Politics," which espoused the principles of a philosophical Whig, "firm to the popular principles of our government, and consequently firm against any encroachment, whether from the monarchical or the democratical side."6 At that time, his allegiance was only theoretical: "I am enrolled in no party, and initiated in no club."7 For some years he kept his distance from the camp of the reviled Scottish Whigs, although his friendship with Horner and other Whig lawyers was drawing him in that direction. He attended Muir's trial, read "democratical books," and wrote to his brother in America of the "destructive violence" of British politics:

> there are three parties, I think, distinguishable enough. The first, which is the loudest, and I believe the most powerful, is that of the fierce aristocrats – men of war, with their swords and their rank – men of property, with their hands on their pockets, and their eyes staring wildly with alarm and detestation – men of indolence and morosity, and, withal, men of place and expectation. The desperate democrats are the second order – numerous enough too, and thriving like other sects under persecution. Most of them are led; so their character is to be taken from that of their leaders. These are, for the most part, men of broken fortunes, and of desperate ambition, and animated by views very different from their professions. To these are joined some, whom a generous and sincere enthusiasm has borne beyond their interest; irritated perhaps excessively at the indiscriminating intolerance of the alarmists, and zealous in the assertion of some truths, which those with whom they co-operate have used as a decoy. The third order is that of philosophers, and of course very small. They necessarily vary in their maxims and opinions, and only agree in blaming something more or less in both parties, and in endeavouring to reconcile their hostility.8

There are times when even moderates must fish or cut bait. By 1800 Jeffrey had made his choice. He was known by the mark of Whig and banished to the dark places of Edinburgh legal life. To further their careers, most of the original *Review* circle left Edinburgh for London. Horner, Smith, and Allen were welcomed into Holland House, the center of the moderate Whigs, while Brougham began his erratic movement toward the party's radical perimeter. Jeffrey remained in Edinburgh and gradually assumed a leading role in local efforts to effect burgh reform. But political life in Dundas's Edinburgh was isolated from that of London and Westminster. Despite his general sympathy with the aims of the Holland House circle, Jeffrey tried to keep the *Edinburgh Review* politically independent in its early years, and Walter Scott felt only slight misgivings in contributing to it. Its first crusade was against the slave trade, essentially a non-party issue. When the short-lived, Whig-dominated "Ministry of All the Talents" advanced a bill to restructure the Scottish Court of Session, Jeffrey led the younger Scottish Whigs in opposition to it, on the grounds that the bill was but another form of that jobbery from which Scottish public life had traditionally suffered. "What is thought of the bill now?" he wrote to Allen, who was close to the counsels of Holland House. "I am myself most anxious for reform and for great change; but I cannot dissemble my suspicions of jobbism. It is nonsense to say that this kind of opposititon endangers the whole measure. It is infinitely more endangered by the doings to which we are opposed. I shall believe that the supporters of the scheme are seriously persuaded of the utility of a Scottish Chancellor and Court of Review, when I hear that they are to offer it to Blair [Robert Blair, a Tory], who is best entitled to it. At the same time, you know that I love the Whigs, and it grieves me to see that they will act like placemen."[9]

As the Napoleonic war dragged on and popular discontent increased in England, Jeffrey came to believe that the best interests of the country would be served by the triumph of the Whig party, and the *Review* became more partisan in tone. By 1808, when Jeffrey published the "Don Pedro Cevallos" article, the *Review* was generally regarded as a voice of Opposition. In 1809 Scott and Gifford began the *Quarterly Review* to counter the *Edinburgh Review*'s influence. Jeffrey, in his own writings, attempted to shape Whig policy, especially in the areas of electoral and economic reform. But as editor he accepted many articles that contained specific doctrines with which he disagreed. In 1815, when Horner questioned the *Review*'s position on renewed hostilities, Jeffrey attempted to justify his editorial policy:

Perhaps it would have been better to have kept more to general views. But in such times as we have lived in, it was impossible not to mix them, as in fact they mix themselves, with questions which might be considered as of a narrower and more factious description. In substance it appeared to me that my only absolute duty as to political discussion was, to forward the great ends of liberty, and to exclude nothing but what had a tendency to promote servile, sordid, and corrupt principles. As to the *means* of attaining these ends, I thought that considerable latitude should be indulged, and that unless the excesses were very great and revolting, every man of talent should be allowed to take his own way of recommending them. In this way it has always appeared to me that a considerable diversity was quite compatible with all the consistency that should be required in a work of this description, and that doctrines might very well be maintained in the same number which were quite irreconcilable with each other, except in their common tendency to repress servility, and diffuse a general spirit of independence in the body of the people.[10]

The major political issues with which Jeffrey was concerned were the conduct of the war and the question of economic and electoral reform. On these issues the Whig party was split into hostile and ineffective factions, and their split became more serious after Charles Fox's death in 1806 deprived the party of its one charismatic leader. Burke's *Reflections on the Revolution in France* (1790), the excesses of the French National Convention, the fate of the Venetian Republic, the invective of the *Anti-Jacobin* – all conspired to turn British public opinion against France and to frighten the government into conservative reaction. Thus, the events and ideas that shaped opinion on the war were those which shaped opinion on reform, and the men who opposed the former were often those who espoused the latter. For the sake of clarity, however, it is best to concentrate first upon the question of the conduct of the war.

Among the Whigs, Fox and his followers were long faithful to their own idealization of the French Revolution. They believed that Britain's interference in Continental affairs was ill-advised, and they supported the anti-war petitions and mass peace rallies conducted by the London Corresponding Society in 1795. After the Pitt government broke off negotiations with Napoleon in 1800, Fox assured the Commons that the British people wished for peace: "Believe me, they are friends to peace; although, by the laws which you have made, restraining the expression of the sense of the people, public opinion cannot now be heard as loudly and unequivocally as heretofore."[11] The war continued, and Fox and his followers were caught in what now seems a recurrent anti-war dilemma. While they attempted to excuse the excesses of the enemy, the enemy acted even more inexcusably. Although they continued to press for peace, their infatuation with Napoleon gradually waned. By 1804 the *New Annual Register,* long sympathetic to the French cause, had announced its disappointment: "A tyranny far more extensive and severe than that which was destroyed, has been established in France . . . . The friend of liberty, and even the republican, must therefore be no longer the advocate of France: he may, without a violation of principle, wish to see restored that milder form of despotism which existed under an ancient and on the whole illustrious dynasty."[12]

The ranks of Opposition were swelled in 1801 when Lord Grenville and his followers allied themselves with Fox. They were united on the issue of Catholic emancipation but not on the question of the war. While Fox continued to believe in the possibility and necessity of peace, it was Grenville who had broken off negotiations with Napoleon in 1800, while acting as Foreign Secretary in the Pitt administration. Grenville subsequently opposed the brief Peace of Amiens and called for renewed British action. When Fox, Grey, and Grenville entered the coalition "Ministry of All the Talents" in 1806, only Fox was confident that peace could be negotiated. Negotiations lapsed with Fox's death, and the fall of the Talents in 1807 dashed hopes for an early peace. From that year until 1815, the policy of the Whigs toward the war was vacillating and contradictory. They had, in fact, no party policy at all. Grey, Grenville, and Lord Holland consistently expressed their desire for an honorable peace and consistently denied that such a peace was possible. While Holland supported the Peninsular campaign, Grey and Grenville opposed it. On the party's left, Samuel Whitbread and his followers pressed for peace on almost any terms.

Jeffrey's private letters before the Peace of Amiens express his horror at the war and his suspicion that Britain and Napoleon were equally at fault. He rejoiced in the temporary peace — "What are victories to rejoice at, compared with an event like this?"[13] — and was deeply troubled by the resumption of hostilities. "It is most clearly and unequivocally a war of our own seeking, and an offensive war upon our part, though we have no means of offending. The consular proceedings are certainly very outrageous and provoking, and, if we had power to humble him, I rather think we have had provocation enough to do it. But with our means, and in the present state and temper of Europe, I own it appears to me like insanity."[14] Nonetheless, he believed that "we must all turn out." He enlisted in the local volunteer militia, where Scott was making boyhood dreams come true as organizer and chief saber-rattler of the Edinburgh Light Horse. In his first major article on the conduct of the war, an 1803 review of Frédéric Gentz's *De l'état de l'Europe* (1802), Jeffrey expressed the hope that the European balance of power might yet be restored through an Austro-Prussian coalition and through the resurgent resistance of those countries which were temporarily under French control.[15]

Mack's surrender at Ulm, the Austro-Russian defeat at Austerlitz, and the Treaty of Tilsit sufficed to destroy that hope. When new negotiations between France and Britain collapsed in 1807, Jeffrey suspected that Britain was at least partially responsible. He was not alone. Whitbread within the Commons and the *Independent Whig* without assailed government policy, and there were many who shred Hazlitt's belief that it was not fear of invasion that had produced the taking-up of arms "but the determination to take up arms which produced the fears of invasion."[16] Jeffrey did not share Hazlitt's high opinion of Napoleon, but he believed that immediate peace was essential to Britain's survival. With that conviction, he wrote in 1807 a long essay on "The Dangers of the Country" — a discussion of the basic principles of British foreign policy.

The war was begun, he noted, to counter the aggressive intentions of the French. But most campaigns had ended in new conquests for France and new humiliations for Britain's allies. Why continue? There were four objectives that government supporters had cited to justify continuing hostilities. The first was the restoration of the Bourbon monarchy; the second, the restoration of the losses of the faithful allies; the third, the retention of the territory already conquered in the war; the fourth, to better secure Britain against the enormous power and rooted hostility of France. Jeffrey argued that the first two objectives must be abandoned as "desperate and unattainable": "Every attack that has been made upon France has ended in adding to her power. The wars which her neighbours have waged against her have been the sole causes of her greatness. . . . The game, we fear, is decidedly lost, as to the Continent of Europe; and for our allies to persist in it, will only be to push their bad fortune. They had better take up the remaining stakes, if they can; and endeavour to acquire a little more skill and contrivance, before they choose partners for a new party." The third objective — in effect, the extension of the British Empire — was not sufficient reason for continuing. "We have more foreign settlements already than we have any good use for; and it would be the height of imprudence to think of keeping all that are now in our hands, even if their original owners were quite willing to relinquish them."[17]

It followed, then, that the only plausible justification for continued war was the belief that Britain's own security would be better strengthened through war than through temporary peace. Jeffrey acknowledged that Napoleon would have in mind only temporary peace. He would agree to peace only to strengthen his resources, to strike again at a more advantageous moment. But, in admitting this, "we do not admit much more than may be safely assumed as to the purposes and dispositions with which nations in general leave off an indecisive war." "We are but little moved with the common declamatory invectives against the perfidiousness of our enemy, and the impossibility of trusting to any promises or engagements he may come under. We conceive that all nations are perfidious in this sense of the word; and that they neither do, nor can trust to the good faith of each other, when they enter into compacts and agreements." The only relevant agrument concerned which nation would profit most from even a temporary cessation of hostilities. The advantages to Britain were clear. Peace would buy time, time to develop a home army sufficient to defend its shores, time to placate the Irish and render Ireland secure. An interval of peace would be "like a truce obtained, while Orlando was recovering from his insanity; or a parley prolonged, till Jupiter could be aroused from his amorous slumbers." And time might work a change on France, despite the militant ambitions of Napoleon. "By making peace . . . even with the intention of renewing the war at a convenient opportunity, France will eventually be seduced into pacific habits, and lose many of those advantages which she now enjoys as a belligerent. To improve her commerce, as the rival of ours, and the basis of her future navy, must be the first great object of her ruler; but a commercial people, and, above all, a people just beginning the tempting career of commercial prosperity, must naturally be averse to war."[18]

By 1808 British attention had turned to the Iberian Peninsula. Despite the Convention of Cintra and the near-disastrous retreat of the British army under John Moore, there were many who believed that an effort should yet be made to aid the Spanish people. The Whigs were predictably divided on the question of a Peninsular campaign. Lord Holland saw it as a moral crusade; Grey and Grenville believed it to be tactically unwise; Whitbread published his *Letter to Lord Holland* in June 1808, professing enthusiasm for the Spanish patriots and pressing for renewed negotiations. "I must say," Jeffrey wrote to Horner, "that a temperate, firm, and enlightened article on Spain, would, of all other things, be the most serviceable and restorative to us at this crisis."[19] He might well wish for it. The crisis was of his and Brougham's making. In October 1808 the *Review* had included their collaboration, the notorious "Don Pedro Cevallos" article, the most intemperate political piece the *Review* had yet published.[20] Holland House was horrified; Tory pamphleteers responded; Walter Scott canceled his subscription; and the Earl of Buchan kicked the offending issue into the street, that its pages and principles might be trod unto dust.

Jeffrey and Brougham had not only suggested that the Peninsula was doomed. They had suggested that the English masses might follow the example of Spanish popular revolt. That second, explosive suggestion is better discussed in the context of Jeffrey's writings on reform. The Peninsular predictions were provoking of themselves. The reviewers predicted defeat. Although the early Spanish efforts were inspiring, Jeffrey-Brougham noted that the Spaniards had been fighting a French occupation-army. Eventually, Napoleon would send a larger force into Spain, and past experience seemed to indicate that Napoleon would win the field. The reviewers were strong on sympathy for the gallant Spanish masses. "Something, we would fain hope, may be done, even yet, to protract the defeat of that great and good cause, and to obtain better terms for the patriots, if they ultimately fail." But Jeffrey and Brougham were not sanguine on the chances of a British crusade into Spain. Rather, they recommended the type of negotiated settlement that Whitebread had proposed in his *Letter.* "Would it be impossible to offer . . . a dereliction of every one *British object*, an oblivion of all our separate causes of quarrel with France, on condition that good terms should be granted to the patriots? Would not such an offer, if successful, be the salvation of Europe, and, though it failed, strengthen our union with Spain?"[21]

Wellington's subsequent success on the Peninsula belied the reviewer's gloomiest predictions. But Wellington on the Peninsula was a long way from Waterloo. The war dragged on, and Jeffrey's disgust only deepened. In 1810 he wrote two articles on the war, both of which raised the specter of a discontented and potentially violent British people. For twenty years, he argued, the British had given up a third of their income in taxes to support the war. After twenty years, the country was left without a single effective ally, in imminent danger of invasion and conquest. Could sane men wonder why there had spread "through the body of the nation a great disposition to despise and distrust their governors, and to judge unfavourably of the form of government itself which could admit of such gross ignorance or imposition?" It was the hostility of other European states that had first given focus and discipline to French revolutionary energies. And those same Continental governments had proved to be no match for the France that Napoleon and their own incompetent hostility had shaped:

> Vigour and rapidity are its characteristics; and, despotic as its constitution undoubtedly is, it is of all the despotisms that history has described, the most active, energetic, and compact. The frame of that constitution is not disordered by inveterate factions, nor clogged with bloated aristocracies. All is bone and muscle: there is no sluggish smoothness, no sleek imbecility: every nerve is braced to its firmest tension, and preserved in perpetual vigour, by the most severe training and unremitting exercise. Perhaps the regimen may be too painful to be perpetual; perhaps a proportionate exhaustion may be expected to succeed: but, as long as the system does retain its present energy, so long, at least, it must continue to triumph over the diseased and decrepit masses of corpulent impotence, that erect themselves upon the Continent with an empty show of resistance, and totter under the weight of the very arms which they affect to wield in their defence.[22]

"As long as the system does retain its present energy" — that was the key. Britain had a chance, but only if its government would give up the vision of decisive military victory. "We do think, then, that there is no chance of our being able to *crush* the power of France by direct hostility and aggression; but still we are of opinion, that by skillful and cautious policy, we may reasonably hope to *disable* it. This, however, we must do by gradual and cautious means; and trust to the natural and regular . . . course of human affairs, for that effectual co-operation, which cannot be hoped from alliances and intrigues." If negotiated peace was impossible while Napoleon held power, let Britain abandon the Continent and concentrate upon a defensive maritime campaign. Having humbled Continental enemies, the French would soon grow restive under Bonaparte's reign. "Would not the multitude soon begin to discover, that, though their burthens remained, the equivalents for which those burthens were borne were totally withdrawn? – that the government was still seizing their persons, draining their purses, checking the cultivation of their lands? . . . in a word, persisting to bear down the rights and the liberties of a great people, without performing any one achievement that could extend the public dominion, or recompense the national pride?" Peace and commercial prospects would succeed where Allied armies had failed. They would dissipate Napoleonic energy:

we should never forget, that the constitution of modern society is eminently favourable to the internal freedom and external independence of nations. The use of printing – the diffusion of commercial opulence – and the full and ready intercourse which now connects all parts of the civilized world – have given a weight and an intelligence to public opinion, which it never possessed in any former period of history . . . . While the war continues, and especially while it is possible to impute its continuance to the restless hostility of England, the vanity and impetuosity of the French people may second the ambition of their ruler; but if they be ever allowed to settle into the habits and enjoyments of peace, all the natural interests and reflections which are generated by the very structure of modern society, will expand with tenfold vigour, and oppose a most formidable resistance to the tyranny which would again repress them for the purposes of its own extension.[23]

Jeffrey was unable to enjoy a war, even from the sidelines. He understood the psychological attractions that war holds for some men, but he was by nature a domestic sort. "You admire greatness much more than I do," he wrote to Horner of Napoleon, "and have a far more extensive taste for the *sublime* in character."[24] In 1810 France was still the master of the field, and Jeffrey did not wish to waste more lives by playing France's game. But events took an unexpected turn. In 1812 the Russian winter withered French forces. By 1814 British and Allied armies had battered Bonaparte into submission. The Emperor was sent to Elba, the Treaty of Paris was signed, and Castlereagh began the work of reestablishing "the order of things." With no illusions about the Allies' intentions, Jeffrey wrote an essay on "the State and Prospects of the European Commonwealth," encouraging Continental monarchs to incorporate more liberal measures into the order of things.[25]

Then, for a moment, the old nightmare revived. Napoleon escaped from Elba, the Bourbons fled France, and the Liverpool Administration pressed for renewed British action. True to form, the Whigs were divided. Grenville was for war, while Grey, Whitbread, and the Holland House circle urged Liverpool to recognize Napoleon and learn to live with him. They had no desire to begin another decade of war in defense of Bourbon monarchy. Horner expressed their sentiments against the "new war" to Jeffrey in June of 1815, two weeks before Waterloo. Jeffrey's reply was personal and candid:

I am mortally afraid of the war, and I think that is all I can say about it. I hate Bonaparte too, because he makes me more afraid than anybody else, and seems more immediately the cause of my paying income-tax, and having my friends killed with dysenteries and gun-shot wounds, and making my country unpopular, bragging, and servile, and everything that I do not wish it to be. I do think, too, that the risk was, and is, far more imminent and tremendous, of the subversion of all national independence, and all peaceful virtues, and mild and generous habits, by his insolent triumph, than by the success of the most absurd of those who are allied against him . . . . I prefer, upon the whole, a set of tyrants, if it must be so, that we can laugh at, and would rather mix contempt with my political dislike, than admiration or terror.[26]

In the autumn of 1815 Jeffrey crossed to the Continent and visited the battleground of Waterloo. The war was over, and he was grateful. But he found the paths of glory very melancholy. "Half of the ground is now ploughed up; and except the broken trees and burnt offices at Hugomont, there is nothing to mark the scene of so much havoc and desolation. The people are ploughing and reaping, and old men following their old occupations, in their old fields, as if 60,000 youths had not fallen to manure them within these six months. The tottering chimney tops are standing, the glass unbroken in the windows, the roads and paths all winding as before, the grass as green, and the trees as fresh, as if this fiery deluge of war had not rolled over the spot on which they are standing. I picked up a bit of cloth and a piece of a bridle."[27]

Jeffrey and the *Edinburgh Review* suffered losses of their own from the war. For many Englishmen the struggle with France had become a holy war — a jihad for God, King, and Country. In Scotland, the circle that surrounded Walter Scott had fused anti-French feeling with a new, romantic nationalism. Jeffrey tried to keep alive the memory of an older, Enlightenment tradition — "the full and ready intercourse which now connects all parts of the civilized world" — the spirit of those days before the deluge when Hume and Adam Smith were welcomed into French salons. He distrusted a swaggering John Bull. He knew that, at some time in the future, the French and British people would have to come to some rapprochement. But Jeffrey's position was unpopular: it lacked the proper passionate conviction. By war's end, both the *Edinburgh Review* and its editor had become objects of suspicion in the minds of many influential Britons.

Politics — Reform

In politics his views are clear;
Oppressions's sway we need not fear,
For Liberty — to Scotsmen dear —
*   Is sacred to Frank Jeffrey.*
*   — from "Hurrah! For Francis Jeffrey,"*
*   an election song of 1832*

Although Fox and Grey had worked for parliamentary reform in the late eighteenth century, the leading Whigs of Jeffrey's day were hardly democrats. It was the frequent practice of eighteenth-century Opposition to court public opinion in support of its attack upon ministers in power. The Whigs had some historical and philosophical excuse for this tactic. They considered themselves to be the custodians of the principles of 1688 — the protectors of the rights of the people and the opponents of usurping monarchy. But the public opinion that they courted and to which they were willing to defer was not that of town mobs or rural laborers. It was, to quote a Whig M.P., the opinion of "the intelligent class of the English public, those who from property, and from education and from place in society, are entitled to sway the opinion of the legislature."[1]

The late eighteenth- and early nineteenth-century Whigs inherited a potent mythology. They saw themselves as the party of landed property, of "Earl Grey of spotless character, followed by the Russells and the Cavendishes, by all the ancient nobility, and all the great property of the realm."[2] When such men condescended to hear public opinion, they did so with the attitude of Lord John Russell: " . . . if great changes accomplished by the people are dangerous, although sometime salutary, great changes accomplished by an aristocracy, at the desire of the people, are at once salutary and safe."[3] The Whigs looked upon themselves as men of enlightened public sympathy, the custodians of British liberty, giving direction and tone to a potentially disruptive and often misguided public opinion. Except for Samuel Whitbread, they turned a deaf ear to calls for parliamentary reform in the early nineteenth century. They listened, at last, because they realized that public sentiment was slipping out of their control.

It was also common practice for eighteenth-century Opposition to rally popular support by a call for economical reform. The Whigs of Jeffrey's day had a special interest in that cause. They believed that the abolition of unnecessary offices and sinecures would reduce the influence of the throne, an influence that the long war had increased. Significantly, it was their preoccupation with the power of the throne, rather than concern for the welfare of the people, that disposed them to press for economical reform. The Whigs, in fact, backed into the nineteenth century, their eyes fixed upon the great issues of 1688. It was only after 1815 that the party in any numbers recognized that economical reform must include tax reform, that such reform was necessary to relieve public distress and to forestall civil violence. But their efforts were hindered by the presence in their midst of Grenville and his followers. The wealth of the Grenville family was derived in part from offices and sinecures secured while Grenville was a member of Pitt's first administration, and the Grenville group was hostile to any plan that endangered their income. Grenville's own political mentality belonged wholly to the eighteenth century. More than any other man in Parliament, he hindered his party's reluctant and confused attempts to deal with the new social and political forces of the new century.

When Jeffrey wrote his 1793 essay on "Politics," those

forces had already begun to take alarming shape. Godwin's *Political Justice* was published in that year. The London Corresponding Society had been formed in the preceding year, and the second part of Paine's *Rights of Man* had appeared. The Corresponding Society held large open-air meetings in 1793-94, pressing for annual parliaments and universal suffrage. Thomas Hardy and Horne Tooke were brought to trial, and Dundas's Committee of Secrecy produced its first frightening *Report*. In this heady atmosphere Jeffrey's "Politics" discussed the problem of "the multitude": "The violence of the multitude is indeed to be dreaded, but it will not be violent unless it is uninformed. It is superfluous to add, that a people who are enlightened are likely to be in the same proportion contented; and that the diffusion of knowledge is yet more essential, perhaps, to their tranquillity, than it is to their freedom."[4] It was important, then, to give direction to the multitude — important for their tranquillity, important for their freedom. Paine would have objected that tranquillity and freedom are often, temporarily, very disparate goals. But after 1795 the multitude was reduced to silence, if not tranquillity, by less subtle influences than the instruction of enlightened Whigs. A reactionary panic had gripped the Pitt administration. Habeas corpus had been suspended; the Treasonable Practices and Seditious Meetings Bills of 1795 scattered the Corresponding Society; the Newspaper Act of 1798 choked the radical press.

When popular agitation revived in 1800, the cause was a severe bread shortage, and a series of bad harvests increased that agitation through the early years of the century. In 1802, in the *Review's* first issue, Jeffrey expressed the hope that Britons might soon recover from unthinking horror at the excesses of the French Revolution and "begin to study the *moral* of that great tragedy."[5] The moral was that violence ensues when government fails to ascertain or disregards the opinions of the people. The core of Jeffrey's mature political philosophy was his belief that "all political power, even the most despotic, rests at last, as was profoundly observed by Hume, upon Opinion."[6] Hume's observation is contained in his essay "Of the First Principles of Government." Jeffrey's sometimes contradictory statements on contemporary politics were his attempts to understand the implications of Hume's observation for nineteenth-century political society.

Jeffrey gave the problem lengthy exposition in his review of an argument for absolute monarchy, the *Essay on the Practice of the British Government* (1812) of Gould Francis Leckie. He began the review with a discussion of the historical evolution of hereditary monarchy, concluding that the chief advantage of such a monarchy consists in the insurance of orderly succession to the first place in the state. Granted, the monarchy must be given enough power to make it effectively the first place in the state and to discourage lesser officers from endangering the general peace by their contentions, "for, otherwise, the whole evils which its institution was meant to obviate would recur with accumulated force, and the same fatal competitions be renewed among persons of disorderly ambition, for those situations, by whatever name they might be called, in which, though nominally subordinate to the throne, the actual powers of the sovereignty were embodied." But the sovereign should be granted no powers beyond those which were clearly required for the public good. He should be granted no powers that were not subject to some efficient control. "It is in the reconciling of these two conditions that the whole difficulty of the theory of a perfect monarchy consists. If you do not control your sovereign, he will be in danger of becoming a despot; and if you do control him, there is danger, unless you choose the depository of this control with singular caution, that you create a power that is uncontrolled and uncontrollable — to be the prey of audacious leaders and outrageous factions, in spite of the hereditary settlement of the nominal sovereignty."[7]

To wisely choose the mechanics of this means of control, it was necessary to understand both the nature of the powers to be controlled and the methods of control that had been employed in the past. Whatever powers kings possess "must be powers conferred upon them by *the consent* of the stronger part of their subjects." The power of the sovereign in any age is only the power that a certain faction of his subjects chooses to lend in order that the sovereign's decisions might be put into practice. The ultimate check to the power of the throne has always been the refusal of that faction to act any longer as instruments of their sovereign's will. "The check, therefore, is substantially the same in kind, in all cases whatever; and must necessarily exist in full vigour in every country in the world, though the likelihood of its beneficial application depends greatly on the structure of society in each particular nation; and the possibility of applying it with safety must result wholly from the contrivances that have been adopted to make it bear at once gradually and steadily on the power it is destined to regulate. It is here accordingly, and here only, that there is any material difference between a good and a bad constitution of Monarchical government."[8]

What of "the structure of society" in different nations? Where does effective power of control rest in different stages of political development? "If every individual were equally gifted, and equally situated, the answer would be, In the numerical majority: But as this never can be the case, this power will frequently be found to reside in a very small proportion of the whole society." In the first stages of political development, power usually belongs to small bands of disciplined brigands. The king, their commander, reigns only through their consent and support. "The check upon the royal authority is the same in substance as in the best administered monarchies, viz. the refusal of the consent or cooperation of those who have the natural power of the community; but from the unfortunate structure of society, which vests this substantial power in a few bands of disciplined ruffians, the check will scarcely ever be interposed for the benefit of the nation, and will merely operate to prevent the king from doing any thing to the prejudice or oppression of the soldiery." In time, political power is assumed by a feudal aristocracy, and the check on royal authority comes to lie in their refusal to cooperate in measures that do not serve their interests. But it is only with the wide diffusion of wealth and education that a structure of society develops in which the interest of the body of the people can be effectively maintained:

when society has attained its full measure of civility and intelligence, and is filled from top to bottom with wealth and industry, and reflection; when every thing that is done or felt by any one class, is communicated in the instant to all the rest, — and a vast proportion of the whole population takes an interest in the fortunes of the country, and possesses a certain intelligence as to the public conduct of its rulers, — then the substantial power of the nation may be said to be vested in the nation at large; or at least in those individuals who can habitually command the good-will and support of the greater part of them; and the ultimate check to the power of the sovereign comes to consist in the general unwillingness of The People to comply with those orders which, if at all united in their resolution, they may securely disobey and resist.[9]

That development brought political theory to a contemporary question. How, in modern times, was the people's opinion to be effectively expressed to those in authority? "It is still of infinite importance to consider what provisions are made by the form of the government for the ready operation of those interests and inclinations upon the immediate agents of public authority. . . . The whole difference, indeed, between a good and a bad government, appears to us to consist in this particular, viz. in the greater or the less facility which it affords for the early, the gradual and steady operation of the substantial power of the community upon its constituted authorities." For a modern exemplum, the reader might study eighteenth-century France. It was partly a failure in communication that brought France to bloody revolution. "If there had been any provision in the structure of the government, by which the increasing power of the lower orders had been enabled to make itself distinctly felt, and to bear upon the constituted authorities as gradually as it was generated, the great calamity which has befallen that nation might have been entirely avoided."[10]

To Jeffrey's mind, the French experience revealed the central truth of political science — the necessity for communication between the officers of government and that body in which the effective power of the state resides. The chief distinction between a good and bad form of government consists in the degree to which it allows such communication. "The main end of government to be sure is, that wise laws should be enacted and enforced; but such is the condition of human infirmity, that the hazards of sanguinary contentions about the exercise of power is [*sic*] a much greater and more imminent evil than a considerable obstruction in the making or execution of the laws; and the best government therefore is, not that which promises to make the best laws . . . but that which guards best against the tremendous conflicts to which all administrations of government, and all exercise of political power is apt to give rise." Fortunately, the arrangements that most effectively ensure the peace of society are often those which provide for wise and efficient legislation. "But we do not hesitate to look upon their negative or preventive virtues as of a far higher cast than their positive and active ones; and to consider a representative legislature to be incomparably of more value when it truly represents the efficient force of the nation in controlling and directing the executive, than when it merely enacts wholesome statutes in its legislative capacity."[11]

And what of Britain? Jeffrey was content with hereditary monarchy. Society was thereby spared the chaos that accompanies the periodic struggles of individuals or factions for first place in the state. The mechanics of political control were his chief concern. In the early nineteenth century the efficient power of the British state resided "in the great body of the people, and especially among the more wealthy and intelligent in all the different ranks of which it consists." It was in the interest of the people that their opinion find a steady and orderly expression. What modern Britain needed was a parliament "which really and truly represents the sense and opinions — we mean the general and mature sense, not the occasional prejudices and fleeting passions — of the efficient body of the people, and which watches over and effectually controls every important act of the executive magistrate." Such a parliament was necessary for the peace of the country, necessary for the security of monarchy itself.[12]

Jeffrey stood within the mainstream of the Whig liberal tradition, but he believed that the function of parliamentary government was essentially a "negative or preventive" one. By giving orderly expression to public opinion, parliament safeguards the state against violent contentions between that public and the forces of the throne. Jeffrey was no egalitarian. His remarks on the power of the people had their oligarchic side. In modern societies substantial power rests with the people "or at least in those individuals who can habitually command the good-will and support of the greater part of them." Again, the power of the modern state resides "in the great body of the people, and especially among the more wealthy and intelligent in all the different ranks of which it consists." That was Whig writing. Jeffrey's problem — and the Whigs' problem — was adapting that political vision to the realities of the nineteenth-century British life.

Before 1808 there was nothing in Jeffrey's writings to alarm the moderate Whigs at Holland House. His political reviews were primarily concerned with works on the French Revolution and the European scene. He was obviously committed to the interest of "property," and he repeatedly described the dangers of violent social revolution. "The international law with regard to power, is . . . like the municipal law with regard to property. Its object is, not to establish a fantastic and irksome equality, like the Agrarian schemes of antiquity, but to protect and secure the irregularities to which fortune has given existence: to make wealth and poverty alike safe and independent; to defend the weak and the humble against the rapacity of their superiors; and to maintain legitimate power and authority against the combinations of discontented inferiors."[13] He believed it to be tragic that "notions of regulated freedom" could not satisfy the ardor of the French republicans.[14] The French Assembly should have been aware of "the most obvious and important lesson in the whole volume of history, that the nation which has recourse to arms for the settlement of its internal affairs, necessarily falls under the iron yoke of a military government in the end, and that nothing but the most evident necessity can justify the lovers of freedom in forcing it from the hands of their governors."[15] Jeffrey had himself found that lesson in the closing sentences of chapter 60 of Hume's *History of England*, a passage that he believed to be "deserving of the most profound meditation."[16]

John Clive has written of the occasional echoes of "Burke's veneration for established institutions" to be heard in the early numbers of the *Edinburgh Review*.[17] In Jeffrey's case the echoes were of Hume. Jeffrey attacked the innaccuracies and Stuart bias of Hume's *History of England*, but he considered Hume to be "the most profound and philosophical of historians," and he recommended to his readers "the great and eternal truths" to be found in passages of the *History*.[18] There are echoes of Hume's *Essays, Moral and Political* (1741-42) throughout Jeffrey's essays, published and unpublished, and in his private letters.[19] Unlike Hume, Jeffrey was involved in the day-to-day affairs of British politics. He attacked the existing social order when that order clearly hindered social progress. "It is among the worst consequences of a system of injustice and oppression," he argued against Catholic Disabilities, "that it in some measure justifies itself by communicating to its victims the vices which it imputes to them. Those who have been long objects of distrust will in the end, I fear, be not trustworthy . . . . Those who are ruled by force will soon require force to rule them."[20] But Jeffrey was, like Hume, a pragmatist, and pragmatists are wary of untested innovation. Just as he believed that individual moral judgments should be evaluated within the context of the experiential "common impressions of morality," so he believed that political wisdom is both cumulative and experiential. "Mr. Bentham must certainly be conscious that no one ever pretended that the mere antiquity of a law was a sufficient reason for retaining it in spite of its evident utility; but when the utility of parting with it is doubtful, its antiquity may fairly be urged as affording a presumption in its favour."[21]

Jeffrey's first detailed article on parliamentary reform was

his 1807 review of William Cobbett's *Political Register.*
Beginning as an ardent anti-Jacobin in the *Porcupine* (1800-
1801), Cobbett had undergone a striking metamorphosis. He
had by 1804 turned his *Register* into a voice of opposition to
all the machinery of political corruption — placement,
sinecures, and rotten boroughs. Through his association with
Francis Burdett and through his firsthand experience of
electoral corruption in the Honiton by-election of 1806, he
had been converted to the cause of radical parliamentary
reform. The Middlesex and Westminster contests of 1806 had
revealed that a vocal and disciplined public opinion was hostile
to both Whigs and Tories, and Cobbett's *Register* had helped
to shape that opinion. Reviewing the recent numbers of the
Register, Jeffrey concluded that "they are all obviously
intended to beget a distrust and contempt of every individual
connected with public life, except only Sir Francis Burdett
and his adherents, — to spread abroad a general discontent
and disrespect for the constitution, usages, principles, and
proceedings of Parliament, — to communicate a very exag-
gerated and unfair impression of the evils, abuses, and inconveniences, which arise from the present system of government,
— and to hold out the absolute impossibility of correcting or
amending these, without some great internal change, of the
nature of a political revolution."[22]

Jeffrey reduced Cobbett's argument for reform to a single
proposition: the evils of British politics could be traced to
the improper composition of the House of Commons, in
which members owe their places to the influence of great
families or to a junta of venal electors. Jeffrey admitted that
there was too much scrambling for place and emolument
both in and out of Parliament. He admitted that the nation
suffered from the scramble. But he denied that the evils of
public life were primarily produced by venal boroughs or by
Peers interfering in elections. Placemen, he believed, are
always with us, and their influence is more effectively contained in Parliament than in areas of influence that are not so
vulnerable to an aroused and enlightened public criticism.
The influence of great families in the election of members is
rather beneficial than injurious to public life,[23] and the sale

of boroughs, although dishonorable to those concerned, is not so widespread as to cripple the effective functioning of Parliament. Defects and irregularities exist, but many of them are inseparable from the practical machinery of representative government and are not susceptible to legislative remedy. Advantageous changes in the system of election might be made, "but these advantages . . . would be extremely inconsiderable compared with those which we at present enjoy; and certainly would not be worth purchasing at the price of any great discontent, or hazard to the general system." After all, the best legislature is that which reunites in itself the greatest proportion of the "effective aristocracy" — those individuals who actually shape the opinions of the people through their birth, wealth, or talents. In this way, the nation is governed by the same individuals who, even out of public office, would direct the majority opinion:

> Now, upon this footing alone, as it is evident that rank, fortune, and official situation, are among the most powerful of the means by which men are enabled individually to influence the opinions and conduct of those around them, so it follows that those qualifications should have their due share in returning members of the Legislature; and that the government could not otherwise be either stable or respectable. The real power of every country is vested in what we have called its effective aristocracy; and that country is the happiest, in which the aristocracy is most numerous and most diversified as to the sources of its influence; that government the most suitable, secure and beneficial, which is exercised most directly by the mediation of this aristocracy. In a country where rank, wealth and office, constitute the chief sources of influence over individuals, it is proper that rank, wealth and office, should make the greatest numbers of its legislators.[24]

Was Jeffrey as complacent as the general tone of these remarks suggests? Evidently not, for in apologizing to "the higher classes of our readers" for bestowing so much time and attention "on a writer of this description," he warned that the higher orders were unaware "either of the great influence which such a writer possesses, or of the extent to which many of his sentiments prevail among the middling classes of the community."[25] In fact, Jeffrey was sympathetic to the call for economic and electoral reform. But Cobbett called for immediate and radical reform. Convinced that politics was an experiential game, Jeffrey thought that precipitant and untested reforms were unwise. Cobbett's slashing and sarcastic indictments of both Whigs and Tories led the public to believe that their interests and opinions were ignored in Parliament. Jeffrey believed that the people's trust in Parliament was, in a modern society, an essential bulwark against civil violence. And so, in order to combat Cobbett's influence with "the middling classes of the community," Jeffrey drew a picture of British representative government in which, as his private letters of this period reveal, he himself did not wholeheartedly believe. In letters to Horner he complained that British politics was closed, as Cobbett claimed, to much of the best talent in the nation:

> I agree with you entirely in thinking that there is in the opulence, intelligence, and morality of our middling people a sufficient quarry of materials to make or to repair a free constitution; but the difficulty is in raising them to the surface. . . . The actual government of the country is carried on by something less, I take it, than 200 individuals, who are rather inclined to believe that they may do any thing they please, so long as the more stirring part of the community can be seduced by patronage, and the more contemplative by their love of ease and their dread of violence and innovation. . . . The antiquity of our government, to which we are indebted for so many advantages, brings this great compensating evil along with it; there is an oligarchy of great families — borough-mongers and intriguing adventurers — that monopolizes all public acitvity, and excludes the mass of ordinary men nearly as much as [do] the formal institutions of other countries. How can you hope to bring the virtues of the people to bear on the vices of the government, when the only way in which a patriot can approach to the scene of action is by purchasing a seat in Parliament?[26]

Fifteen months after the attack upon Cobbett, the *Review* published Jeffrey's and Brougham's review of Don Pedro Cevallos's *Exposition of the Practices and Machinations Which Led to the Usurpation of the Crown of Spain* (1808). The article was not so dizzying a volte-face as it appeared to some. Stating their belief that the Spanish popular revolt would fail, the reviewers allowed themselves to contemplate the effects of the struggle on the cause of civil liberty, "and we do so the rather, that a part of those good consequences are likely to ensue from the glorious efforts already made, although it should terminate unsuccessfully." The resistance to Napoleon had been begun and carried on by the Spanish people, a people whose king and aristocracy had betrayed them:

> The people, then, and, of the people, the middle, and, above all, the lower orders, have alone the merit of raising this glorious opposition to the common enemy of national independence. Those who had so little of what is commonly termed *interest* in the country, — those who had *no stake* in the community (to speak the technical language of the aristocracy,) — the persons of *no consideration* in the state, — they who could not pledge *their fortunes*, having only lives and liberties to lose, — the bulk — the mass of the people, — nay, the very odious, many-headed beast, the multitude — the mob itself — alone, uncalled, unaided by the higher classes . . . raised up the standard of insurrection, — bore it through massacre and through victory, until it chased the usurper away, and waved over his deserted courts. Happen what will in the sequel, here is a grand and permanent success, — a lesson to all governments, — a warning to all oligarchies, — a cheering example to every people.[27]

Supposing for a moment that the popular revolt succeeded, would the Spanish people allow the restoration of such a tyrannical and decadent monarchy as that which had once betrayed them? "That they should have a king, every one must admit, who believes that an hereditary monarch, well fettered by the constitution, is the best guardian of civil liberty." A king would be found — either Charles or Ferdinand or "a new stock" brought from Germany "for a breed." But the Spanish people would carry reform through all the departments of their state. That happy progress, once begun, would be met by the warm approbation of the English people. "And who then shall ever more presume to cry down popular rights, or tell us that the people have nothing to do with the laws, but to obey them, — with the taxes, but to pay them, — and with the blunders of their rulers, but to suffer from them? What man will now dare to brand his political adversary with the name of revolutionist, — or to hunt those down, as enemies of order, who expose the follies and corruptions of an unprincipled and intriguing administration? These tricks have had their day, — a day unmeasurably disastrous in its consequences to England and to Europe."[28]

It was possible, then, to anticipate a salutary change in English politics if the efforts of the Spanish people proved successful. The measures of the government would be more freely canvassed. The voice of the country would be no longer stifled. "Reforms in the administration of our affairs must be adopted, to prevent more violent changes; and some radical improvements in our constitution, will no longer be viewed with horror; because they will be found essential to the permanence of any reformation in the management of the national concerns." Even if the Spanish popular revolt should prove unsuccessful, "still enough has been performed by the Spanish people to raise the spirit of the middle and lower classes, both in this country and the rest of Europe." A feeling of power had been communicated to the people in every part of Europe, "and any such shameless aggressions as those which first raised up this feeling in Spain, will in all likelihood give rise to revolutionary movements elsewhere." In answer to "insinuations which have reached us . . . of [the *Review's*] coldness and unwillingness towards the cause of the patriots," the reviewers concluded their remarks in the rich and righteous cadences of Johnsonian prose:

We sincerely believe, that the success of that cause would

not only save the rest of the Continent from France, — from the enemy of both national independence and civil liberty, but would infallibly purify the internal constitution both of this and the other countries of Europe. Now, if any man thinks, that we should not extravagantly rejoice in any conceivable event which must reform the constitution of England, — by reducing the over-grown influence of the Crown, — by curbing the pretensions of the privileged orders, in so far as this can be effected without strengthening the Royal influence, — by raising up the power of real talents and worth, the true nobility of a country, — by exalting the mass of the community, and giving them, under the guidance of that virtual aristocracy, to direct the councils of England, according to the spirit, as well as the form of our invaluable constitution; — whoever believes, that an event, leading to such glorious consequences as these would not give us the most heartfelt joy, must have read but few of the pages of this Journal, or profited but little by what he has read.[29]

The fat was in the fire. "Had it appeared in a popular form in 1794 instead of in 1808," Arthur Aspinall believed, "little short of a miracle would have saved the author from the hands of the hangman and his head from reposing on Temple Bar."[30] Outrage was loud and unanimous among government supporters. The *Courier* called the *Review* "a quarterly Cobbett" and declared that "Thomas Paine never published any thing more seditious than the last No. of the Edinburgh Review."[31] A Tory M.P. labeled the reviewers "as absurd as Sir F. Burdett, and as blackguard as Cobbett."[32] "Mentor," in a pamphlet entitled *The Dangers of the Edinburgh Review*, charged the reviewers with "*infidelity* in Religion; *licentiousness* in Morals; and . . . *seditious and revolutionary principles* in Politicks."[33] Horner and Holland House were alarmed: "Are all the fruits of a long continuous study of politics, great opportunities of seeing both affairs and men very near at hand, and the best talents nature had to give, to be thrown away upon slashing declamations to suit a temporary purpose or give vent to the humour & fit of the day?"[34]

The rhetoric was certainly inflammatory for the *Edinburgh*

Review. But the Holland House circle might have recognized that, at the core of the article, in the quoted closing paragraph, the old Whig attitudes remained. The reforms advocated were, first of all, "reducing the over-grown influence of the Crown." The pretensions of the privileged orders were to be curbed, but only "in so far as this can be effected without strengthening the Royal influence." The mass of the community was to be exalted, but under the guidance of "the true nobility" of the country. To be sure, the true nobility were now men "of real talents and worth" rather than the "effective aristocracy" of the Cobbett article, of which "rank, wealth and office" formed the greatest part. But, in an editorial note following this passage, Jeffrey described the Whig leaders as "the only class of statesmen who have ever showed that great talents and acquirements are not incompatible with pure and virtuous principles."[35] If "real talents and worth" were to nominally replace "rank, wealth and office" in the *Review*'s pantheon, the shift in personnel would clearly not unseat many of the Whigs.

Jeffrey apologized to Horner and to Walter Scott for the rhetorical excesses of the Cevallos article. For a time Scott believed that Jeffrey was planning to resign from the *Review*. But there was nothing in the article that was inconsistent with the basic tenet of his political philosophy — his belief that the best form of government for a country in which real power lay in the opinion of the body of its citizens was a representative parliament that could steadily and effectively bring the power of that opinion to bear upon the officers and person of the Crown. Jeffrey had come out for reform because he realized that the disaffected opinion of the British people was *not* being effectively communicated to the administration then in power — that the Parliament, as then constituted, was *not* representative — and that, if public opinion was any longer denied an orderly avenue of influence, it would soon find other and more socially disruptive channels.

Jeffrey's public recognition of this situation may appear sudden and belated, but his private letters indicate his awareness, even while he castigated Cobbett, that all was not well with the country and Westminster. What brought that awareness into public print was probably the widespread agitation caused by revelations of corruption within the government and Royal Family. Colonel Wardle had exposed to the Commons and the nation the role of the Duke of York's mistress, Mrs. Clarke, in the sale of military commissions. The Duke's acquiescence in this business was clear. Public opinion condemned him, but the Commons did not. At the same time, Castlereagh's misuse of public funds in connection with the East India Writership was revealed. Again, the Commons failed to act on behalf of the people. Radical reformers like Cobbett and Burdett and more moderate voices like the *Independent Whig* joined in the same question — Was public opinion to have no effective voice in Parliament? In Westminster, an unruly public meeting was held to express thanks to Colonel Wardle, while the borough of Southwark called a public rally to demand of its representatives justification for their conduct and pledges of support for parliamentary reform. The cry for reform, electoral and economic, was growing stronger. But among the parliamentary Whigs, only Whitbread and his followers supported it.

The situation grew worse in 1809. "The present cry for reform," wrote the *Morning Chronicle* in April, "comes from the most respectable part of the elective Body of the United Kingdom."[36] The ranks of Westminster reformers were joined by a number of influential men from the London City Council. Later in the year, news of the Walcheren disaster[37] further undermined public confidence in the foreign policy of the Portland administration, and the economic distress caused in some quarters by the long war supplied even more threatening domestic support for the radical Burdett. By the fall of 1809 Jeffrey was genuinely alarmed, not only by the increase in popular discontent, but also by the Whigs' insensitivity and incapacity to deal with it. He wrote a series of letters to Horner and Allen in the fall and winter, attempting to bring some pressure to bear upon the party:

> In the first place, you admit now that *there is* a spirit of discontent . . . among the people, which must be managed and allayed, in some way or other, if we wish to preserve

tranquility. And, in the next place, you admit that the leading Whigs belong to the aristocracy, and have been obliged to govern themselves a great deal by the necessity of managing this aristocracy. Now, all I say is, that there is a radical contest and growing struggle between the aristocracy and the democracy of this country; and agreeing entirely with you, that its freedom must depend in a good measure on their coalition, I still think that the aristocracy is the weakest, and ought to give way, and that the blame of the catastrophe will be heaviest on those who provoke a rupture by maintaining its pretensions. . . . The people are both stronger, and wiser, and more discontented than those who are not the people will believe. Let the true friends of liberty and the constitution join with the people, assist them to ask, with dignity and with order, all that ought to be granted, and endeavour to withhold them from asking more.[38]

What Jeffrey was proposing was a tactic, a maneuver that might enable the Whigs to regain a moderating influence over public opinion. "You must lay aside a great part of your aristocratical feelings, and side with the most respectable and sane of the democrats; by so doing, you will enlighten and restrain them."[39] He repeated this advice in an article that appeared in the January 1810 number of the *Edinburgh Review*. His aim in that article, more clearly than in any theretofore, was the education of his own party. He was no longer trying to mollify the middle class by attacks upon Cobbett. He was careful to avoid the offending rhetoric of the Cevallos article, but he purposely drew a picture of impending crisis in the darkest tones.[40] At the same time, he described the Whigs in terms that might flatter them into acquiescence with his proposed strategy. There was, he argued, only one way in which the impending conflict between courtiers and democrats might be avoided. The "friends of liberty and of order — the old constitutional Whigs of England — " must "unbend from their cold and repulsive neutrality, and . . . join themselves to the more respectable members of the party to which they have the greatest affinity; and thus, by the weight of their character, and the force of their talents, to temper its violence and moderate its excesses, till it can be guided in safety to the defence, and not to the destruction of our liberties." If the Whig leaders remained aloof from the popular party — "if they do not save them from the leaders they are already choosing in their own body, and become themselves their leaders, by becoming their patrons, and their cordial, though authoritative advisers; — they will in no long time sweep away the Constitution itself, the Monarchy of England, and the Whig aristocracy, by which that Monarchy is controlled and confirmed, and exalted above all other forms of polity."[41]

If there should be a popular revolt, Jeffrey wrote, its triumph would be almost certain. But that triumph would itself be the ruin of English liberty, peace, and prosperity:

Those who have merely lived in our times, must have seen, and they who have read of other times, or reflected on what Man is at all times, must know . . . how much *chance*, and how much *time*, must concur with genius and patriotism to form a good or a stable government. . . . The stability of the English Constitution depends upon its monarchy and aristocracy; and their stability, again, depends very much on the circumstance of their having grown naturally out of the frame of society — upon their having struck their roots deep through every stratum of the political soil, and having been moulded and impressed, during a long course of ages, by the usages, institutions, habits and affections of the community. A popular revolution would overthrow the monarchy and the aristocracy; and, even if it were not true that revolution propagates revolution, as waves give rise to waves, till the agitation is stopped by the iron boundary of despotism, it would still require ages of anxious discomfort, before we could build up again that magnificent fabric, which now requires purification rather than repair.

If revolution were to be avoided, it could be avoided only through the wise public conduct of the Whigs — "men who, without forgetting that all government is from the people, and for the people, are satisfied that the rights and liberties of the people are best maintained by a regulated hereditary monarchy, and a large, open aristocracy; and who are as much averse, therefore, from every attempt to undermine the Throne, or to discredit the nobles, as they are indignant at every project to insult or enslave the people."[42]

Having flattered the collective Whig ego, Jeffrey confronted his party with a program of reform. In the area of economic retrenchment, let sinecures be abolished and all expenditure be closely watched. When compared with the total sum of necessary expenditure, such retrenchments as were practically possible might appear to Whig leaders to be insignificant. "But, at the same time, it is of infinite importance that they should be adopted; — both because they cut off one source of almost avowed corruption — and because they remove a most provoking and invidious spectacle from the eyes of a suffering and indignant people." On the question of ministerial responsibility, some arrangement must be made to insure the punishment of guilty ministers. Repeatedly the British people had heard delinquent ministers attacked by parliamentary opponents, only to see those ministers, when temporarily removed from office, resume place and retain power in the Parliament. The moral of such musical chairs was not lost on the people. They "are naturally apt to conclude, or at least are easily taught to believe, that neither party have any real concern for the wrongs of the country; that the whole object of the accusers is to get into the place of the delinquent . . . and thus the character of all public men is vilified and degraded, and an universal distrust or despair of public virtue is propagated through the whole mass of the people."[43]

On the central question of reform in parliamentary representation, Jeffrey argued that the Whigs must bend or break. "Though we can neither approve of *such* a reform as some very popular persons [Burdett and Cobbett] have suggested, nor bring ourselves to believe that any reform would accomplish the objects that seem to be in the view of its most zealous advocates," some reform must be encouraged. The reason for supporting reform at that moment was clear and overpowering — "the people are zealous for its adoption, and are entitled to this gratification at the hands of their representatives." Regarding the supposed danger of yielding to the demands of the people, "we can only say, that we are much more strongly impressed with the danger of thwarting them." The English people were possessed of more wealth and intelligence than at any previous time in English history, "and therefore they ought to have, and they must have, more political power." The real danger lay not in yielding to this social change but in attempting to resist it:

> We, in short, are for the monarchy and the aristocracy of England, as the only sure supports of a permanent and regulated freedom; but we do not see how either is now to be preserved, except by surrounding them with the affection of the people. The admirers of arbitrary power, blind to the great lesson which all Europe now holds out to them, have attempted to dispense with this protection; and the demagogues have taken advantage of their folly to excite the people to withdraw it altogether. The friends of the constitution must now bring it back; and must reconcile the people to the old monarchy and the old Parliament of their land, by restraining the prerogative within its legitimate bounds, and by bringing back Parliament to its natural habits of sympathy and concord with its constituents.[44]

Thus, through threats and flattery, Jeffrey tried to nudge the Whigs into the nineteenth century. On one level, his theme and rhetoric were traditionally Whig — a development of the Whigs' traditional appeal to public opinion in support of their opposition to the throne. But Jeffrey realized that monarchical encroachment was a secondary danger.[45] The immediate nineteenth-century concern was widespread public discontent and loss of faith in all politicians. Although he justified his call for reform by citing the increasing wealth and intelligence among the people, the "chief and over-powering reason" for its adoption was that "the people are zealous for its adoption." There is none of Paine's republican enthusiasm or of Godwin's utopian optimism to be found in Jeffrey's politics. Studying the lesson of the French experience and the growth of democratic forces in his own country, he had concluded that some reform was a practical necessity. "Reforms in the administration of our affairs must be adopted, to prevent more violent changes."

Something like the alliance he advised was attempted when Whitbread, Creevey, and their followers among the Whigs made cautious overtures to Burdett, Cartwright, and the Westminster reformers. In May of 1810, four months after the publication of Jeffrey's article, Thomas Brand moved in the Commons the first comprehensive Whig plan for parliamentary reform to be heard since 1797. But all this came to grief. The mob violence following Burdett's arrest in April caused a new wave of conservative reaction in Parliament. Many moderate members, fearful that a censure of ministers at that moment would encourage the extremists, voted to dismiss the censure motion in the Walcheren inquiry. Cobbett was imprisoned, and the abiding Whig aversion to radical reformers was expressed in Grey's speech of June 1810: "The path they are treading is dangerous in the extreme, and demands the most vigilant caution to prevent it from leading to a fatal termination. Whenever this great question shall be taken up by the people of this country seriously and affectionately, — (for, notwithstanding all we everyday hear, I doubt much whether there exists a very general disposition in favour of this measure,) there will then be a fair prospect of accomplishing it, in a manner consistent with the security of the constitution."[46]

With the defeat of Brand's second reform measure in 1812, the parliamentary Whigs dropped reform altogether, and the question was not raised again in the Commons until 1817. The reform cause itself was not dead. Economic distress kept the issue very much alive outside of Parliament, but neither the Liverpool administration nor Opposition would support it. Brand was silent; Whitbread dissipated his energy and influence in the cause of the Princess of Wales; Brougham's evolution as an effective influence on the Whigs had only begun. And Jeffrey, tiring of his role as Whig Cassandra, gradually withdrew from the arena of political journalism. As a result of changes in the Scottish legal system, his career as an advocate consumed more time and attention. In the *Review* he began to concentrate upon imaginative and travel literature. When he wrote on political subjects, he generally confined himself to reviews of works on European politics, repeatedly citing "the moral" of the French Revolution and the wisdom of Hume's *History*.

But he could not sever his political connections. When the war ended Scottish politics revived, and Jeffrey's aid was sought by advocates of various reforms. In 1816 he chaired a meeting called in opposition to the income tax. In 1817 he defended the Scottish reformers, Maclaren and Baird, against charges of sedition. He was now the proprietor of Craigcrook, a country estate to the northwest of Edinburgh, and Craigcrook soon rivaled Scott's Abbotsford as a retreat for men of politics and letters. Walking on the lawns or lingering over dinner in Tusculan disputes, the company at Craigcrook pressed Jeffrey to take a place of leadership among the Scottish Whigs. "Seeing the course that the current was taking, and the certainty of its being at last irresistible," wrote Cockburn, who was working closely with him, "he thought the slowness of its motion, which gave more time for knowledge, no misfortune; and therefore seldom originated active proceedings. But, so as his uniform recommendation of uniting reasonableness of object with temperance of means, was acceded to, he never shrank from coming forward when required; and, consequently, was always in the van."[47]

If Jeffrey continued to lend himself to the cause of political reform, he did so from a genuine concern for civil liberties and from a no-less-genuine fear that other, more radical reformers might take his place. Writing of Madame de Staël in 1818, he admitted that he could only envy "that sanguine and buoyant temper of mind which, after all she has seen and suffered, still leads her to overrate, in our apprehension, both the merit of past attempts at political amelioration, and the chances of their success hereafter."[48] In his private letters he was voicing the fear that would grow upon him until his death: "It is very plain to me," he wrote to Charles Wilkes, an American, "that the French revolution, or rather perhaps the continued operation of the causes which produced that revolution, has laid the foundations, over all Europe, of an inextinguishable and fatal struggle between popular rights and ancient establishments — between democracy and tyranny — between legitimacy and representative government, which may involve the world in sanguinary conflicts for fifty years, and *may* also end, after all, in the establishment of a brutal and military despotism."[49] In the *Review* he argued that liberal Britons must cultivate more friendly and less condescending relations with the new American republic, "a condition upon which I cannot help thinking that not only our own freedom and prosperity, but that of the better part of the world, will ultimately be found to be more and more dependent."[50]

In 1829, upon election as Dean of the Scottish Faculty of Advocates, Jeffrey retired from the *Edinburgh Review*. When the Whigs returned to power in 1830, he was elected to Parliament and appointed Lord Advocate of Scotland, assuming a leading role in the passage of the First Reform Bill.[51] "To the question, therefore, of What are the actual evils of the present system, and what the actual benefits you expect from its reform," he told the Commons, "I now answer, boldly, that the evil is the grievous discontent, gradually passing into disaffection, which it produces in those who suffer from it, and that the inestimable benefit to be derived from its reformation, is the cure of that discontent — the redemption of great bodies of meritorious citizens from the hazard of being seduced into fatal disorders and excesses."[52] The Bill passed, but Jeffrey's experience at Westminster evoked no paeans for the British parliamentary system. The radical members grew more outrageous as the session drew to its close, "in order, I suppose, that they may go to their constituents with the sweet savour of these offences fresh upon them, to counteract any odour of reason or moderation they may have contracted in other parts of their course."[53] He watched his own Scottish Burgh Committee "chatter, and wrangle, and contradict, and grow angry, and read letters and extracts from blockheads of town-clerks, and little fierce agitators; and . . . go on speculating, and suggesting, and debating, more loosely, crudely, and interminably, than a parcel of college youths in the first novitiate of disceptation."[54] In forestalling a revolution of despair, the First Reform Bill had produced a revolution of rising expectations. Jeffrey was instrumental in guiding that Bill through the Commons and the Lords. But the subsequent call for immediate and widespread restructuring of British institutions fell upon his ears with all the accents of doctrinaire enthusiasm. "What intense apes our provincial censors, and thorough, simple, sweeping reformers are!"[55]

A writer in the *Oxford History of English Literature* has dismissed Jeffrey as "a born reformer."[56] Jeffrey's mentality was more complex and interesting than that. He entered public life with certain influences strong upon him: the Enlightenment attack upon irrational social prejudice; the belief shared by the majority of eighteenth-century Scottish thinkers that the rise of the modern capitalist system encouraged the progress of civil liberty; the tendency of parliamentary Whigs to appeal to popular opinion for support in their opposition to the power of the throne. To the extent that these influences worked upon him, Jeffrey was a liberalizing and reforming force in British life. But other factors influenced his thinking. There was, first and funda- mental, his early conviction that human life is essentially a difficult affair, that suffering of some order is inescapable, and that a measure of contentment can be won only through the discipline of personal desires. "There are evils, in every human lot, for which Governments are no way responsible, and for which laws can provide no effectual remedy."[57] As the effects of the industrial revolution upon the lower classes became evident, Jeffrey came to doubt the benefits of the new capitalist order. He never doubted that an increase of wealth and education among the middle class was essential to the growth of civil liberties, but he recognized by 1813 that middle-class education and independence were won at the cost of sordid and suffering labor among a large part of the population.

Finally, he recognized that the French Revolution — "or rather perhaps the continued operation of the causes which produced that revolution" — had fundamentally affected the dynamics of British and European politics. "The people *has* increased in consequence, in power, and in political importance. Over all Europe, we verily believe, that they are everywhere growing too strong for their governments; and that, if these governments are to be preserved, *some* measures must be taken to accommodate them to this great change in the condition and interior structure of society."[58] Mindful of "what Man is at all times," Jeffrey wrote without millennial or egalitarian enthusiasm. He fought for reform in the hope that Britain might be spared civil violence. In 1848, two years before his death, the new outbreak of Continental revolutions provided fresh proof of the wisdom of that principle which he had followed through the maze of early nineteenth-century politics. "It strikes me," he wrote at the conclusion of a long letter to his son-in-law, "that this furious outbreak is truly to be traced to the want of that very electoral reform which its authors were so unwisely baffled in seeking by other means — it being but one more example of the general truth, that in all intelligent communities, public opinion, if refused its legitimate vents, will burst its way through the close system of the government; but here, luckily for you, is dinner."[59]

Aesthetics and Literary History

*Is there any thing that can be called a standard
of Taste, by appealing to which we may distinguish between a good and a bad Taste? Or,
is there in truth no such distinction; and are
we to hold that, according to the proverb,
there is no disputing of Tastes; but that whatever pleases is right, for that reason that it
does please? This is the question, and a very
nice and subtile one it is, which we are now to
discuss.*

— *Hugh Blair,* Lectures on Rheroric
and Belles Lettres *(1783)*

When eighteenth-century Scottish literati turned to questions of aesthetics, they employed the same inductive,
empirical method that shaped their studies of the mind and
moral sentiments. Kames's "plan," as he explained it in the
Introduction to his *Elements of Criticism,* was "to ascend
gradually to principles, from facts and experiments; instead
of beginning with the former, handled abstractedly, and
descending to the latter."[1] "The rules of Criticism," Blair
noted, ". . . are not formed by a train of abstract reasoning,
independent of facts and observations. Criticism is an art
founded wholly on experience."[2] This methodology effected
a significant change in eighteenth-century Scottish literary
culture.[3] In a manner analogous to their rejection of a priori

reasoning in questions on the moral sentiments, the Scottish writers rejected the formal study of rhetorical rules for a comparative study of belles lettres. "It is evident," wrote Hume, "that none of the rules of composition are fixed by reasonings *a priori,* or can be esteemed abstract conclusions of the understanding, from comparing those habitudes and relations of ideas, which are eternal and immutable. Their foundation is the same with that of all the practical sciences, experience; nor are they any thing but general observations, concerning what has been universally found to please in all countries and in all ages."[4] The attempt to establish rules without regard to practice, Adam Smith complained, had produced the endless divisions and subdivisions of ancient and modern rhetorical systems. "They are generally a very silly set of books and not at all instructive."[5] "Taste and Judgment joined together are above all rules whatever," Reid advised his students at Aberdeen. "A man will be more profited and succeed better by endeavouring to copy exactly the most eminent and noble examples, than by paying the strictest attention to any rules."[6]

The Scottish aestheticians acknowledged the wide diversity of taste apparent among men, and they recognized that taste is partly shaped by national character and "custom." But they were certain that a common standard of taste could be discovered. It was necessary to accumulate sufficient data, to read widely, but a wide and sympathetic study of belles lettres was certain to discover certain literary qualities that please all men in all ages. Their confidence in this approach arose from their dual conviction that men share a common nature and that men instinctively appeal to the standard of that common nature to justify individual moral and aesthetic judgments. "This conviction of a common nature or standard and of its perfection," Kames argued, "accounts clearly for that remarkable conception we have, of a right and a wrong sense or taste in morals. It accounts not less clearly for the conception we have of a right and a wrong sense or taste in the fine arts. A man who, avoiding objects generally agreeable, delights in objects generally disagreeable, is condemned as a monster: we disapprove his taste as bad or wrong, because we have a clear conception that he deviates from the common standard."[7] Hutcheson, Kames, Smith, Blair, and Alexander Gerard were thus able to develop variations of a common-sense aesthetic, based upon those qualities of "Uniformity amidst Variety" or "propriety" or "utility" which please all men.[8] "What pleases universally," wrote Blair, "must on that account be held to be truly beautiful; and . . . no rules or conclusions concerning objects of Taste, can have any just authority, if they be found to contradict the general sentiments of men."[9]

This methodology was compromised, however, by the teleological assumptions that influenced Scottish thinking on epistemology and morals. Kames, Smith, Blair, and Hutcheson maintained that men feel pleasure in perceiving regularity or propriety or utility because it is an essential instinct of human nature to so respond to those qualities. And human nature is so constituted that men might attempt to realize those qualities in their own conduct or better understand the universe in which they live, thus acting in accordance with the wise design of a benevolent Creator.[10] In Scotland as in England, the empirical approach to aesthetic problems usually involved associationist psychology. But the Scots were somewhat cautious in their use of that psychology because their aesthetic and moral philosophies were so closely allied. Through his *Inquiry into the Original of Our Ideas of Beauty and Virtue* (1725), Hutcheson had introduced into Scottish aesthetics Shaftesbury's concept of man's intuitive response to moral and aesthetic qualities. The influence of this near-synthesis of ethics and aesthetics was profound upon Beattie, Kames, and Blair. They cited feeling as the basic agent in aesthetic response, and Adam Smith effectively combined moral and aesthetic responses in his concept of "sympathy." These men were willing to use associationist psychology to the extent that it aided them in discovering objective and universal standards of aesthetic common sense. But the relativistic implications of associationist aesthetics were recognized as dangerous when the line between morals and aesthetics was so dimly defined. If *de gustibus non est disputandum*, Kames warned, it must follow that "there is

not such a thing as a *good* or a *bad,* a *right* or a *wrong;* that
every man's taste is to himself an ultimate standard without
appeal; and consequently that there is no ground of censure
against any one, if such a one there be, who prefers Black-
more before Homer, selfishness before benevolence, or
cowardice before magnanimity."[11]

Hume's position was, predictably, somewhat different.
Although he believed that men share basic appetites and
emotions, he refused to explain men's moral sentiments or
aesthetic responses in terms of the designs of a benevolent
Creator. Free of teleological commitments, he could un-
reservedly admit that men's notions of "beauty" and
"deformity," like their notions of virtue and vice, develop
from subjective responses. But Hume stopped short when
faced with logical conclusion of his subjectivist aesthetic —
the conclusion that one man's taste is as good as another's.
Although we differ among ourselves in our subjective associational responses, we can agree, Hume argued, that a certain
type of man is the best judge of beauty. These men are the
great critics, men of impartial and experienced judgment, and
a standard of taste can be developed by analyzing those
works which such critics agree in admiring.[12] Perhaps sensing
the difficulties involved in this argument, Hume added an
appeal to the test of time — "the durable admiration, which
attends those works, that have survived all the caprices of
mode and fashion, all the mistakes of ignorance and envy."[13]
Hume might have worked out a detailed associationist
aesthetic if he had been willing to give the subject more
attention. But that task was left till the end of the century,
when a Scottish Episcopalian clergyman named Archibald
Alison published *Essays on the Nature and Principles of Taste*
(1790).

Jeffrey came to know Alison through the meetings of the
Edinburgh Friday Club, a group that included Walter Scott,
Henry Mackenzie, and Dugald Stewart. If Alison and Jeffrey
discussed aesthetics there, conversation must have come
easily. Jeffrey had been applying associationist psychology
to aesthetic questions since undergraduate days.[14] In his
general indictment of the "philosophy of mind," he had

singled out investigations of the workings of association as the only significant contribution of formal eighteenth-century epistemology.[15]   In his writings on the moral sentiments, he had acknowledged the subjective, associational basis of men's notions of virtue and vice. Like Hume, Jeffrey was free of teleological commitments, and his own pragmatic thinking on the moral sentiments was not threatened by the relativistic implications of associationist psychology.

Thus, Jeffrey could appreciate the achievement of Alison, who had developed an associationist aesthetic to logical subjectivist conclusions.[16] It was Alison's thesis that the aesthetic emotions that men experience in contemplating works of nature or of art are not directly produced by any quality intrinsic in the work being contemplated. The complex aesthetic emotions are produced through the imaginative recollection or conception of other objects or experiences, objects and experiences that are associated in men's minds with the work being contemplated. These emotional associations are suggested by some quality in nature or in art, but the works of nature or of art are not beautiful or sublime in themselves. A mountain storm, a landscape by Lorrain, a passage from Handel or from Milton — all are beautiful or sublime only in the sense that they trigger the associative imagination of man and produce those peculiar, complex emotions that we call *aesthetic*.[17]

When a second edition of the *Essays* appeared in 1810, Jeffrey gave the work a detailed and enthusiastic review. "It is the opinion of this excellent writer, to express it in one sentence, — that the emotions which we experience from the contemplation of sublimity or beauty, are not produced by any physical or intrinsic quality in the objects which we contemplate; but by the recollection or conception of *other* objects which are associated in our imaginations with those before us . . . and which are interesting or affecting, on the common and familiar principle of being the natural objects of love, or of pity, or of fear or veneration." Thus, the seasons of spring and autumn, the hours of the morning and the evening, suggest the beginning and the end of human life. The sound of thunder suggests that danger and uncontrolled power which are the natural objects of fear and awe. An English landscape — "green meadows with fat cattle" — "humble antique church, with churchyard elms, and crossing hedge-rows" — produces pleasure through its association with human comfort and simplicity. By Alison's theory, "all objects are beautiful or sublime which signify or suggest to us some simple emotion of love, pity, terror, or any other social or selfish affection of our nature; and . . . the beauty or sublimity which we ascribe to them, consists entirely in the power which they have acquired, by association or otherwise, of reminding us of the proper objects ["the feelings or condition of sentient beings"] of these familiar affections."[18]

Jeffrey recognized problems in Alison's approach. Certain combinations of sounds and of colors, for example, seem to appeal directly to our senses, without the agency of associative imagination.[19] Although Alison contended that aesthetic pleasure can be distinguished from "every other pleasure of our nature,"[20] the sympathetic emotions evoked by certain passages of poetry are difficult to distinguish from the direct every-day emotions of tenderness and pity. The pleasures of a poem like Keats's *Endymion* could be explained through Alison's theory of imagination, but the pleasures of a poem like Crabbe's *Tales* involved the sympathetic imagination described by Smith and Hume. Admitting these problems, Jeffrey still believed that Alison's theory allowed a more comprehensive explanation of the diversity of men's aesthetic responses than any theory had allowed theretofore. The *Essays* might serve, he believed, as a resolution to many of the arguments in British eighteenth-century aesthetics. Where Burke and Hogarth had singled out certain physical qualities as the bases of sublimity or beauty, other aestheticians had cited the perception of utility. Their common error lay not in citing these as sources of sublimity or beauty but in holding that there are no other sources. They had attempted to identify beauty or sublimity with one quality of the object contemplated or with one associative response.

Is it not notorious, on the contrary, that there are almost as many kinds of beauty as there are varieties of mental emotion; that some are melancholy, and some cheerful, — some humble and simple, and others commanding and magnificent; — and that we are moved accordingly, by the contemplation of all those varied species, either to pensive tenderness, — to love, pity and regret, — or to gay and airy imaginations, — or to still and tranquil thought, — or to admiration, humility and awe? But if it be true, that the emotions which we receive from beauty are thus various in themselves, and that they partake thus largely of the character of other emotions, why should we not conclude, that they are but modifications of these more familiar affections, — and that the beauty which we impute to external objects, is nothing more than their power of reflecting these several inward affections?[21]

Jeffrey thought that Alison's theory had established "the substantial identity" of those hallowed eighteenth-century categories, the Beautiful, the Sublime, and the Picturesque. If most works of nature or of art affect us in the same associative manner, those categories have meaning only as they serve to distinguish the different emotions men can feel. And Alison's theory, if generally adopted, might put an end to the long dispute about the standard of taste. "If things are not beautiful in themselves, but only as they serve to suggest interesting conceptions to the mind, then every thing which does in point of fact suggest such a conception to any individual, *is beautiful* to that individual; and it is not only quite true that there is no room for disputing about tastes, but that all tastes are equally just and correct, in so far as each individual speaks only of his own emotions." To be sure, a man with warm affections, active imagination, and habits of attentive observation will be more deeply and more often moved by art and nature. But insofar as a sense of beauty is regarded as merely a source of individual enjoyment, "the only cultivation that taste should ever receive, with a view to the gratification of the individual, should be through the indirect channel of cultivating the affections and powers of observation."[22]

Then who needs critics? If, after all, there is no disputing about taste, how could Jeffrey hold forth as the champion of Crabbe and the nemesis of Wordsworth? "All tastes," he argued, ". . . are equally just and true, in so far as concerns the individual whose taste is in question; and what a man feels distinctly to be beautiful, *is beautiful* to him, whatever other people may think of it. . . . If we aspire, however, to be *creators*, as well as observors of beauty, and place any part of our happiness in ministering to the gratification of others — as artists, or poets, or authors of any sort — then, indeed, a new distinction of tastes, and a far more laborious system of cultivation, will be necessary." This new distinction of tastes involves the recognition of different types of associative relationships. There are certain universal relationships between inward feelings and external objects "where the object is necessarily and universally connected with the feeling by the law of nature." The Elizabethan and Jacobean dramatists had richly used these universal relationships. In the process they had created a body of dramatic poetry that was unmatched by the drama of any other age or nation. "Their illustrations and figures of speech, are more borrowed from rural life, and from the simple occupations, or universal feelings of mankind. They are not confined to a certain range of dignified expressions, nor restricted to a particular assortment of imagery, beyond which it is not lawful to look for embellishments. Let any one compare the prodigious variety, and wide-ranging freedom of Shakespeare, with the narrow round of flames, tempests, treasons, victims, and tyrants, that scantily adorn the sententious pomp of the French drama, and he will not fail to recognise the vast superiority of the former, in the excitement of the imagination, and all the diversities of poetical delight." True, Shakespeare would have done well to blot a thousand lines. But the man remained a wonder: ". . . that indestructible love of flowers and odours, and dews and clear waters — and soft airs and sounds, and bright skies, and woodland solitudes, and moonlight bowers, which are the material elements of Poetry — and that fine sense of their undefinable relation to mental emotion, which is its essence and vivifying soul."[23]

There are, then, associative relationships that are felt by all men, "where the object is necessarily and universally connected with the feeling by the law of nature." There are also accidental relationships, where "this perception of beauty is not universal, but entirely dependent upon the opportunities which each individual has had to associate ideas of emotion with the object to which it is ascribed; — the same thing appearing beautiful to those who have been exposed to the influence of such associations, and indifferent to those who have not." These accidental associations affect the tastes of individuals and of entire social classes. An individual may find beauty in his childhood home, in the type of feminine expression with which he was first enamored, in the form of verse that first gave him pleasure. The study of classical culture had shaped the taste of Europe's upper class, and associations thus developed lent a charm to the remains of classical antiquity that men who were not so schooled could not always feel. The comfortable German burghers who bought books at the Frankfurt Fair found nothing so enchanting as a novelist's description of the cooking, eating, and drinking that were the chief delights of their circumscribed lives. The Highland Scots actually enjoyed bagpipes.[24]

Jeffrey believed that it was part of the critic's function to distinguish between these universal and accidental associations, because the artist is not, or should not be, a man who "speaks only of his own emotions":

A man who pursues only his own delight, will be as much charmed with objects that suggest powerful emotions, in consequence of personal and accidental associations, as with those that introduce similar emotions by means of associations that are universal and indestructible. . . . But if he conceive the ambition of creating beauties for the admiration of others, he must be cautious to employ only such objects as are the *natural* signs and *inseparable* concomitants of emotions, of which the greater part of mankind are susceptible; and his taste will *then* deserve to be called bad and false, if he obtrude upon the public, as beautiful, objects that are not likely to be associated in common minds with any interesting impressions.

An artist, like any other man, will necessarily be moved by

personal and accidental associations. "For those who make no demands on public admiration, however, it is hard to be obliged to sacrifice this source of enjoyment; and, even for those who labour for applause, the wisest course, perhaps, if it were only practicable, would be, to have two tastes, — one to enjoy, and one to work by, — one founded upon universal associations, according to which they finished those performances for which they challenged universal praise, — and another guided by all casual and individual associations, through which they looked fondly upon nature, and upon the objects of their secret admiration."[25]

This was Jeffrey's standard of aesthetic common sense, the standard by which he judged contemporary poetry and prose fiction, and it was consistent with the standard of moral common sense to which he appealed in his writings on the moral sentiments. If men's individual notions of virtue and vice develop from subjective, associational assessments of the pleasure or pain involved with any attitude of mind or course of conduct, there are "common impressions of morality" that can still serve erring mortals as a pragmatic moral standard. If individual notions of beauty are based upon subjective, associational responses, there are common associational relationships that can serve the artist and the critic as a practical aesthetic standard. Thus, out of the nettle of subjectivism did Jeffrey pluck the flower of a public standard. All private tastes may be "equally just and correct." But the man who aspires to provide pleasure for others "must be cautious to employ only such objects as are the *natural* signs and *inseparable* concomitants of emotions, of which the greater part of mankind are susceptible."

In 1816 Jeffrey mused over Walter Scott's edition of and commentary on *The Works of Jonathan Swift* (1814). It was published by Constable, who also published the *Review*, and Constable had made an unusual request that Jeffrey give the book public notice. Jeffrey was willing because the subject was intriguing. Scott on Swift — the present on the past. It moved Jeffrey to reflection:

> By far the most considerable change which has taken place in the world of letters, in our own days, is that by which the wits of Queen Anne's time have been gradually brought down from the supremacy which they had enjoyed, without competition, for the better part of a century. When we were at our studies, some twenty-five years ago, we can perfectly remember that every young man was set to read Pope, Swift, and Addison, as regularly as Virgil, Cicero, and Horace. All who had any tincture of letters were familiar with their writings and their history; allusions to them abounded in all popular discourses and all ambitious conversation; and they and their contemporaries were universally acknowledged as our great models of excellence, and placed without challenge at the head of our national literature.[26]

Jeffrey thought that the subordination of the Queen Anne wits could be justified, and his discussion of their failings led him into a sketch of English literary history, a task he had begun in an earlier review of Jacobean drama.[27] These histories are of interest to anyone concerned with the literary attitudes of the early nineteenth century. In them Jeffrey moved from abstract considerations of the duties of "the artist" to a discussion of the problems of English writers in specific periods of literary culture. In citing the relationship of writers to their cultural milieu, he was following the lead of eighteenth-century Scottish aestheticians.[28] And, in his enumeration of the forces that had produced a revolution in taste in his own time, he gave a valuable, firsthand account of the rise of what later literary historians would label "Romanticism."

Jeffrey argued that the same cultural ferment that had produced the Reformation had helped to develop in Elizabethan and Jacobean England a "distinct, original, and independent" English literature, a "native stock." Classical learning had not yet become the exclusive study. The models of antiquity had not yet subdued men's minds to a sense of inferiority or condemned English writers to the lot of imitators. The Elizabethan and Jacobean writers neither feared nor affected the derision of fastidious ages. They were poets, whether writing in verse or in prose, and a modern reader finds in their work "more fine fancy and original imagery — more brillant conceptions and glowing expressions — more new figures, and new applications of old figures — more, in short, of the body and the soul of poetry, than in all the odes and epics, that have since been produced in Europe." The works of Shakespeare, Marlowe, Ralegh, and Jeremy Taylor share a common character. "They are the works of Giants — and of Giants of one nation and family; — and their characteristics are, great force, boldness and originality; together with a certain raciness of English peculiarity, which distinguishes them from all those performances that have since been produced upon a more vague and general idea of European excellence. Their sudden appearance, indeed, in all this splendour of native luxuriance, can only be compared to what happens on the breaking up of a virgin soil, — where all indigenous plants spring up at once with a rank and irrepressible fertility, and display whatever is peculiar or excellent in their nature, on a scale the most conspicuous and magnificent."[29]

The fanaticism and civil war of the Commonwealth period touched the literature of England with a darker tone. But what was truly native in that literature survived until the time of Charles II and his Gallophile court. "The Restoration . . . broke down the barriers of our literary independence, and reduced us to a province of the great republic of Europe. The genius and fancy which lingered through the usurpation, though soured and blighted by the severities of that inclement season, were still genuine English genius and fancy; and owned no allegiance to any foreign authorities. But the Restoration brought in a French taste upon us, and what was called a classical and a polite taste; and the wings of our English muses were clipped and trimmed, and their flights regulated, at the expense of all that was peculiar, and much of what was brightest in their beauty." Partly through the influence of Continental standards, partly in reaction to the religious and republican enthusiasm of the recent English past, the Restoration writers introduced a new style. "It was more worldly, and more townish, — holding more of reason, and ridicule and authority — more elaborate and more assuming —addressed more to the judgment than to the feelings, and somewhat ostentatiously accommodated to the habits, or supposed habits, of persons in fashionable life." The peculiar excellence of native English literature — its "luxuriant negligence" — was lost on the taste-makers of the Restoration court. "The grand and sublime tone of our greater poets, appeared to them dull, morose and gloomy; and the fine play of their rich and unrestrained fancy, mere childishness and folly: while their frequent lapses and perpetual irregularity were set down as clear indications of barbarity and ignorance." What was needed was a voice of refined and independent judgment, a poet to combine the rich irregularity of the older literature with the regular refinement of Continental modes.

"The result seemed at one time suspended on the will of Dryden — in whose individual person the genius of the English and of the French school of literature may be said to have maintained a protracted struggle." But Dryden trimmed his sails to the prevailing wind, subjecting Shakespeare to lifeless adaptations. "Carried by the original bent of his genius, and his familiarity with our older models to the cultivation of our native style, to which he might have imparted more steadiness and correctness — for in force and in sweetness it was already matchless — he was unluckily seduced by the attractions of fashion, and the dazzling of the dear wit and gay rhetoric in which it delighted, to lend his powerful aid to the new corruptions and refinements; and to prostitute his great gifts to the purposes of party rage or licentious ribaldry."[30]

The wits of Queen Anne's age continued in the Restoration style, purging its grossest indecencies and polishing its pleasantry and sarcasm. "Coming into life immediately after the consummation of a bloodless revolution, effected much more by the cool sense, than the angry passions of the nation, they seem to have felt, that they were born in an age of reason, rather than of fancy; and that men's minds, though considerably divided and unsettled upon many points, were in a much better temper to relish judicious argument and cutting satire, than the glow of enthusiastic passion, or the richness of luxuriant imagination." Accordingly, the Queen Anne wits won their laurels through correct judgment and cool common sense rather than through strong emotion and imagination. Addison's poetry is the most correct and lifeless product of the age; Pope's is the most spirited. What Pope set out to do, he did well. His writings set the tone for poetry through most of the century, as Addison's *Spectator* papers set the style for prose. "But Pope is a satirist, and a moralist, and a wit, and a critic, and a fine writer, much more than he is a poet. . . . There are no pictures of nature or of simple emotion in all his writings. He is the poet of town life, and of high life, and of literary life; and seems so much afraid of incurring ridicule by the display of natural feeling or unregulated fancy, that it is difficult not to imagine that he thought such ridicule would have been very well directed." There were stirrings as the century wore on. The poetry of Thomson, Young, and Goldsmith — the prose of Junius and Johnson — Percy's *Reliques of Ancient English Poetry* (1765) and Warton's *History of English Poetry* (1774-81)) — all recalled an English literature of deeper feeling and more active fancy. But the times were not ripe for a literary revolution. "There never was, on the whole, a quieter time than the reigns of the first two Georges, and the greater part of that which ensued. There were two little provincial rebellions indeed, and a fair proportion of foreign war; but there was nothing to stir the minds of the people at large, to rouse their passions, or excite their imaginations — nothing like the agitations of the Reformation in the 16th century, or of the civil wars in the 17th. . . . And certainly there was never so remarkable a dearth of original talent — so long an interruption of native genius — as during about 60 years in the middle of the last century."[31]

Then came a change. Jeffrey had only to look up to his shelves for evidence, to his reviewer's copies of the *Lyrical Ballads* (1798), *Childe Harold's Pilgrimage* (1812-18), and *Waverley* (1814). The change was not a purely literary phenomenon. The literature was itself a reflection of the change in British attitudes:

> The agitations of the French revolution, and the discussions as well as the hopes and terrors to which it gave occasion — the genius of Edmund Burke, and some others of his country — the impression of the new literature of Germany, evidently the original of our lake-school of poetry, and of many innovations in our drama — the rise or revival of a general spirit of methodism in the lower orders — and the vast extent of our political and commercial relations, which have not only familiarized all ranks of people with distant countries, and great undertakings, but have brought knowledge and enterprise home, not merely to the imagination, but to the actual experience of almost every individual. — All these, and several other circumstances, have so far improved or excited the character of our nation, as to have created an effectual demand for more profound speculation, and more serious emotion than was dealt in by the writers of the former century, and which, if it has not yet produced a corresponding supply in all branches, has at least had the effect of decrying the commodities that were previously in vogue, as unsuited to the altered condition of the times.[32]

All this was part of what Hazlitt and Shelley would later call "the spirit of the age." As Jeffrey described it, the condition of contemporary imaginative literature was very like the condition of contemporary politics. In politics, the people's growing sense of power was threatening the eighteenth-century institutions that attempted to ignore them. "This is the stage of society in which fanaticism has its second birth, and political enthusiasm its first true development — when plans of visionary reform, and schemes of boundless ambition are conceived, and almost realized by the energy with which they are pursued — the era of revolutions and projects — of vast performances and infinite expectations." Jeffrey tried to control that political energy, tried to direct it toward the making of both popular and stable institutions. In literature, the excited sensibility of the British people had led them to discard eighteenth-century literary models. "Instead of ingenious essays, elegant pieces of gallantry, and witty satires all stuck over with classical allusions, we have the dreams of convicts, and the agonies of Gypsy women, and the exploits of buccaneers, freebooters, and savages. . . . And as they agree in nothing but in being the vehicles of strong and natural emotions, and have generally pleased, nearly in proportion to the quantity of that emotion they conveyed, it is difficult not to conclude, that they have pleased only for the sake of that quality — a growing appetite for which may be regarded as the true characteristic of this age of the world." In his criticism of imaginative literature, Jeffrey would try to control that emotional and imaginative energy — try to direct it toward the making of a literature of wide and lasting associational appeal.[33]

Poetry and Prose Fiction

Health to immortal Jeffrey! once, in name,
England could boast a judge almost the same;
In soul so like, so merciful, yet just,
Some think that Satan has resign'd his trust,
And given the spirit to the world again,
To sentence letters, as he sentenced men.
— Lord Byron, *English Bards and
Scotch Reviewers* (1809)

*My natural foible is to admire and be pleased
too easily, and I am never severe except from
effort and reflection. I am afraid some people
would not believe this; but you will, when I
tell you that I say it quite in earnest.*
— Jeffrey to Thomas Moore, 28 May 1816

Jeffrey believed that imaginative literature should provide pleasure and instruction for the audience that reads it. This was a traditional view — the orientation of British criticism since the time of Sidney. But the audience whose pleasure and instruction were involved was not the traditional audience assumed in Renaissance and Neoclassical criticism. The reading public of the early nineteenth century was not a homogeneous body. It was a larger audience than that which Sidney, Dryden, or even Johnson had known, an audience for whom classical literature no longer served as such a dominant standard.[1] Among the multitudes who read Scott and Byron there were many men and women who turned to poetry with the same spirit and expectations with which twentieth-century readers turn to popular novels. And there were some, already, who really preferred novels to any poetry at all.

Jeffrey is interesting as a critic of imaginative literature because he faced a new problem — the relationship of literature and a large, powerful, and heterogeneous reading public. As he saw it, the relationship was symbiotic. If the cultural milieu of any given age determines to a significant degree the kind of literature that will be written, the reading public's taste is a significant element in any cultural milieu. For glory or for guineas, a poet writes with an audience in mind, and those who live to please must please to live. "Present popularity, whatever disappointed writers may say, is, after all, the only safe presage of future glory; — and it is really as unlikely that good poetry should be produced in any quantity where it is not relished, as that cloth should be manufactured and thrust into the market, of a pattern and fashion for which there was no demand."[2] But if the reading public's taste is good — if they appreciate and demand rich imagination, forceful expression, and universal associations — the writers of the age will be encouraged, or compelled, to try to satisfy them. In turn, a literature of rich imagination, forceful expression, and universal associations will confirm or improve the taste of the reading public.[3]

And the critic? The critic has value insofar as he encourages a healthy relationship between writers and their public. The potential audience for Byron's poetry was large, but that same large audience might give reward and encouragement to hacks like Bernard Barton.[4] To Jeffrey, the emergence of a large reading public was both a hopeful and disheartening prospect. If educated, they might encourage a literature of more forceful expression and of wider associational appeal than that of any age since Shakespeare's. If uneducated or uneducable, they would provide a growing market for sensational and hackneyed trash. In his criticism, Jeffrey followed the practical and pedagogic instincts of enlightened Scotland. He tried to confirm or improve the taste of the large reading public, judging Wordsworth and Crabbe by his standard of aesthetic common sense, measuring contemporary favorites like Byron, Scott, and Moore against what was best in the British literary past.

Those were worthy projects. For modern readers, however, Jeffrey's long campaign against the "Lake Poets" is confusing reading. In several reviews he treated Wordsworth, Coleridge, and Southey as a coherent poetic "sect" — aesthetic radicals and doctrinaires who had recently emerged upon a cultural stage already crowded with shallow minds excited by the innovative spirit of the times.[5] In the sheer dialectical delight of responding to Wordsworth's Advertisement and Prefaces, Jeffrey sometimes worked himself into positions that he later quietly abandoned. But a consistent theme runs throughout his criticism: Wordsworth had misunderstood the sources of poetic pleasure and offered to the public a poetry of limited associational appeal. Jeffrey struck that theme in his review of Southey's *Thalaba* (1801) in the first number of the *Edinburgh Review*, opening with a sentence that has made later critics wince: "Poetry has this much, at least, in common with religion, that its standards were fixed long ago, by certain inspired writers, whose authority it is no longer lawful to call in question; and that many profess to be entirely devoted to it, who have no *good works* to produce in support of their pretensions." Those sentiments from the "dear Pyrrhonist" must have made even Smith and Horner blink. But the sentence turns out to be only an excuse for a long, half-whimsical string of metaphors — "the catholic poetical church," its "corruptions and reformation," its "heresies" and "sects." Wordsworth, Coleridge, and Southey appear as *"dissenters* from the established systems in poetry and criticism," and their prophets are Schiller and Rousseau.[6]

In the Advertisement to the first edition of the *Lyrical Ballads,* Wordsworth had announced that he was attempting a radical experiment "to ascertain how far the language of conversation in the middle and lower classes of society is adapted to the purposes of poetic pleasure." Jeffrey thought the experiment a risky one, remarking that poetry written by such a system must be initially distasteful to many readers.

"The language of the higher and more cultivated orders may fairly be presumed to be better than that of their inferiors; at any rate, it has all those associations in its favour, by means of which a style can ever appear beautiful or exalted, and is adapted to the purposes of poetry, by having been long consecrated to its use. The language of the vulgar, on the other hand, has all the opposite associations to contend with. . . . A great genius indeed may overcome these disadvantages; but we scarcely conceive that he should court them."[7] Jeffrey had lamented since university days the absence of "simplicity and naturality of expression" in eighteenth-century poetry.[8] He praised Cowper for having revived a more natural poetic language, and he found "something very noble and conscientious" in Wordsworth's plan of composition.[9] But he doubted that the new sect really understood the implications of their innovative system. The natural expression of passion will always interest, but there remain parts of most poems — the narrative and descriptive sections — that must appear flat without a more intense and figurative language than "the language of conversation in the middle and lower classes of society." The poor may be made interesting through the poet's fresh or pathetic treatment of their situation, but a truly accurate record of any sentiments and diction that are *peculiar* to them must be either boring or disgusting. "In serious poetry, a man of the middling or lower order *must necessarily* lay aside a great deal of his ordinary language; he must avoid errors in grammar and orthography; and steer clear of the cant of particular professions, and of every impropriety that is ludicrous or disgusting: nay, he must speak in good verse, and observe all the graces in prosody and collocation. After all this, it may not be very easy to say how we are to find him out to be a low man, or what marks can remain of the ordinary language of conversation in the inferior orders of society."[10] In time, Coleridge would agree.[11]

Jeffrey recognized in Wordsworth's announced experiment another symptom of revolutionary fever. To use Hazlitt's later phrase, Wordworth's was a leveling muse — "a pure emanation of the Spirit of the Age."[12] The issue was not simply an aesthetic one: there were political and social implications. And Jeffrey's argument was not simply an aesthetic one:

> A splenetic and idle discontent with the existing institutions of society, seems to be at the bottom of all their [the "Lake Poets'"] serious and peculiar sentiments. . . . For all sorts of vice and profligacy in the lower orders of society, they have the same virtuous horror, and the same tender compassion. While the existence of these offences overpowers them with grief and confusion, they never permit themselves to feel the smallest indignation or dislike towards the offenders. The present vicious constitution of society alone is responsible for all these enormities. . . . It is not easy to say whether the fundamental absurdity of this doctrine, or the partiality of its application, be entitled to the severest reprehension. If men are driven to commit crimes, through a certain moral necessity; other men are compelled, by a similar necessity, to hate and despise them for their commission. . . . Wealth is just as valid an excuse for the one class of vices, as indigence is for the other.[13]

Apparently, rumor had reached Edinburgh of the Lake Poets' early Jacobin enthusiasms. Jeffrey's remarks hint at more than *Thalaba* or the *Lyrical Ballads* themselves could have revealed. When Southey's *Madoc* (1805) appeared, Jeffrey discussed "the ambition of Mr. Southey and some of his associates" in language that was both political and aesthetic. "The *ambition* . . . is not, our readers will understand, of that regulated and manageable sort which usually grows up in old established commonwealths, either political or literary — which aspires at distinction through a just gradation of honours, and, looking at first with veneration to those who have previously attained the heights of fame, ventures by degrees to follow their footsteps, and to emulate or surpass their achievements." The Lakers' ambition was of a different kind, "of a more undisciplined and revolutionary character," one which "looks, we think, with a jealous and contemptuous eye on the old aristocracy of the literary world, and refuses the jurisdiction of its constituted authorities." In the 1802 version of his Preface to the *Lyrical Ballads*,

Wordsworth had claimed that the acceptance of his doctrines would radically affect "our judgments concerning the works of the greatest Poets both ancient and modern." Jeffrey thought that damnable presumptuous and unempirical. The aim of poetry is pleasure, and men cannot be mistaken as to what has pleased them. Accidental associations may sway the public taste for a season, but that poetry which has given pleasure to successive generations is the surest index to the sources of poetic pleasure. "The ancient and uninterrupted possession of the great inheritors of poetical reputation, must be admitted therefore as the clearest evidence of their right, and renders it the duty of every new claimant to contend with them as lawful competitors, instead of seeking to supplant them as usurpers." Wordsworth and company would turn mankind's aesthetic experience upon its head.[14]

Perhaps Jeffrey should have interpreted Wordsworth's Preface in the manner that Coleridge advised — "by the purpose and object, which he may be supposed to have intended, rather than by the sense which the words themselves must convey, if they are taken without this allowance."[15] But that dubious exegesis was left to Coleridge and later critics. Jeffrey and most of Wordsworth's contemporaries took the poet at his word. "'Pedlars,' and 'Boats,' and 'Wagons!'" Byron moaned. "Oh! ye shades/Of Pope and Dryden, are we come to this?"[16] Even Scott, who was more sympathetic, feared that the Lake group's "unfortunate idea of forming a New School of Poetry" had led them to dissipate their energies "in trying to find not a better but a different path from what has been travell'd by their predecessors."[17] When Jeffrey took up Wordsworth's *Poems in Two Volumes* (1807) for review, the poet's doctrines were still very much in his mind. He found some things in the *Poems* to admire. He also found "Alice Fell," "To the Small Celandine," and "The Kitten and Falling Leaves," all of which exemplified the weaknesses of Wordsworth's system of poetic diction. There are, the critic argued, certain unavoidable linguistic facts that determine the language that a poet can profitably use. Certain words carry associations of tenderness or dignity; certain words carry associations of coarseness or insipidness.

Wordsworth's egalitarian aesthetic might soothe his own social conscience, but that aesthetic had led him to write many poems that would bore his readers stiff. "We do not mean, of course, to say any thing in defence of the hackneyed common places of ordinary versemen. Whatever might have been the original character of these unlucky phrases, they are now associated with nothing but ideas of schoolboy imbecility and vulgar affectation. But what we do maintain is, that much of the most popular poetry in the world owes its celebrity chiefly to the beauty of its diction; and that no poetry can be long or generally acceptable, the language of which is coarse, inelegant, or infantine."[18] Caught in the toils of his own doctrinaire system, Wordsworth had sometimes confused "simple" with "insipid," "natural" with "mean."[19]

Jeffrey read Wordsworth's poetry as it came off the presses, the gold with the dross, without the intercessions of a sympathetic editor or the benefit of Wordsworth's later deletions and revisions. If the titles of some of the poems that bothered Jeffrey are unfamiliar, the reason is that no one, voluntarily, reads those poems any more. To Jeffrey, to other critics in contemporary periodicals, and to the modern editors of the *Oxford Book of Children's Verse*, some of Wordsworth's poems appeared to be "verses that have been written for children."[20] Jeffrey was himself highly sensitive to beauty in the natural world. His botanical descriptions in private letters are as detailed as anything in Wordsworth's poems. But both the sentiments and diction of "To the Daisy" and "To the Small Celandine" struck him as affected. Wordsworth had, after all, become a mannerist, as much a mannerist as "the poetasters who ring changes on the common places of magazine versification." Even when the sentiments expressed were patently sincere, Wordsworth had sinned against associational propriety, "connecting his most lofty, tender, or impassioned conceptions, with objects and incidents, which the greater part of his readers will probably persist in thinking low, silly, or uninteresting." "It is possible enough, we allow, that the sight of a friend's garden-spade, or a sparrow's nest, or a man gathering leeches, might really have suggested to such a mind ["a mind of extraordinary sensibility, habituated to solitary meditation"] a train of powerful impressions and interesting reflections; but it is certain, that, to most minds, such associations will always appear forced, strained, and unnatural; and that the composition in which it is attempted to exhibit them, will always have the air of parody, or ludicrous and affected singularity."[21]

To most minds, perhaps. But Scott, Coleridge, and Crabb Robinson thought that Jeffrey's criticism of Wordsworth's poetry was something less than honest. "I have often wondered," Scott wrote, "that a man who loves & admires Poetry as much as he does can permit himself the severe or sometimes unjust strictures which he fulminates even against the authors whom he most approves of & whose works actually afford him most delight."[22] Jeffrey's and Horner's correspondence indicates that Jeffrey did admire many of the *Lyrical Ballads*.[23] But Jeffrey's personal taste was his *personal* taste. "The only thing on which I am at all disposed to differ from you," he wrote to the Italian poet Ugo Foscolo, "is in the confidence with which you appeal to the scales or principles of taste, as something precise and certain. That many things are certainly *bad* may indeed be affirmed with tolerable safety — but for my own part I never can be quite sure that what appears to me *good*, may not have that effect in consequence of some whim or prejudice of my own."[24] Jeffrey was reviewing poetry for a large reading public that still read poetry, and he consistently subordinated his personal taste to what he understood to be the legitimate demands of that public. It is the artist's duty, he wrote in his review of Alison, "to employ only such objects as are the *natural* signs and *inseparable* concomitants of emotions, of which the greater part of mankind are susceptible"; and, "even for those who labour for applause, the wisest course . . . would be, to have two tastes, — one to enjoy, and one to work by, — one founded upon universal associations, according to which they finished those performances for which they challenged universal praise, — and another guided by all casual and individual associations, through which they looked fondly upon nature, and upon the objects of their secret admiration."[25]

Wordsworth was writing cult poetry, poetry of limited associational appeal. "The current of his feelings," Hazlitt noted, "is deep, but narrow."[26] Jeffrey himself was easily moved by poetry of rural life, sensitive to what he once described as that "force of imagination" by which poets have "connected with human emotions, a variety of objects, to which common minds could not discover the relation." That was part of Wordsworth's definition of a poet. But Jeffrey believed that Wordsworth's egotism had led him to waste "a great deal of genius" on an introverted poetry that only a small coterie could enjoy. It was Wordsworth's inconsistent but undeniable genius that troubled Jeffrey most: the man might influence other poets to follow his example. And Wordsworth could write good poetry, publicly accessible poetry, "when, by any accident, he is led to abandon his system." The Miltonic sonnets were evidence in point. At the end of his review of *Poems in Two Volumes*, Jeffrey expressed the hope that Wordsworth might find a style and a subject that would win him a larger audience.[27]

But *The Excursion* (1814) would never do. In 1814 Jeffrey was no longer troubled by the political implications of Wordsworth's innovations. Wordsworth, Coleridge, and Southey had long since lost their Jacobin enthusiasms. They were now the champions of Church, State, and landed aristocracy. Jeffrey thought their metamorphosis ridiculous, but he no longer saw their poetry as dangerous.[28] His brief against *The Excursion* was argued on aesthetic grounds: the poem showed all the worst and little of the best in Wordsworth's wayward genius. "It is longer, weaker, and tamer, than any of Mr. Wordsworth's other productions; with less boldness and originality, and even less of that extreme simplicity and lowliness of tone which wavered so prettily, in the Lyrical Ballads, between silliness and pathos." Wordsworth had crossed imitations of Milton and Cowper with wordy, mind-wearying blank verse that was the curse of Southey, developing a hybrid of triteness and obscurity that he could justly claim as all his own. "The volume before us, if we were to describe it very shortly, we would characterize as a tissue of moral and devotional ravings, in which innumerable changes are rung upon a few very simple and familiar ideas: — but with such an accompaniment of long words, long sentences, and unwieldly phrases — and such a hubbub of strained raptures and fantastical sublimities, that it is often extremely difficult for the most skilful and attentive student to obtain a glimpse of the author's meaning — and altogether impossible for an ordinary reader to conjecture what he is about."[29]

"Your opinion of Jeffrey is just," Wordsworth wrote to a friend; " — he is a depraved Coxcomb; the greatest Dunce, I believe, in this Island, and assuredly the Man who takes most pains to prove himself so."[30] At this stage in the game, litotes was neither Wordsworth's nor Jeffrey's strong card. But to anyone who has recently read through *The Excursion,* Jeffrey's criticism has a healthy sound. There are long passages in the poem that are maddeningly prolix or obscure. Jeffrey noticed Wordsworth's predilection for "mysterious and unintelligible language" in the early years, a strange predilection for a champion of natural poetic language. In *The Excursion* predilection had become obsession — a "rapturous mysticism which eludes all comprehension, and fills the despairing reader with painful giddiness and terror." To a critic whose epistemology was Hume's brand of common sense, Wordsworth's mysticism appeared more muddled than profound. And Jeffrey found the passages of "hubbub" exasperating because Wordsworth had shown, in other passages, that he could treat common human feelings with pathos and insight. Jeffrey singled out for praise what must be, for many readers, the best part of the poem — the tale of the ruined cottage. He recommended in the Solitary's tale the accounts of bereavement and of hopes raised and dashed by the French Revolution. But the poem as a whole revealed Wordsworth as the prisoner of his own ego, "finally lost to the good cause of poetry." Jeffrey, a clubbable man, wondered at the effects of long habits of seclusion among lakes and mountains: "Solitary musings, amidst such scenes, might no doubt be expected to nurse up the mind to the majesty of poetical conception . . . . But the collision of equal minds, — the admonition of prevailing impressions — seems necessary to reduce its redundacies, and repress that tendency to extravagance or puerility, into which the self-indulgence and self-admiration of genius is so apt to be betrayed, when it is allowed to wanton, without awe or restraint, in the triumph and delight of its own intoxication."[31]

What did Jeffrey believe to be "the good cause of poetry"? Primarily, he hoped that poetry would be read, encouraged, kept alive by the growing reading public. In the early nineteenth century that cause appeared to be still viable, and Jeffrey criticized Wordsworth's poetry in its support. But Jeffrey learned from Wordsworth. In working out the dialectic of Wordsworth's publicly announced position, he came to better understand the implications of his own associationist aesthetic. "A man will borrow a part from his opponent the more easily," Coleridge noticed, "if he feels himself justified in continuing to reject a part."[32] Jeffrey continued to reject Wordsworth's experiments in poetic style, but he gradually revised his theory on the proper subject of poetic imitation. In his 1802 review of *Thalaba* he had argued "that the arts that aim at exciting admiration and delight, do not take their models from what is ordinary, but from what is excellent; and that our interest in the representation of any event, does not depend upon our familiarity with the original, but on its intrinsic importance, and the celebrity of the parties it concerns."[33] But his study of Wordsworth's occasional successes in treating humble subjects and his subsequent study of the poetry of Crabbe helped him to develop a more comprehensive position on the proper subject of poetic imitation.

In *The Village* (1783), *Poems* (1807), and *The Borough* (1810), Crabbe had mocked the pastoral illusions of those "gentle souls, who dream of rural ease,/Whom the smooth stream and smoother sonnet please."[34] Reading Crabbe's accounts of struggling tradesmen and broken peasants, Jeffrey suspected that Crabbe's poetry might succeed where Wordsworth's poetry had often failed. "By the mere force of

his art . . . he forces us to attend to objects that are usually
neglected, and to enter into feelings from which we are in
general but too eager to escape; — and then trusts to nature
for the effect of the representation." Sometimes Crabbe had
missed the mark. His prostitutes and alcoholics were too
dehumanized to be the object of most readers' sympathies.
His petty smugglers and cheats were too insignificant and
weak to excite a reader's fear or indignation. In those cases,
Crabbe's poetry evoked not pity but disgust. In his narratives
of ordinary tradesmen and artisans, however, Crabbe was
clearly onto something:

> Now, the delineation of all that concerns the lower and
> most numerous classes of society, is, in this respect, on a
> footing with the pictures of our primary affections, — that
> their originals are necessarily familiar to all men, and are
> inseparably associated with a multitude of their most
> interesting impressions. . . . Many diligent readers of
> poetry know little, by their own experience, of palaces,
> castles or camps; and still less of princes, warriors and
> banditti; — but every one thoroughly understands every
> thing about cottages, streets and villages; and conceives,
> pretty correctly, the character and condition of sailors,
> ploughmen and artificers. If the poet can contrive, there-
> fore, ["by his judicious selection of circumstances, — by
> the force and vivacity of his style"] to create a sufficient
> interest in subjects like these, they will infallibly sink
> deeper into the mind, and be more prolific of kindred
> trains of emotion, than subjects of greater dignity.[35]

Jeffrey recognized in the best of Crabbe's poetry the
possibilities of a contemporary poetry of wide associational
appeal. On the general level of aesthetic theory, he could
recommend Crabbe's poetry to "all persons of taste and
sensibility" for its treatment of "affections that belong to
our *universal* nature." But Crabbe's subjects were particularly
fitted to the associations of a growing middle-class reading
public. "In this country," he wrote in his review of Crabbe's
Tales (1812), "there probably are not less than two hundred
thousand persons who read for amusement or instruction

among the middling classes of society. In the higher classes, there are not as many as twenty thousand. It is easy to see therefore which a poet should choose to please for his own glory and emolument, and which he should wish to delight and amend out of mere philanthropy." In the cause of mere philanthropy, Crabbe had given an account of all ranks of rural life, trying to interest his readers' sympathies for that suffering which is the common lot of all. "He aims at an important moral effect by this exhibition; and must not be defrauded either of that, or of the praise which is due to the coarser efforts of his pen, out of deference to the sickly delicacy of his more fastidious readers."[36]

Wordsworth must have groaned. Jeffrey knew that Wordsworth was writing to produce a similar effect, to broaden the associational sympathies of the reading public. But Jeffrey did not think that the majority of Wordsworth's rustics were real men and women. They were personifications of a peculiar philosophic system, a system that most readers in any age would be hard pressed to understand. Should Crabbe and other poets succeed in overcoming the fastidiousness of polite readers, Wordsworth's "hysterical schoolmasters" and "metaphysical pedlars" would still appear unnatural:

Mr. Crabbe, in short, shows us something which we have all seen, and may see, in real life; and draws from it such feelings and such reflections as every human being must acknowledge that it is calculated to excite. He delights us by the truth, and vivid and picturesque beauty of his representations, and by the force and pathos of the sensations with which we feel they ought to be connected. Mr. Wordsworth and his associates show us something that mere observation never yet suggested to any one. They introduce us to beings whose existence was not previously suspected by the acutest observors of nature; and excite an interest for them, more by an eloquent and refined analysis of their own capricious feelings, than by any obvious or very intelligible ground of sympathy in their situation. The common sympathies of our nature, and our general knowledge of human character, do not enable us either to understand or to enter into the feelings of their characters.[37]

In 1810, the year in which he praised Crabbe's *Borough*, Jeffrey was recommending that the Whigs adopt a plan of moderate parliamentary reform. Democratic forces were at work in British culture, and Jeffrey's politics and aesthetics were affected. Crabbe's poetry was itself a moderate reform — democratic subjects in heroic couplets. In truth, Jeffrey was never completely comfortable with *The Village* or *The Borough*. He admitted to Horner that he had overpraised the poet, and he later described Moore and Crabbe as "the antipodes of our present poetical sphere," representing "the extreme points of refinement and homeliness that can be said to fall within the legitimate dominion of poetry."[38] But Crabbe's poetry did allow Jeffrey an opportunity to recommend a contemporary poetry of "*universal* nature," "the just representation of common feelings and common situations,"[39] without Wordsworth's impropriety or mysticism or doctrinaire scheme of aesthetic innovation. Crabbe's poetry was humanitarian, but realistically humanitarian, designed to show "that poverty, in sober truth, is very uncomfortable; and vice is by no means confined to the opulent."[40]

In contrasting Crabbe's poetry to contemporary tales of "palaces, castles . . . princes, warriors and banditti," Jeffrey had in mind the poetic narratives of Walter Scott. He criticized Scott's poetry and the later Eastern narratives of Byron and Moore by his standard of aesthetic common sense, searching for that "just representation of common feelings and common situations" to which the majority of readers in any age must sympathetically respond. Throughout his reviews there are echoes of Samuel Johnson's edict that "nothing can please many, and please long, but just representations of general nature." Jeffrey's criticism was more explicitly associational than Johnson's. In the tradition of eighteenth-century Scottish aesthetics, he was concerned with the reader's sympathetic emotional response to, rather than intellective grasp of, just representations of the common experience.

But reviewing Scott's *Lay of the Last Minstrel* (1805) was a touchy assignment. "You must do it," Horner advised, "but you will of course do it with a little of the partiality, which we all feel for the author, and which it would be both disagreeable to yourself and affected to attempt to avoid."[41] Scott and Jeffrey had been young advocates together. They were members of the same clubs, and Scott was a contributor to the *Edinburgh Review* before political disagreements forced him to initiate the *Quarterly*. Jeffrey's affection for Scott survived politics, but he did not share the poet's antiquarian enthusiasms. Jeffrey valued the study of the past insofar as it taught practical lessons for the present. Writing detailed chivalric romances in the early nineteenth century seemed to him a bizarre business, "much such a fantasy as to build a modern abbey, or an English pagoda."[42] Reviewing the *Lay*, he praised Scott for having improved upon his medieval models. Scott's style was more concise, his imagery was more striking, and the emotions that he attributed to his characters were more appealing to contemporary readers. But Scott had sometimes fallen into "such combinations of metre, as must put the teeth of his readers, we think, into some jeopardy,"[43] and his antiquarian detail sometimes brought a glaze to gentle readers' eyes. When Scott continued to accumulate detail in *Marmion* (1808), Jeffrey lodged a protest "in the name of a very numerous class of readers," including many twentieth-century readers who have tried to appreciate Scott's poetry, "against the insufferable number, and length, and minuteness of those descriptions of antient dresses; and manners, and buildings; and ceremonies, and local superstitions, with which the whole poem is overrun, — which render so many notes necessary, and are, after all, but imperfectly understood by those to whom chivalrous antiquity has not hitherto been an object of particular attention."[44]

Jeffrey knew that Scott's poetry was already stimulating an enthusiasm for medieval minutiae among those same resolutely au courant readers who had babbled of botany in the heyday of Erasmus Darwin. He did not think that such enthusiasms last. "The world will never be long pleased with what it does not readily understand; and the poetry which is destined for immortality, should treat only of feelings and events which can be conceived and entered into by readers of all descriptions."[45] But the literary world of the early nineteenth century was very pleased with Scott's poetry. When the *Lady of the Lake* (1810) made its debut, Jeffrey acknowledged that any critical caveats on his part would be but a whistle in the wind. In fact, Scott was improving as a poet as his audience increased. The *Lady* was more lively in its narrative, more varied in its characters, and less laden with antiquarian detail than were his earlier romances. Yielding to that "partiality" which the Scottish literati felt for Scott, Jeffrey wished his fellow advocate the joys of his current popularity. "He has *the jury* hollow in his favour; and though *the court* may think that its directions have not been sufficiently attended to, it will not quarrel with the verdict."[46] As Scott and Jeffrey knew, juries and the reading public could be swayed. Within a few years Scott would lose poetic place to Byron.

Jeffrey bore Byron no grudge for *English Bards and Scotch Reviewers.* He enjoyed clever satires on the *Edinburgh Review:* a clever satirist might be enlisted as a clever contributor.[47] When the first two cantos of *Childe Harold's Pilgrimage* appeared in 1812, Jeffrey found "something piquant" in its moody, misanthropic hero. Byron's poetry, he thought, surpassed that of any other contemporary poet in the expression of passionate emotion and disturbing ideas. "He alone has been able to *command* the sympathy, even of reluctant readers, by the natural magic of his moral sublimity, and the terrors and attractions of those overpowering feelings, the depths and heights of which he seems to have so successfully explored." But when Childe Harold was succeeded by *The Giaour* (1813), *The Corsair* (1814), and *Manfred* (1817), Jeffrey grew a bit restive. The heroes all turned out to be the same person. Byron seemed unable to identify with personalities that differed from his own. "The very intensity of his feelings — the loftiness of his views — the pride of his nature or his genius, withhold him from this identification; so that in personating the heroes of the scene,

he does little but repeat himself." When Byron attempted
dramatic poetry in *Sardanapalus* and *The Two Foscari*
(1821), Jeffrey had a stong sense of déjà vu:

> A man gifted as he is, when he aspires at dramatic fame,
> should emulate the greatest of dramatists. Let Lord B.
> then think of Shakespeare — and consider what a noble
> range of character, what a freedom from mannerism and
> egotism, there is in him! How much he seems to have
> studied nature; how little to have thought about himself;
> how seldom to have repeated or glanced back at his own
> most successful inventions! Why indeed should he? Nature
> was still open before him, and inexhaustible; and the
> freshness and variety that still delight his readers, must
> have had constant attractions for himself . . . . Lord Byron,
> in Shakespeare's place, would have peopled the world with
> black Othellos![48]

In *Lalla Rookh* (1817) Tom Moore turned his hand to that
vein of Eastern narrative which Byron had already worked
with commercial success. Jeffrey thought that Moore's
imagery was "the finest orientalism we have had yet," but he
wondered if the poem's impassioned caliphs and demented
harem girls would please many and please long. "In order to
avoid the debasement of ordinary or familiar life, the author
has soared to a region beyond the comprehension of most of
his readers. All his personages are so very beautiful, and
brave, and agonizing — so totally wrapt up in the exaltation
of their vehement emotions, and withal so lofty in rank, and
so sumptuous and magnificent in all that relates to their
external condition, that the herd of ordinary mortals can
scarcely venture to conceive of their proceedings, or to
sympathize freely with their fortunes." Jeffrey admitted that
the narratives that deeply interest us are often those which
represent headier events and passions than those found in
ordinary life. "But, in order that this very elevation may be
felt, and produce its effect, the story must itself, in other
places, give us the known and ordinary level, — and, by a
thousand adaptations and traits of *universal* nature, make us
feel, that the characters which become every now and then

the objects of our intense sympathy and admiration, in great emergencies, and under the influence of rare but conceivable excitements, are, after all, our fellow creatures — made of the same flesh and blood with ourselves, and acting, and acted upon, by the common principles of our nature." That associational common touch lends human interest to the most exalted doings in Homer, Chaucer, Ariosto, and Shakespeare, "and will be found to occur, we believe, in all poetry that has been long and extensively popular, or that is capable of pleasing very strongly, or stirring very deeply, the common sensibilities of our nature."[49]

As it happened, *Lalla Rookh* sold well. But the market for narrative poetry was very soon to dwindle. British publishing suffered a severe slump in the mid-1820s. The market had been glutted with poetry, and almost overnight medieval and Eastern narratives were dead.[50] Later in the century individual poets such as Longfellow, Macaulay, and Tennyson would find a large reading public in Britain. By the 1830s, however, the novel was fast replacing poetry as the vehicle of narrative excitement, and poetry was accelerating its evolution into the modern lyric mode. Scott's *Waverley* (1814) was the shape of things to come. When the novel appeared, Jeffrey noticed that it had assumed a place "rather with the most popular of our modern poems, than with the rubbish of provincial romances."[51] As Scott churned out successful novels with a dizzying facility, Jeffrey recognized that contemporary novelists were in a cultural position similar to that of the dramatists of Elizabethan times.[52] Unlike early-nineteenth-century poets, novelists did not have to have to carry or reject the burden of the past. There were no intimidating models to discourage them; few critics bothered to consider their artistic merits.[53] They had all the freedom of poets in an earlier time, and Jeffrey thought that some of them were very good:

We have often been astonished at the quantity of talent — of invention, observation, and knowledge of character, as well as of spirited and graceful composition, that may be found in those works of fiction in our language, which are generally regarded as among the lower productions of our literature, upon which no great pains is understood to be bestowed, and which are seldom regarded as titles to a permanent reputation. If Novels, however, are not fated to last as long as Epic poems, they are at least a great deal more popular in their season; and, slight as their structure, and imperfect as their finishing may often be thought in comparison, we have no hesitation in saying, that the better specimens of the art are incomparably more entertaining, and considerably more instructive.[54]

Jeffrey guessed that the novel might fundamentally affect the traditional dynamics of literary life. He himself enjoyed "pure poetry," poems like *Endymion* (1818), "where a number of bright pictures are presented to the imagination, and a fine feeling expressed of those mysterious relations by which visible external things are assimilated with inward thoughts and emotions, and become the images and exponents of all passions and affections."[55] But he knew that the majority of readers demanded coarser stuff — narrative excitement, humor, pathos. If talented writers continued to turn to the novel, they might provide even discriminating readers with that ready human interest which he had always felt compelled to demand from contemporary poets. By the early 1840s, when he was preparing his reviews for republication, he found it necessary to explain the tone of some of his reviews of Scott, John Galt, and Maria Edgeworth. "As I perceive, I have, in some of the following papers, made a sort of apology for seeking to direct the attention of my readers to things so insignificant as *Novels*, it may be worthwhile to inform the present generation that, *in my youth*, writings of this sort were rated very low with us — scarcely allowed indeed to pass as part of a nation's permanent literature — and generally deemed altogether unworthy of grave critical notice." As he recognized, the situation in the 1840s was very different. In Britain, in America, and on the Continent, the novel stood "at the head of all that is graceful and instructive in the productions of modern genius."[56] But Jeffrey was no longer an active reviewer when the nineteenth-century novel came to flower. He resigned as editor in 1829 and left the reading public to its own devices. When court and Parliament were out of session, he was free to indulge his private taste, free to "lounge about" and "read idle snatches of Shakespeare, and Fletcher, and Keats, and Shelley."[57]

Perhaps he retired with relief. His concept of a periodical critic's role — the role of culture-broker between writers and the public — is a concept that still deserves respect. But the role had proved very hard to play. Because he believed that the level of literary culture was determined partly by the reading public's taste, Jeffrey had attempted to expose "the middling classes" to the best authors, ancient and modern. Believing that the public's taste was shaped by what they read, he had insisted that poets such as Wordsworth and Keats should turn from fit audience though few, to try to reach a larger audience. In effect, a book was valued insofar as it was read — read by the middle-class reading public who were destined to determine the character of British culture. In his efforts to influence that public, Jeffrey had become at times their prisoner and spokesman. His demand for literature of wide associational appeal became a demand for literature that triggered middle-class associations. And the portion of the British middle class that he knew best were the merchants and professionals and blue-stockinged ladies of Edinburgh, a group whom he once described to Hazlitt as full of "conceit and fastidiousness," "very ready to find fault and decry."[58]

Educated Edinburgh — proud of its philosophy, but still insecure and self-consciously correct in its use of written English — loomed very large in Jeffrey's mind. Much as he admired the "luxuriant negligence" that he found in Elizabethan literature, he compulsively censured contemporary poets for muddled metaphysics or "low" diction. Even as he analyzed the general British hunger for new literary excitements, he was reluctant to express his own catholic taste. In a letter to Moore he admitted that he often found "something to love and admire in works which I could never have courage or conscience to praise."[59] Once, in a rare confessional mood, he struck the same note in the *Edinburgh Review*: "We have often been indebted for a very considerable gratification to works which we should be somewhat ashamed to praise, and not very proud of having written — works too humble, or too full of faults, to be tolerated by critical readers, or recommended with safety to those who are not critical."[60]

Was the game worth the candle? Would not Jeffrey's reputation be more secure today if he had not concerned himself with what was acceptable in Edinburgh, London, or Bristol? Perhaps it would — but Jeffrey could not play the game in any other way. For philosophic reasons he could not use periodical reviews as a means of expressing a purely private taste. The logic of his own associationist aesthetic forced him to appeal to some aesthetic consensus. Neither did he wish to confine himself to general theoretical remarks. Jeffrey's critical intelligence was practical: his interest in aesthetic theory was always secondary to his concern with the promise and the danger inherent in the growth of a large reading audience. His reviews are the record of a moment that is now long past — when poetry, for better and for worse, was read by a large reading public. Since Matthew Arnold's time, major British critics have ignored that public. And that public now ignores poetry.

In the Preface to his collected *Contributions to the Edinburgh Review* (1843), Jeffrey asked to be remembered for having made "the Moral tendencies of the works under consideration a leading subject of discussion."[61] Critics of his day often mixed moral with aesthetic criticism, but the habit was particularly strong in Scotland. Eighteenth-century Scottish aestheticians had been deeply influenced by Hutcheson's and Shaftesbury's theories of man's innate moral and aesthetic senses, senses instilled by a wise and benevolent Creator. "In this respect," Kames argued, "a taste in the fine arts goes hand in hand with the moral sense, to which indeed it is nearly allied: both of them discover what is right and what is wrong: fashion, temper, and education, have an influence to vitiate both, or to preserve them pure and untainted: neither of them are arbitrary nor local; being rooted in human nature, and governed by principles common to all men."[62] If moral and aesthetic "tastes" were so nearly allied, it was logical for Scottish aestheticians to judge literature in terms of its moral influence. The best poetry, Beattie believed, is that "which awakens our pity for the sufferings of our fellow-creatures; . . . makes vice appear the object of indignation or ridicule; inculcates a sense of our dependence upon Heaven; fortifies our minds against the evils of life; or promotes the love of virtue and wisdom, either by delineating their native charms, or by setting before us in suitable colours the dreadful consequences of imprudent and immoral conduct."[63]

Jeffrey was wary of the Hutcheson-Shaftesbury meta-physic.[64] He did not accept the theory of a specific moral or aesthetic sense, nor did he think that an honestly empirical moral or aesthetic philosophy could appeal to the supposed designs of a benevolent Creator.[65] But Jeffrey's philosophy was shaped in basic ways by the thought of eighteenth-century Scottish moralists and aestheticians. He believed that men's notions of virtue and vice develop from subjective emotional responses, and he recognized the role of sympa-thetic imagination in our enjoyment of poetry and prose fiction. There was the rub. A writer could manipulate his reader's sympathetic emotions to good or ill effect. Scott could make tolerance and magnanimity attractive, but Byron could seduce a generation into moody misanthropy. In combating the intolerance, restlessness, and cynicism born of revolution, a long war, and a dissolute Regency, Jeffrey did not carry many of the moralist's traditional weapons. His own skeptical intelligence denied him the authoritative assistance of Scripture. He could not offer the teleological assurances of eighteenth-century Scottish moral philosophy or of Renaissance theories of right reason. He could only appeal to experiential moral wisdom, to those pragmatic virtues which he thought might best serve the majority of men, "the ways and means of ordinary happiness."

He recognized in Byron's poetry the war-weary cynicism that he himself felt in darker moments. Byron's heroes were, on first encounter, the most compelling figures in contemporary poetry. But Byron's "fierce and magnificent misanthropy" was a form of psychic suicide. He taught his fascinated readers that a courageous, independent spirit must end in misery and guilt, that only hypocrites and cowards can succeed in the world. "Lord Byron's poetry, in short, is too attractive and too famous to lie dormant or inoperative; and therefore, if it produce any painful or pernicious effects, there will be murmurs, and ought to be suggestions of alteration." The Byronic hero, Jeffrey noted, ends as a burnt-out case. The majority of men find what fulfillment life allows them only through the practice of those conventional virtues which Byron's poetry taught them to view with contempt. When *Cain* (1821) provoked howls from pious readers and reviewers, Jeffrey counseled Byron as one Scottish skeptic to another:

> Now, we can certainly have no objection to Lord Byron writing an Essay on the Origin of Evil — and sifting the whole of that vast and perplexing subject with the force and the freedom that would be expected and allowed in a fair philosophical discussion. But we do not think it fair, thus to argue it partially and *con amore*, in the name of Lucifer and Cain; without the responsibility or the liability to answer that would attach to a philosophical disputant — and in a form which both doubles the danger, if the sentiments are pernicious, and almost precludes his opponents from the possibility of a reply.[66]

Death works wonders for some men's reputations. Byron passed into myth at Missolonghi, and Burns became a Scottish culture-hero. When Jeffrey reviewed the *Reliques of Robert Burns* (1808), the majority of Scottish literati had already forgiven or forgotten those indiscretions which had once denied Burns entrée to their drawing rooms. Jeffrey admired Burns's songs and tender poetry of rustic life. Unlike Wordsworth, Burns had treated humble subjects without sliding into insipidity.[67] But Jeffrey was troubled by Burns's "contempt, or affectation of contempt, for prudence, decency, and regularity; and his admiration of thoughtlessness, oddity, and vehement sensibility; — his belief, in short, in *the dispensing power* of genius and social feeling, in all matters of morality and common sense."[68] Jeffrey suspected that an irregular life-style might be essential to creative genius,[69] but Burns had overplayed the role of the roaring boyo. A poet is still a man, and a man has responsibilities to more than his muse and the demimonde. "It requires no habit of deep thinking, nor any thing more, indeed, than the information of an honest heart, to perceive . . . that it is a vile prostitution of language, to talk of that man's generosity or goodness of heart, who sits raving about friendship and philanthropy in a tavern, while his wife's heart is breaking at her cheerless fireside, and his children pining in solitary poverty."[70] Burns's ways were not the ways and means of ordinary happiness.

This may read like pure priggery today, and it gave offense to Burns's admirers when it was published.[71] But Jeffrey knew that Burns was a leading figure in the Scottish cult of sentiment, and his remarks illustrate his ambivalent attitude toward the whole sentimental movement. In eighteenth-century France and Britain, *bienfaisance* or sentimentalism involved belief in the natural goodness of uncorrupted man and concern with the nonintellective side of human personality. In Scotland, moral philosophers cited the emotions as the basic element in moral life, and moral philosophers turned aestheticians praised that literature which deepened and purified the culture of the heart. Their emphasis on sympathetic emotion and an uncorrupted heart passed from philosophy to Scottish pulpits, poetry, and prose fiction. Hugh Blair's sermons charmed even Samuel Johnson, although Johnson knew that "the dog is a Scotchman, and a Presbyterian, and every thing he should not be."[72] In imaginative literature, sentiment was all. Henry Mackenzie's *Man of Feeling* (1771), *Man of the World* (1773), and *Julia de Roubigné* (1777) set the tone of "moral weeping" for contemporary Scottish novelists. John Home's *Douglas* (1757) proved, at least to some Scottish minds, that Shakespeare and Scottish sentiment were reconcilable. The anonymous lyrics of Scottish songs and the poetry of Allan Ramsay,

Robert Fergusson, and James Macpherson all prepared the way for Robert Burns.

Jeffrey did his share of moral weeping, especially when reading of unhappy children or domestic love. "I know no one of more domestic habits," Mrs. Anne Grant wrote of him, "nor any one to whom the charities of home and kindred seem more endeared. If the world were not full of inconsistency, I would say it was almost impossible to reconcile the asperity of his criticisms with the general kindness of his disposition."[73] He was deeply moved by the pathos of Thomas Campbell's *Gertrude of Wyoming* (1809) and of Samuel Rogers's *Human Life* (1819).[74] His letters to Dickens on *Dombey and Son* (1846-48) are embarrassing.[75] In an essay "On the Present State of Periodical Criticism" in the *Edinburgh Annual Register* of 1809, Scott concluded that sentiment was the only constant factor in Jeffrey's literary criticism: "Were we to attempt to make any general deduction from a style of criticism so shadowy and variable, we should say, that subjects of pathos, bearing immediate reference to domestic feelings and affections, seem to come most home to the critic's bosom."[76]

But Jeffrey knew that strong sensibility is often used as an excuse for self-indulgence. He found something mawkish in the novels of Richardson and Sterne, and he recognized the dangers of "sentimental rant" in a revolutionary age.[77] Mackenzie might indulge in moral weeping and still support, sometimes ruthlessly, Henry Dundas's attempt to maintain the political and social status quo. In France, however, the theorists of revolution had put the doctrine of man's natural goodness to a test. In England, the Lake Poets' early poetry revealed the pervasive influence of Rousseau's "antisocial principles, and distempered sensibility, . . . his perpetual hankerings after some unattainable state of voluptuous virtue and perfection."[78] All this Rousseauist rant on uncorrupted man countered Jeffrey's basic concept of the human condition — "*considerably* lower than angels," something short of perfectible. He preferred a mixture of sense and sensibility, the balance that he found in Crabbe's poetry and Scott's novels — a benevolence that encouraged tolerance and compromise, a benevolence that admitted the essential flaws in human nature.[79]

Jeffrey's concern with the moral aspects of imaginative literature has earned him the contempt of modern critics and literary historians whose concern is exclusively aesthetic.[80] But Jeffrey was a critic of contemporary life, not just contemporary literature. He believed that "the great art is the art of living; and the chief science, the science of being happy."[81] He knew that powerful literature does practically affect men's attitudes, and he recognized that the authors of the *Lyrical Ballads, Waverley*, and *Don Juan* had written in the same belief. Poetry — the suggestive power of words — delighted him. As a young man at Oxford and Edinburgh, he thought to make his living as a poet. As a judge and a member of Parliament, he took Elizabethan verse to the court and the Commons, to read when law or politics allowed. Jeffrey was not a Philistine, but he did believe that poetry and prose fiction are of value, finally, as means of promoting human happiness. Studying the spirit of his time, he recognized a basic restlessness — a rejection of more than eighteenth-century literary models. And he was wary. Like the mature Goethe, Jeffrey believed that any new freedom of the spirit must be matched by a corresponding gain in self-discipline. His basic concern was the strength of those personal and civic ties which Cicero called *duties*.

Conclusion

In his *Reminiscences* Carlyle recalled the case in which Jeffrey first won a wide reputation as an advocate. He was defending one Nell Kennedy of Dumfriesshire, who was accused of having poisoned her neighbor and his household. "Horror was universal in those solitary quiet regions," Carlyle remembered, and there was widespread conviction of poor Nell's guilt:

> in the Border regions, where it was the universal topic, perhaps not one human creature doubted but Nell was the criminal, and would get her doom. Assize-time came, Jeffrey there; and Jeffrey, by such a play of advocacy as was never seen before, bewildered the poor jury into temporary deliquium, or loss of wits (so that the poor foreman, *Scotticé* "chancellor," on whose casting-vote it turned, said at last, with the sweat bursting from his brow, "Mercy, then, Mercy!"), and brought Nell clear off, — home that night, riding gently out of Dumfries in men's clothes to escape the rage of the mob. The jury-chancellor, they say, on awakening next morning, smote his now dry brow, with a gesture of despair, and exclaimed, "Was I mad?"[1]

Jeffrey affects some readers in the same way. He was an able advocate, in and out of court, at a time when lawyers dominated Scottish letters. A liberal education and his own curiosity encouraged him to study a wide range of subjects, and he wrote his reviews with the same sharp analysis and sometimes with the same legal language that he used in preparing courtroom briefs. We read him, we are persuaded, and in the morning we awake with second thoughts. Jeffrey was quick-minded, and those of us who find epistemology or politics somewhat harder going may suspect that he was

177

also superficial. But Jeffrey was raised in a community where criticism was a way of life. At the Speculative Society, the Academy of Physics, and the Friday Club, clergymen, physicians, geologists, and aestheticians educated one another in the methodology and basic data of different disciplines. Jeffrey absorbed it all. He read hard, thought hard, and in the process he developed a pragmatic critical response to the innovative and reactionary movements of his time.

Hazlitt once described Jeffrey as "a person in advance of the age, and yet perfectly fitted both from knowledge and habits of mind to put a curb upon its rash and headlong spirit."[2] Hazlitt knew his man, and the description fits. Jeffrey was a skeptical thinker, shaped by the most subjectivistic elements in British thought. He believed that mankind's fundamental epistemological and ontological assumptions are finally unverifiable — that moral approbation and aesthetic pleasure are essentially subjective, associational responses. But the skeptic was a critic, and the critic was a Scotsman, with all the practical instincts of the Scottish intellectual milieu. As a critic, Jeffrey proposed working standards for the conduct of life and the practice of art. Without elevating the epistemological and ontological assumptions of mankind to the status of philosophical first principles, he settled for the basic common sense on mind and matter, working by that chastened empiricism which would serve as a counterpoint to philosophical idealism for the remainder of the nineteenth century. In matters of private conduct and public legislation, he recommended the common impressions of morality as a salutary guide, and he argued that a literature of wide and lasting appeal must be based on those associational responses which are shared by the majority of men.

Judging Jeffrey's politics was and is a problem of perspective. In the eyes of the radical *Westminster Review*, the *Edinburgh Review* and its editor appeared as the champions of oligarchic Whig control.[3] But to conservative journals like *John Bull*, the *Edinburgh Review* was a kind of Caledonian antichrist, the "prolific parent of all that is base in principle and mischievous in morals, . . . originally established for the purpose of conveying the poison of the French philosophism to the hearts of the British people."[4] Jeffrey and his *Review* did carry on the Enlightenment attack upon religious bigotry and social prejudice, campaigning against Catholic Disabilities, against the slave trade, and for a more liberal policy in Ireland. But Jeffrey was a moderate, a pragmatist, practicing the art of the possible. In his political reviews, he sidestepped the issue of the abstract rights of man and concentrated upon the practical machinery of representative government. Measured by modern democratic standards, his political thinking was elitist. Measured by the general level of political intelligence in the early nineteenth century, his thinking was enlightened.

There are more heroic virtues than pragmatism, and Jeffrey knew it. There are more exciting modes of thought than the cool empiricism he publicly espoused. But Jeffrey deserves a more comprehensive reading than that which literary historians have been inclined to grant. Coleridge recognized that the *Edinburgh Review* was a major force in public education — a source of that "diffusion of knowledge"[5] which led to and partly justified the passing of the First Reform Bill. For that pedagogic service the public was in Jeffrey's debt. In the years when the British middle class for whom he wrote were assuming control of British culture, he analyzed contemporary problems in terms of philosophical first principles. Through his own essays and through the editorial additions that he made to the work of his contributors, he brought to English parsonages, clubs, and country houses the critical experience of Scotland in her prime.

But Scotland's prime was passing. By the late 1820s, when Jeffrey retired from the *Review*, forces were at work that would weaken the enlightened Scottish culture he had known. A wave of Evangelical enthusiasm had begun to embitter and divide the ranks of Scottish men of letters. At the same time, a Royal Commission was established to inquire whether Scottish undergraduate instruction should be revised to conform to the Oxford-Cambridge models, with less general training in philosophy and more detailed training in Greek and mathematics. By mid-nineteenth century both religious enthusiasts and academic specialists had combined to undermine that critical, encyclopedic culture which Jeffrey's generation had inherited from Smith, Kames, and Hume. An old man, Jeffrey saw the changes and regretted them. He knew that something valuable in Scottish life was lost.

Notes

CHAPTER 1

1. Edward Topham, *Letters from Edinburgh in 1774 and 1775* (1776; reprint ed. Edinburgh: James Thin, 1971), p. 208.

2. Sir James Mackintosh, quoted in Henry Lord Cockburn's *Life of Lord Jeffrey, with a Selection from His Correspondence* (Philadelphia: Lippincott, 1852), 1: 45.

3. On population, see James Gray Kyd's *Scottish Population Statistics,* Publications of the Scottish Historical Society, 3d series, no. 44 (Edinburgh: Constable, 1952). For information on Scottish club life, I am indebted to Henry Gray Graham, *The Social Life of Scotland in the Eighteenth Century,* 4th ed. (London: Black, 1937); John M. Lothian, ed., *Lectures on Rhetoric and Belles Lettres Delivered in the University of Glasgow by Adam Smith,* Landmarks in Rhetoric and Public Address (Carbondale and Edwardsville, Ill.: Southern Illinois University Press, 1963), pp. xiii-xxxix; D. D. McElroy, "The Literary Clubs and Societies of Eighteenth Century Scotland," Dissertation, Edinburgh University 1952; Ernest Campbell Mossner, *The Life of David Hume* (Austin: University of Texas Press, 1954).

4. John Gregory, *A Father's Legacy to His Daughters* (Edinburgh: Creech, 1788), pp. 39, 41.

5. For Hume's correspondence with Reid and Campbell, see *The Letters of David Hume,* ed. J. Y. T. Greig (Oxford: Clarendon Press, 1932), 1: 360-61, 375-76.

6. Reid to David Hume, 18 March 1763, *The Works of Thomas Reid,* ed. Sir William Hamilton, 6th ed. (Edinburgh: Maclachlan and Stewart, 1863), 1: 92.

7. Thomas Reid, "Of Mr. Hume's Opinion of the Idea of Power," *Essays on the Active Powers of the Human Mind* (1815; reprint ed. Cambridge, Mass. and London: M.I.T. Press, 1969), p. 29.

8. Preface quoted in McElroy's "The Literary Clubs," p. 105.

9. Monboddo's remark is quoted in Henry Gray Graham's *Scottish Men of Letters in the Eighteenth Century* (London: Black, 1901), p. 181. The proposals of the Edinburgh Society, an offshoot from the Select Society, are quoted in McElroy's "The Literary Clubs," pp. 147, 148, 155.

10. Hume to Gilbert Eliot of Minto, 2 July 1757, *Letters of David Hume,* 1: 255.

11. The phrase is Hume's, from the Introduction to *A Treatise of Human Nature,* ed. L. A. Selby-Bigge (Oxford: Clarendon Press, 1896), p. xx.

12. Tobias Smollett, *The Expedition of Humphrey Clinker* ("Matthew Bramble to Dr. Lewis, 8 August").

13. See Alexander Law, *Education in Edinburgh in the Eighteenth Century* (London: University of London Press, 1965), p. 150.

14. See Robert Kerr, *Memoirs of the Life, Writings, & Correspondence of William Smellie* (Edinburgh: Anderson, 1811), 2: 213.

15. *Scots Magazine,* July 1761, p. 390.

16. Thomas Somerville, *My Own Life and Times, 1741-1814* (Edinburgh: Edmonston & Douglas, 1861), p. 56.

17. From *Notes and Speeches on Questions Debated in the Belles Lettres Society,* quoted in McElroy's "The Literary Clubs," p. 204.

18. The primary source of biographical information on Jeffrey is Cockburn's *Life of Lord Jeffrey.* Unless otherwise indicated, biographical information is taken from Cockburn's book, cited hereafter as *Life.*

19. Cockburn, *Life* 1: 126, 127.

20. Sydney Smith to John George Clarke, 5 December 1798, quoted in G. C. Heseltine's "Five Letters of Sydney Smith," *London Mercury* 21 (March 1930): 513-14.

21. See Law, *Education in Edinburgh.* pp. 59, 78; Graham, *The Social Life of Scotland,* pp. 435-47.

22. See Henry Lord Cockburn, *Memorials of His Time,* ed. Harry A. Cockburn (Edinburgh: Foulis, 1910), pp. 3-11; John Gibson Lockhart, *Memoirs of the Life of Sir Walter Scott* (Boston: Houghton, Mifflin, 1901). 1: 22-28, 78-84 (Chaps. 2 and 3).

23. Quoted in Cockburn's *Life,* 1: 12.

24. Jeffrey to John Jeffrey, 20 May 1796, Cockburn's *Life,* 2: 26.

25. The *Dictionary of National Biography* states that Jeffrey studied under *John* Jardine at Glasgow. But George Jardine was Professor of Logic at Glasgow from 1787 to 1824. John Jardine (1716-66), a Presbyterian minister, was a friend of Adam Smith and a contributor to the first *Edinburgh Review.*

26. John Gibson Lockhart, writing as "Peter Morris," *Peter's Letters to His Kinsfolk,* 2d ed. (Edinburgh: Blackwood, 1819), 3: 191. Lockhart had himself studied under Jardine at Glasgow.

27. George Jardine, *Outlines of Philosophical Education* (Glasgow: Anderson, 1818), p. iii.

28. Ibid., p. v.

29. Ibid., p. 178.

30. Cockburn, *Life,* 1: 13.

31. Jardine, *Outlines,* p. 240.

32. Cockburn mentions these topics among the ones assigned to Jeffrey, *Life,* 1: 22-23. See Jardine, *Outlines,* p. 358.

33. Haldane is quoted in Cockburn's *Life,* 1: 16-17.

34. Jardine, *Outlines,* p. 407.

35. Quoted in Cockburn's *Life,* 1: 14.

36. See Jeffrey's reviews of later editions of Millar's works in the *Edinburgh Review* (cited hereafter as *ER*) 3 (October 1803) Art. 13: 154-81; *ER* 9 (October 1806) Art. 5: 83-92. References to the *Edinburgh Review* and other nineteenth-century periodicals have been abbreviated in the following manner: *ER* 3 (January 1802) Art. 1: 216 refers to vol. 3 of the *ER*, the January 1802 number, article 1 within that number, and the page. Jeffrey's description of Millar's lecturing style reads very much like the account of an eye-witness. But Cockburn insists that Jeffrey was not one of Millar's students. For lack of stronger evidence against Cockburn's claim, we must conclude that Jeffrey's description was based upon accounts by friends who had studied under Millar.

37. The literature on Millar is not extensive. A comprehensive study of his thought is William C. Lehmann's *John Millar of Glasgow,* Publications of the Department of Social and Economic Research, University of Glasgow, no. 4 (Cambridge: Cambridge University Press, 1960). Lehmann's volume includes Millar's *Origin of the Distinction of Ranks* (the title of the 3d ed. of *Observations Concerning the Distinction of Ranks in Society)* and a selection from Millar's other writings.

38. See Millar's *Observations,* pp. 290, 292, 294-295, 316, and the selections from his *Historical View,* pp. 348-54, 357, 326, included in Lehmann's *John Millar.*

39. *ER* 135 (April 1872) Art. 5: 207.

40. Alexander Carlyle, *Autobiography of Dr. Alexander Carlyle of Inveresk, 1722-1805,* ed. John Hill Burton (London and Edinburgh: Foulis, 1910), p. 516.

41. Cockburn, *Life,* 1: 15.

42. Jardine, *Outlines,* p. 262.

43. Jeffrey, quoted in Cockburn's *Life,* 1: 30.

44. Quoted in ibid., 1: 29-30.

45. Ibid., 25.

46. George Saintsbury, *Essays in English Literature, 1780-1860,* 3d ed. (London: Rivington, 1906), p. 103.

47. Jeffrey to Mary Jeffrey, 6 March 1792, quoted in Cockburn's *Life,* 1: 36.

48. Ibid., 25 October and 7 December 1791, quoted in Cockburn's *Life,* 1: 59.

49. Anne Grant to Miss C. M. Fanshawe, 6 October 1810, *Memoir and Correspondence of Mrs. Grant of Laggan,* ed. J. P. Grant (London: Longman, 1844), 1: 270-71.

50. Jeffrey to John Jeffrey, 20 May 1796, Cockburn's *Life,* 2: 26.

51. Jeffrey to Robert Morehead, 22 December 1795, Cockburn's *Life,* 2: 23.

52. Ibid., 26 November 1796, Cockburn's *Life,* 2: 31.

53. Quoted in Peter Mackenzie's *Life of Thomas Muir* (Glasgow: M'Phun, 1831), p. 107. Mackenzie dedicated his biography of Muir to Jeffrey, whom he described as "the Eloquent Advocate of Civil and Religious Liberty." At the time of the book's publication, Jeffrey was Lord Advocate of Scotland.

54. Jeffrey to John Jeffrey, 30 March 1793, Cockburn's *Life,* 2: 17.

55. Jeffrey to Robert Morehead, 15 January 1798, quoted in Cockburn's *Life,* 1: 82.

56. See Lockhart, *Life of Scott,* 1: 160 (chap. 6).

57. Mentioned in Cockburn's *Life*, 1: 48.

58. Henry Lord Brougham, *The Life and Times of Henry Lord Brougham* (New York: Harper & Brothers, 1871), 1: 175.

59. Quoted in William K. Dickson's *The History of the Speculative Society, 1764-1904* (Edinburgh: Constable, 1905), pp. 28-29.

60. Cockburn, *Life,* 1: 49.

61. Lockhart, *Life of Scott,* 5: 244 (chap. 41).

62. Lockhart, *Peter's Letters,* 1: 210.

63. Walter Scott, *The Heart of Midlothian,* chap. 1.

64. Ibid.

65. Jeffrey to John Jeffrey, 4 March 1799. Cockburn's *Life*, 2: 37.

66. David Welsh, *Account of the Life and Writings of Thomas Brown* (Edinburgh: Tait, 1825), p. 77. Thomas Brown (1778-1820) was a physician who became a joint-Professor, with Dugald Stewart, in Moral Philosophy at Edinburgh.

67. For an analysis of the confusing circumstances surrounding the conception of the *Review,* see John Clive, *Scotch Reviewers* (Cambridge, Mass.: Harvard University Press, 1957), pp. 186-97.

68. See Brougham, *Life and Times,* 1: 180. On the dangers of relying exclusively on Brougham's memory of things, see Arthur Aspinall, "Lord Brougham's 'Life and Times,'" *English Historical Review* 59 (January 1944): 81-112. Thomas Thomson (1768-1852) was a lawyer who subsequently made a significant contribution to the study of Scottish antiquities as Deputy Clerk-Register of Scotland and as President, after Walter Scott, of the Bannatyne Club.

69. Brougham, *Life and Times,* 1: 180; Sydney Smith to James Mackintosh, 13 January 1802, a letter in the Mackintosh Collection of the Wedgwood Museum, quoted in A. S. Bell's "An Unpublished Letter on the Edinburgh Review," *Times Literary Supplement,* 9 April 1970, p. 388.

70. Brougham, *Life and Times,* 1: 180.

71. Cockburn, *Life,* 1: 101-2.

72. Sydney Smith, *The Works of the Rev. Sydney Smith* (London: Longman, 1850), p. iii.

73. It was Mounier who proposed the famous Oath of the Tennis Court on 20 June 1789.

74. Mackintosh's remark is quoted in Horner's letter to Francis Jeffrey, 30 May 1803. This letter is part (vol. 2, item 11) of the Horner Collection in the British Library of Political and Economic Science of the London School of Economics. It is not included among the letters published in the official *Memoirs and Correspondence of Francis Horner, M.P.,* ed. Leonard Horner, 2 vols. (Boston: Little, Brown, 1853).

75. *ER* 1 (October 1802) Art. 1: 1-2, 6-7, 7, 7-8, 8, 9, 10, 11, 10. See also Jeffrey's review of Bailly's *Mémoires d'un témoin de la révolution, ER* 6 (April 1805) Art. 12: 137-49.

76. Jeffrey to Robert Morehead, 24 May 1802, Cockburn, *Life,* 2: 57.

77. These figures are taken from Henry Brougham's letter to James Loch, 12 December 1803, *Brougham and His Early Friends,* ed. R.H.M. Buddle Atkinson

and G. A. Jackson (London: Darlington and Pead, 1908), 2: 102; Francis Horner to James Loch, 7 November 1802, *Memoirs and Correspondence of Francis Horner,* 1: 210. See also Clive, *Scotch Reviewers,* p. 30.

78. Scott to George Ellis, 2 November 1808, *The Letters of Sir Walter Scott,* ed. H. J. C. Grierson, Centenary ed. (London: Constable, 1932), 2: 121.

79. Jeffrey to Francis Horner, 11 May 1803, Cockburn's *Life,* 2: 62. Jeffrey was himself quoting Longman. A "sheet" was sixteen printed pages.

80. Ibid., 11 May 1803, Cockburn's *Life,* 2: 63.

81. Horner to Francis Jeffrey, 30 May 1803, Horner Collection (vol. 2, item 11).

82. Brougham, *Life and Times,* 1: 188.

83. *Quarterly Review* 91 (June 1852) Art. 5: 125. The writer was Lockhart.

84. Adam Smith, *An Inquiry into the Nature and Causes of the Wealth of Nations,* Cannan ed. (New York: Modern Library, 1937), p. 748 (bk. 5, chap. 1, pt. 3).

85. Peter Gay, *The Enlightenment: An Interpretation: The Rise of Modern Paganism* (New York: Knopf, 1967), pp. 130, 131.

CHAPTER 2

1. Hume, *Treatise,* pp. xx, 22 (Introduction and bk. 1, pt. 1, sec. 7).

2. Berkeley's purpose was to refute skepticism rather than to advance it. "If the principles, which I here endeavour to propagate, are admitted for true; the consequences which, I think, evidently flow from thence, are, that *atheism* and *scepticism* will be utterly destroyed, many intricate points made plain, great difficulties solved, several useless parts of science retrenched, speculation referred to practice, and men reduced from paradoxes to common sense" (Preface to "Three Dialogues between Hylas and Philonous," *The Works of George Berkeley,* ed. A. A. Luce and T. E. Jessop, vol. 2 [London: Thomas Nelson, 1949]: 168). But eighteenth-century readers understandably interpreted his epistemology as an argument for the skeptic's side.

3. David Hume, "Enquiry Concerning Human Understanding," *The Philosophical Works,* ed. T. H. Green and T. H. Grose (1882: reprint ed. Darmstadt: Scientia Verlag Aalen, 1964), 4: 125-26.

4. Hume, *Treatise,* p. 250 (bk. 1, pt. 4, sec. 5).

5. Ibid., p. 252 (bk. 1, pt. 4, sec. 6). But Hume admitted in an Appendix to the *Treatise* that he was not satisfied with this explanation of the notion of personal identity: "In short there are two principles, which I cannot render consistent; nor is it in my power to renounce either of them, viz. *that all our distinct perceptions are distinct existences,* and *that the mind never perceives any real connexion among distinct existences.* . . . For my part, I must plead the privilege of a sceptic, and confess, that this difficulty is too hard for my understanding."

6. Hume, *Treatise,* pp. 89, 165 (bk. 1, pt. 3, secs. 6 and 14).

7. Hume, "My Own Life," *Philosophical Works,* 3:, 2.

8. Quoted in Mossner's *Life of David Hume,* p. 367.

9. Reid to David Hume, 18 March 1763, *Works of Thomas Reid,* 1: 91;

Reid, "Of the Sentiments of Mr. Hume," *Essays on the Intellectual Powers of Man* (1814; reprint ed. Cambridge, Mass. and London: M.I.T. Press, 1969), pp. 198-99; Reid, "Of Mr. Hume's Opinion of the Idea of Power," *Essays on the Active Powers,* p. 29. Reid found the origin of Locke's theory of knowledge in "the ideal system" of Descartes.

10. Reid, "An Inquiry into the Human Mind on the Principles of Common Sense," *Works,* 1: 106, 209.

11. Reid, "The First Principles of Contingent Truths" and "The First Principles of Necessary Truths," *Essays on the Intellectual Powers,* pp. 622, 641, 652.

12. Reid, "Inquiry into the Human Mind on the Principles of Common Sense," *Works,* 1: 209.

13. Reid, "Of Mr. Hume's Opinion of the Idea of Power," *Essays on the Active Powers,* p. 29.

14. Arthur O. Lovejoy, "The Parallel of Deism and Classicism," *Essays in the History of Ideas* (Baltimore, Md.: Johns Hopkins Press, 1948), p. 78. Lovejoy points out that faith in the *consensus gentium* and a cultivation of independent, analytical reason, both characteristic of Enlightenment philosophy, were potentially incompatible. Coexistence was possible as long as individual reason was turned upon the eccentric beliefs or dogma of a specific age or institution, but Hume turned reason upon the *consensus* itself.

15. Hume, *Treatise,* pp. 269, 273 (bk. 1, pt. 4, sec. 7); "Enquiry Concerning Human Understanding," *Philosophical Works,* 4: 132, 131, 6.

16. Quoted in Cockburn's *Life,* 1: 29-30; *ER* 8 (July 1806) Art. 7: 328.

17. Horner to Francis Jeffrey, 13 August 1804, *Memoirs and Correspondence of Francis Horner,* 2: 272.

18. See *ER* 2 (April 1803) Art. 1: 1; *ER* 4 (April 1804) Art. 1: 1-26; *ER* 1 (October 1802) Art. 7: 63-72.

19. Jeffrey to Thomas Carlyle, 19 - - - - 1827, Jeffrey Correspondence (Ms. 787, letter 9), National Library of Scotland; Jeffrey to Carlyle, 16 May 1831, quoted in David Alec Wilson's *Carlyle to "The French Revolution" (1827-1837)* (London and New York: Kegan Paul, 1924), p. 203.

20. Jeffrey to Macvey Napier, 23 November 1829, *Selection from the Correspondence of the Late Macvey Napier,* ed. by his son, Macvey Napier (London: Macmillan, 1879), p. 70.

21. See *ER* 10 (April 1807) Art. 6: 101-2; *ER* 42 (August 1825) Art. 7: 417.

22. *ER* 9 (October 1806) Art. 9: 157, 158. Stewart's phrase is found in his "Philosophical Essays," *Works of Dugald Stewart* (Cambridge: Hilliard and Brown, 1829), 4: 3. In discussing the Materialist argument, Jeffrey began by admitting that man has "no distinct idea of substance, and that...it is impossible to combine three propositions upon the subject, without involving a contradiction." Materialists and their opponents, in arguing about the identity or radical distinction of the substance of mind and matter, are arguing about a subject, *substance,* of which "we have no distinct notion." We have distinct ideas about the qualities of substance, however, and the controversy can be analyzed on that level. On analysis, Jeffrey found the Materialist's reasoning sometimes inconsistent, sometimes unintelligible: "... it seems a little disorderly and unphilosoph-

ical, to class perception among the qualities of matter, when it is obvious, that it is by means of perception alone that we get any notion of matter or its qualities." The problem was not clarified by the Materialist's claim that perception is the quality of matter by which matter becomes conscious of its own existence: "It is plain that this [perception] is not a quality, but a knowledge of qualities; and that the percipient must necessarily be distinct from that which is perceived by it." The obvious objection to this tenet of Materialism is "that it makes the faculty of perception a quality of the thing perceived, and converts, in a way that must at first sight appear absurd to all mankind, our knowledge of the qualities of matter into another quality of the same substance." For further refinements on this argument, see *ER* 9 (October 1806) Art. 9: 153-60.

23. *ER* 17 (November 1810) Art. 9: 180, 172; *ER* 10 (April 1807) Art. 12: 197; *ER* 3 (January 1804) Art. 1: 277; *ER* 7 (October 1805) Art. 12: 175.

24. *ER* 3 (January 1804) Art. 1: 281; *ER* 7 (October 1805) Art. 12: 172, 172-73. Dugald Stewart noted that the terms *Ideal* and *Idealist* had become ambiguous terms in the epistemological writings of the latter eighteenth century: "In England, the word *Idealist* is most commonly restricted to such as (with Berkeley) reject the existence of a material world. Of late, its meaning has been sometimes extended (particularly since the publications of Reid) to all those who retain the theory of Descartes and Locke, concerning the immediate objects of our perceptions and thoughts, whether they admit or reject the consequences deduced from this theory by the Berkeleians. In the present state of the science, it would contribute much to the distinctness of our reasonings, were it to be used in the last sense exclusively" ("Dissertation," *Works*, 6: 360). In his review of Drummond's *Academical Questions*, Jeffrey used *ideal* in the Berkeleian sense. In his review of Stewart's *Account of the Life and Writings of Thomas Reid*, he used *ideal* as a term to describe Locke's representational theory of ideas.

25. *ER* 7 (October 1805) Art. 12: 173. See also *ER* 3 (January 1804) Art. 1: 282.

26. *ER* 7 (October 1805) Art. 12: 174, 173.

27. *ER* 7 (October 1805) Art. 12: 173, 174, 174-75, 175.

28. *ER* 3 (January 1804) Art 1: 283, 284; *ER* 7 (October 1805) Art. 12: 175.

29. James Beattie, "Essay on the Nature and Immutability of Truth," *Essays* (1776; reprint ed. New York: Garland, 1971), p. 141.

30. Samuel Johnson to James Boswell, 5 July 1773, *Boswell's Life of Johnson*, Oxford Standard Authors ed., new ed. (Oxford: Oxford University Press, 1953), p. 550. Jeffrey commented on the English reception of Beattie and his *Essay:* "The truth is, that the Essay acquired its popularity, partly from the indifference and dislike which has long prevailed in England, as to metaphysical inquiries; partly from the perpetual appeal which it affects to make from philosophical subtlety to common sense; and partly from the accidental circumstances of the author. It was a great matter for the orthodox scholars of the south, who knew little of metaphysics themselves, to get a Scotch professor of philosophy to take up the gauntlet in their behalf" (*ER* 10 [April 1807] Art. 12: 197).

31. *ER* 10 (April 1807) Art. 12: 193).

32. Ibid. pp. 194, 195.

33. Beattie, "Essay on Truth," p. 327.

34. Ibid.

35. *ER* 10 (April 1807) Art. 12: 196.

36. *ER* 3 (January 1804) Art. 1: 273: *ER* 17 (November 1810) Art. 9: 180.

37. See Stewart, "Account of the Life and Writings of Thomas Reid," *Works*, 7: 228-71.

38. *ER* 3 (January 1804) Art 1: 273. Hume does begin the *Treatise* by predicting the establishment of a "solid foundation" for "the science of man," a science "which will not be inferior in certainty, and will be much superior in utility to any other of human comprehension." It was probably Hume's Introduction that Jeffrey had in mind here. But the epistemological section of the *Treatise* closes in chastened tones, and it was the Hume who recognized the limitations of empirical epistemology whom Jeffrey admired.

39. Jeffrey did not review any work by Kant, but he did make passing reference to Kant's "obscurity" in his review of Drummond's *Academical Questions*. Kant did not find a sympathetic Scottish interpreter until Sir William Hamilton began to write for the *ER* in 1829.

40. *ER* 17 (November 1810) Art. 9: 176; *ER* 3 (January 1804) Art. 1: 277.

41. *ER* 17 (November 1810) Art. 9: 184; *ER* 3 (January 1804) Art. 1: 273-74. See also *ER* 17 (November 1810) Art. 9: 177-78.

42. *ER* 3 (January 1804) Art. 1: 275.

43. Horner to Francis Jeffrey, 11 February 1804, Horner Collection (vol. 2, item 43).

44. Jeffrey to Francis Horner, 19 February 1804, Cockburn's *Life*, 2: 75. In his seventies Jeffrey added this footnote to his reprinted review of Stewart's *Philosophical Essays*: "Upwards of thirty years have now elapsed since this was written, during which a taste for metaphysical inquiry has revived in France, and been greatly encouraged in Germany. Yet I am not aware to what useful applications of the science its votaries can yet point; or what practical improvement or increase of human power they can trace to its cultivation" (Francis Jeffrey, *Contributions to the Edinburgh Review* [Boston: Phillips, 1856] , p. 510).

45. *ER* 3 (January 1804) Art. 1: 276.

CHAPTER 3

1. Jeffrey to Mary Jeffrey, 2 November 1791, Cockburn's *Life* 2: 13.

2. Francis Hutcheson, *A Short Introduction to Moral Philosophy* (Glasgow: Foulis, 1747), p. 2.

3. Summaries always do injustice to someone. For a possible corrective the reader may wish to consult three other summaries, somewhat different in emphases: Gladys Bryson, *Man and Society* (Princeton, N.J.: Princeton University Press, 1945), pp. 15-29; Louis Schneider, ed., *The Scottish Moralists on Human Nature and Society* (Chicago and London: University of Chicago Press, 1967), pp. xvi-lxxviii; Paul Stein, "Law and Society in Eighteenth-Century Scottish Thought," *Scotland in the Age of Improvement*, ed. N. T. Phillipson and Rosalind Mitchison (Edinburgh: Edinburgh University Press, 1970), pp. 148-68.

4. Hume, *Treatise*, pp. 414-15 (bk. 2, sec. 3). Hume analyzed what he

believed to be the common misrepresentation of the Reason vs. Passion argument in bk. 2 of the *Treatise*. But Reid believed that Hume's own statement of the argument involved a gross misuse of language. A critical student of Hume's writings and of the Lockean tradition, Reid was wary of the subjectivist elements in contemporary moral philosophy. Among the principles of human action, he included "rational principles." Unlike Hume, who had argued that Reason only guides us in the choice of the means to attain those ends to which the Passions have already impelled us, Reid believed that Reason can select the ends. See Essays 3 and 5 of his *Essays on the Active Powers of the Human Mind*.

5. Francis Hutcheson, *An Inquiry into the Original of Our Ideas of Beauty and Virtue*, 2d ed. (1726; reprint ed. New York: Garland, 1971), p. 216.

6. Hume, "Enquiry Concerning Human Understanding," *Philosophical Works*. 4: 68.

7. Millar, "Observations," p. 176, included in Lehmann's *John Millar*.

8. Adam Ferguson, *An Essay on the History of Civil Society* (1767; reprint ed. New York: Garland, 1971), p. 28.

9. Reid, "Of Desires," *Essays on the Active Powers,* p. 137.

10. Ferguson, *Essay on the History of Civil Society,* p. 12. In his *Treatise,* Hume did argue that justice is not a natural virtue, but, "to avoid giving offence, I must here observe, that when I deny justice to be a natural virtue, I make use of the word, *natural,* only as opposed to *artificial.* In another sense of the word, as no principle of the human mind is more natural than a sense of virtue; so no virtue is more natural than justice."

11. But Smith also adapted Mandeville's idea that "Private Vices" can become "Public Benefits." In pursuing his private good, capitalist man promotes the economic welfare of his society.

12. Hume, "Enquiry Concerning the Principles of Morals," *Philosophical Works,* 4: 208 n.

13. Ferguson, however, was wary of the corruptions of commercial advancement (*Essay*, pp. 282-87). He warned of the effects of division of labor upon the laboring class, a warning that Smith and Millar repeated.

14. *ER* 7 (January 1806) Art. 7: 416; *ER* 10 (April 1807) Art. 6: 89; *ER* 4 (April 1804) Art. 1: 12. See also *ER* 13 (January 1809) Art. 5: 349-50.

15. *ER* 10 (April 1807) Art. 12: 197.

16. See Hume's "The Sceptic," *Philosophical Works,* 3: 213-31. In this essay and its companion pieces ("The Epicurean," "The Stoic," and "The Platonist"), Hume is using philosophical personae. But the arguments of "The Sceptic" are a consistent development of the realtivistic elements in Hume's theory of the moral sentiments. This relativistic aspect was, as Norman Kemp Smith remarks, a side of his argument "to which Hume, very understandably, was not concerned to draw special attention" (Smith, *The Philosophy of David Hume* [London: Macmillan, 1949], p. 200). But it was the aspect that impressed Jeffrey. See Sydney Smith's letter to Jeffrey, April or May 1804, in which Smith mimics Jeffrey's Humean analysis of the moral sentiments (*The Letters of Sydney Smith,* ed. Nowell C. Smith [Oxford: Clarendon Press, 1953], 1: 95-96).

17. *ER* 21 (February 1813) Art. 1: 12, 13; *ER* 10 (April 1807) Art. 12: 197.

18. *ER* 7 (October 1805) Art. 12: 175; *ER* 4 (April 1804) Art. 1: 11; *ER* 7 (January 1806) Art. 7: 418.

19. The *Traités de législation civile et pénale* was an edition of several of Bentham's previously unpublished manuscripts, translated into French by a disciple, Etienne Dumont. Dumont's series of editions and translations were for many years the most influential literary expression of Bentham's ideas.

20. *ER* 4 (April 1804) Art. 1: 10-11.

21. See ibid., p. 12. Bentham claimed that he had learned to see utility as the test of all virtue from reading bk. 2 ("Of Morals") of Hume's *Treatise*. See Jeremy Bentham, *A Fragment on Government and An Introduction to the Principles of Morals and Legislation*, ed. Wilfred Harrison (Oxford: Blackwell, 1948), p. 50 n. 2. In fact, it was Hutcheson who first gave Scottish statement to the utilitarian principle, "that Action is best, which procures the greatest Happiness for the greatest Numbers": *Inquiry into the Original of Our Ideas of Beauty and Virtue*, p. 177.

22. *ER* 4 (April 1804) Art. 1: 11, 13.

23. Ibid., pp. 15, 13, 14-15.

24. *ER* 21 (February 1813) Art. 1: 14, 11, 14-15. See also *ER* 27 (December 1816) Art. 1: 298-99.

25. *ER* 21 (February 1813) Art. 1: 16. See also *ER* 10 (April 1807) Art. 6: 88; *ER* 18 (May 1811) Art. 1: 7; *ER* 16 (April 1810) Art. 2: 36; *ER* 30 (September 1818) Art. 9: 464-65.

26. Jeffrey to Lord Cockburn, 28 March 1833, quoted in Cockburn's *Life*, 1: 270.

27. Quoted in Wilson's *Carlyle to "The French Revolution,"* p. 181.

28. See Horner to Francis Jeffrey, 16 July 1810, *Memoirs and Correspondence of Francis Horner*, 2: 26-27. See also Jeffrey to Lord Cockburn, 28 August 1835, Cockburn's *Life*, 2: 215-16 and *ER* 62 (October 1835) Art. 11: 132-36.

29. Jeffrey to Francis Horner, 9 March 1806, Cockburn's *Life*, 2: 90. See also *ER* 27 (December 1816) Art. 1: 300.

30. *ER* 8 (July 1806) Art. 18: 456.

31. Thomas Moore, *Memoirs, Journal, and Correspondence*, ed. Lord John Russell (London: Longman, 1853), 5: 203-4.

32. Ibid., p. 205.

33. The breakfast was arranged by that master breakfast-giver, the banker-poet Samuel Rogers.

34. Jeffrey to George Joseph Bell, 22 August 1806, quoted in Cockburn's *Life*, 1: 138. Neither Jeffrey nor Moore could hold a grudge. Jeffrey enlisted Moore in the ranks of the Edinburgh Reviewers, and their friendship ripened with the years. "I was surprised this morning," Jeffrey wrote in 1823, "to run against my old friend Tommy Moore, who looks younger, I think, than when we met at Chalk Farm some sixteen years ago." Quoted by Lord Moncreiff of Tulliebole in James Taylor's *Lord Jeffrey and Craigcrook* (Edinburgh: Douglas, 1892), p. 24.

35. Jeffrey to Charles Wilkes, 9 May 1818, Cockburn's *Life*, 2: 144.

36. Jeffrey to Lord Cockburn, 28 March 1833, quoted in Cockburn's *Life*, 1: 270.

37. Quoted in Wilson's *Carlyle to "The French Revolution,"* p. 81.

38. Ibid., p. 35; Thomas Carlyle, *Reminiscences,* ed. Charles Eliot Norton (London: Macmillan, 1887), 2: 273.

39. Jeffrey to Thomas Carlyle, 4 (or 24) January 1829, Jeffrey Correspondence (Ms. 787, letter 22).

40. See *Quarterly Review* 91 (June 1852) Art. 5: 134.

41. Lockhart to John Wilson Croker, 10 April 1852, quoted in Myron F. Brightfield's *John Wilson Croker* (Berkeley: University of California Press, 1940), p. 422.

42. For Smith's articles, see *ER* 11 (January 1808) Art. 5: 341-62; *ER* 12 (April 1808) Art. 9: 151-81.

43. See Horner's letters to John Archibald Murray of 15 February 1796 and 21 March 1797, Horner Collection (vol. 1, items 3 and 33); Brougham to Francis Horner, 27 March 1797, Horner Collection (vol. 1, item 34). A censored version of the 1796 letter is included in the *Memoirs and Correspondence of Francis Horner.*

44. Francis Horner to Thomas Thomson, 10 January 1804, Horner Collection (vol. 2, item 38).

45. Horner to Francis Jeffrey, 28 September 1805 (?), Horner Collection (vol. 2, item 44). In a letter of 29 October 1805, Smith warned Jeffrey against allowing "antichristian sentiments" to appear in the *Review:* ". . . you must be thoroughly aware that the rumor of infidelity decides not only the reputation but the existence of the Review" (*Letters of Sydney Smith,* 1: 109).

46. Quoted in M. J. Holland, Viscountess Knutsford's *Life and Letters of Zachary Macaulay* (London: Edward Arnold, 1900), p. 482.

47. Horner to Francis Jeffrey, 13 August 1804, Horner Collection (vol. 2, item 67). A censored version of this letter is included in the *Memoirs and Correspondence of Francis Horner.*

48. *ER* 7 (January 1806) Art. 7: 434.

49. That suggestion is strongest in his review of Robert Morehead's *A Series of Discourses on the Principles of Religious Belief* (1809), *ER* 14 (April 1809) Art. 7: 82-95. But Morehead was Jeffrey's cousin and close friend, and Jeffrey's remarks on "the Temporal Advantages of Christianity" and "rational religion" could be seconded by any secular humanist.

50. *ER* 1 (January 1803) Art. 3: 304.

51. See *ER* 17 (November 1810) Art. 9: 186; *ER* 20 (July 1812) Art. 1: 26-27; *ER* 46 (June 1827) Art. 2: 43-44.

52. The phrases are Horner's, from a letter to Francis Jeffrey, 16 July 1810, *Memoirs and Correspondence of Francis Horner,* 2: 26-27.

53. Cockburn, *Life,* 1: 282.

54. *ER* 20 (November 1812) Art. 2: 279.

55. Jeffrey to Thomas Carlyle, 16 May 1831, quoted in Wilson's *Carlyle to "The French Revolution,"* p. 204.

56. Jeffrey to Thomas Carlyle, 8 December 1833, quoted in Wilson's *Carlyle to "The French Revolution,"* p. 349.

57. *ER* 5 (January 1805) Art. 1: 260. See Also *ER* 10 (April 1807) Art. 12:

187; *ER* 48 (December 1828) Art. 2: 314-16.

58. *ER* 29 (February 1818) Art. 10: 475. But Jeffrey did admit to "a feeling of something like envy and delighted wonder" in reading of the "child-like innocence, and humble apparatus of enjoyment" of the American Indians described in Washington Irving's *Christopher Columbus* (1828).

59. *ER* 46 (June 1827) Art. 2: 44. See also *ER* 29 (November 1817) Art. 1: 2.

60. *ER* 21 (February 1813) Art. 1: 21; *ER* 17 (November 1810) Art. 9: 169.

61. *ER* 13 (January 1809) Art. 5: 344.

62. *ER* 21 (February 1813) Art. 1: 20.

63. Ibid.

64. But Horner was a critical catechist: "We owe much at present to the superstitious worship of Smith's name; and we must not impair that feeling, till the victory is more complete. There are few practical errors in the "Wealth of Nations," at least of any great consequence; and, until we can give a correct and precise theory of the nature and origin of wealth, his popular and plausible and loose hypothesis is as good for the vulgar as any other" (Horner to Thomas Thomson, 15 August 1803, *Memoirs and Correspondence of Francis Horner,* 1: 237-38).

65. *ER* 5 (October 1804) Art. 1: 16.

66. *ER* 14 (April 1809) Art. 4: 55. See also *ER* 3 (October 1803) Art 13: 175: *ER* 2 (April 1803) Art. 1: 7, 26-27, 29.

67. *ER* 1 (October 1802) Art. 22: 147; *ER* 21 (February 1813) Art. 1: 22.

68. *ER* 21 (February 1813) Art. 1: 23.

69. Ibid. p. 24.

70. Jeffrey to Charles Wilkes, 24 August 1819, Cockburn's *Life,* 2: 153.

71. Francis Jeffrey, *Combinations of Workmen: Substance of the Speech of Francis Jeffrey, Esq. upon introducing the toast, "Freedom of Labour — But let the Labourer recollect, that in exercising his own rights, he cannot be permitted to violate the rights of others" at the Public Dinner Given at Edinburgh to Joseph Hume, Esq. M. P. on Friday the 18th of November 1825* (Edinburgh: Constable, 1825).

72. Jeffrey to Thomas Carlyle, 13 November 1830, quoted in Wilson's *Carlyle to "The French Revolution,"* pp. 185-86.

73. Jeffrey to William Empson, 31 January 1831, Cockburn's *Life,* 2: 187. The word *swing* refers to the fictional Captain Swing, whose signature was affixed to intimidating letters sent to farmers and land-owners in the south of England in 1830-31. The letters were followed by the destruction of farm property.

74. It took two years to edit the material for the first volume of *Das Kapital,* which appeared in 1867.

CHAPTER 4

1. In the period between 1789 and 1815, the labels *Whig* and *Tory* were often replaced by *Ministers* and *Opposition, Ins* and *Outs,* or clique labels such as *Pittites, Foxites,* and *Grenvillites.* But most historians use the *Whig* and *Tory* labels in writing of this period, and I have followed the general practice. For

information on politics I am indebted to the following works: Arthur Aspinall, *Lord Brougham and the Whig Party* (Manchester: The University Press, 1927); Elie Halévy, *England in 1815,* trans. E. I. Watkin and D. A. Barker, 2d ed. (1949; reprint ed. New York: Barnes and Noble, 1968); Simon Maccoby, *English Radicalism, 1786-1832* (London: Allen & Unwin, 1955); Henry W. Meikle, *Scotland and the French Revolution* (1912; reprint ed. New York: Augustus M. Kelley, 1969); Austin Mitchell, *The Whigs in Opposition, 1815-1830* (Oxford: Clarendon Press, 1967); Chester W. New, *The Life of Henry Brougham to 1830* (Oxford: Clarendon Press, 1961); Michael Roberts, *The Whig Party, 1807-1812* (1939; reprint ed. London: Cass, 1965); J. Steven Watson, *The Reign of George III, 1760-1815.* The Oxford History of England, vol. 12 (Oxford: Clarendon Press, 1960).

2. Cockburn, *Life,* 1: 64-65. Cockburn's testimony might be suspect for both political and personal reasons. He was in the unhappy position of being at the same time a Whig and Henry Dundas's nephew. But his description of political Scotland in the *Life* and the *Memorials of His Time* (1856) has been substantially verified by later historians.

3. Cockburn, *Life,* 1: 65.

4. Ibid.

5. Quoted in ibid, p. 57.

6. Cockburn, *Life,* 1: 56.

7. Quoted in ibid., p. 57.

8. Jeffrey to John Jeffrey, 1 June 1794, Cockburn's *Life,* 2: 21-22. At this time, Charles Fox and Charles Grey were on friendly terms with the London Corresponding Society. But, in writing of those "whom a generous and sincere enthusiasm has borne beyond their interest," Jeffrey may have had in mind John Millar. In the early 1790s Millar was a member of the Society of the Friends of the People.

9. Jeffrey to John Allen, 17 March 1807, quoted in Cockburn's *Life,* 1: 141.

10. Jeffrey to Francis Horner, 12 March 1815, Cockburn's *Life,* 2: 124.

11. "Debate in the Commons on the King's Message respecting Overtures of Peace," 3 February 1800, *The Parliamentary Debates (Cobbett's Parliamentary History of England).*

12. *New Annual Register for the Year 1803* (London: Robinson, 1804), p. 4.

13. Jeffrey to Robert Morehead, 7 October 1801, Cockburn's *Life,* 2: 55.

14. Jeffrey to John Jeffrey, 2 July 1803, Cockburn's *Life,* 2: 65-66.

15. *ER* 2 (April 1803) Art. 1: 22-23. Brougham may have had a hand in the writing of this article. See Elisabeth Schneider, Irwin Griggs, and John D. Kern, "Brougham's Early Contributions to the *Edinburgh Review:* A New List," *Modern Philology* 42 (February 1945): 161.

16. William Hazlitt, "Free Thoughts on Public Affairs: or Advice to a Patriot," *The Complete Works of William Hazlitt,* ed. P. P. Howe, Centenary ed., vol. 1 (London and Toronto: J. M. Dent, 1930): 98.

17. *ER* 10 (April 1807) Art. 1: 19, 20.

18. Ibid., pp. 20, 20-21, 24, 25.

19. Jeffrey to Francis Horner, 20 December 1808, quoted in Cockburn's *Life,* 1: 153.

20. There has been some confusion concerning the author(s) of this article, but recent scholarship has established that it was Jeffrey's and Brougham's collaboration. See Schneider et al., "Brougham's Early Contributions," pp. 170-71; New, *Life of Henry Brougham*, p. 445.

21. *ER* 13 (October 1808) Art. 14: 233.

22. *ER* 15 (January 1810) Art. 15: 510; *ER* 16 (April 1810) Art. 1: 18-19.

23. *ER* 16 (April 1810) Art. 1: 26, 27, 27-28.

24. Jeffrey to Francis Horner, 9 June 1815, Cockburn's *Life*, 2: 129.

25. *ER* 23 (April 1814) Art. 1: 1-40.

26. Jeffrey to Francis Horner, 9 June 1815, Cockburn's *Life*, 2: 128-29.

27. Quoted in Cockburn's *Life*, 1: 188.

CHAPTER 5

1. William Plunket, "Motion for a Committee on the Claims of the Roman Catholics," 25 February 1813, *Parliamentary Debates* (Hansard's).

2. Thomas Creevey, *Creevey's Life and Times*, ed. John Gore (London: John Murray, 1934), p. 55.

3. "Reform of Parliament," 25 April 1822, *Parliamentary Debates* (Hansard's).

4. Quoted in Cockburn's *Life*, 1: 58.

5. *ER* 1 (October 1802) Art. 1: 17.

6. *ER* 30 (September 1818) Art. 1: 283.

7. *ER* 20 (November 1812) Art. 4: 325.

8. Ibid., pp. 325, 326. See also *ER* 6 (April 1805) Art. 12: 145-46.

9. *ER* 20 (November 1812) Art 4:326, 326-27, 327. Jeffrey mentioned this part of the Leckie review in a letter to Horner: ". . . there is a good part of that article which I thought in considerable danger of being attacked and ridiculed, as a caricature of our Scotch manner of running every thing up to elements, and explaining all sorts of occurrences by a theoretical history of society" (Jeffrey to Francis Horner, 5 January 1813, Cockburn's *Life*, 2:115). Jeffrey was referring to the kind of history written by Hume, Kames, Millar, et al., in which the early history of society was deduced from certain general laws of society and human nature. He discussed the strengths and weaknesses of this approach in *ER* 2 (April 1803) Art. 23: 206-7 and in *ER* 62 (October 1835) Art. 11:133-34. More recently, Gladys Bryson has analyzed the Scottish historical school in *Man and Society*, pp. 78-113.

10. *ER* 20 (November 1812) Art. 4:328-29, 332. See also *ER* 30 (September 1818) Art. 1:284-89; *ER* 23 (April 1814) Art. 1:19.

11. *ER* 20 (November 1812) Art. 4:333.

12. Ibid., pp. 333-34.

13. *ER* 2 (April 1803) Art. 1:16.

14. *ER* 1 (October 1802) Art. 1:2.

15. *ER* 6 (April 1805) Art. 12:140-41. See also *ER* 11 (October 1807) Art.8: 133; *ER* 30 (September 1818) Art. 1:308.

16. *ER* 6 (April 1805) Art. 12:142 n.

17. Clive, *Scotch Reviewers*, p. 95.

18. *ER* 6 (April 1805) Art. 12:142. For Jeffrey on the strengths and weaknesses of Hume's *History*, see *ER* 40 (March 1824) Art. 5:92-146; Jeffrey to William Empson, 20 March 1849, Cockburn's *Life*, 2:361. Late in life, Jeffrey did describe Burke as "the greatest and most accomplished intellect which England has produced for centuries" (Jeffrey to Lord Cockburn, 4 September 1844, quoted in Cockburn's *Life*, 1:308).

19. Compare, for examples, Cockburn's description of Jeffrey's "On Politics" (*Life*, 1:57-58) with Hume's "That Politics May Be Reduced to a Science" (*Philosophical Works*, 3:98); *ER* 20 (November 1812) Art. 4:322-25 with Hume's "That Politics . . . " (*Works*, 3:100-101); Jeffrey to John Jeffrey, 30 March 1793 (*Life*, 2:17) with Hume's "That Politics . . . " (*Works*, 3:107); *ER* 20 (November 1812) Art. 4:325, passim with Hume's "Of the First Principles of Government" (*Works*, 3:109-13); *ER* 10 (July 1807) Art. 9:413-19 with Hume's "On the Independency of Parliament" (*Works*, 3:117-22).

20. Quoted by Lord Moncreiff of Tulliebole in Taylor's *Lord Jeffrey and Craigcrook*, p. 39. See also *ER* 11 (October 1807) Art. 8:116-44.

21. *ER* 4 (April 1804) Art. 1:18-19. See also *ER* 6 (April 1805) Art. 12:142-43.

22. *ER* 10 (July 1807) Art. 9:399.

23. For Jeffrey's distinction between the "natural" influence of property in elections and the "artificial" influence, see *ER* 17 (February 1811) Art. 1:265-72.

24. *ER* 10 (July 1807) Art. 9:410, 408. See also *ER* 6 (April 1805) Art. 12:146.

25. *ER* 10 (July 1807) Art. 9:421.

26. Jeffrey to Francis Horner, 18 September 1806, Cockburn's *Life*, 2:93-94. Jeffrey indirectly acknowledged the validity of many of Cobbett's arguments in *ER* 10 (April 1807) Art. 1:10-18.

27. *ER* 13 (October 1808) Art. 14:220.

28. Ibid., pp. 221, 222.

29. Ibid., pp. 223, 225.

30. Arthur Aspinall, *Lord Brougham and the Whig Party*, p.19.

31. *Courier* "1 & 2 December 1808," quoted in Clive's *Scotch Reviewers*, pp. 111, 113.

32. Quoted in Roberts's *The Whig Party*, p. 238.

33. "Mentor," *The Dangers of the Edinburgh Review* (London: Rivington, 1808), p. 4.

34. Francis Horner to John Murray, 9 December 1808, Horner Collection (vol. 3, item 131).

35. *ER* 13 (October 1808) Art. 14:234 n.

36. *Morning Chronicle*, 17 April 1809, n.p.

37. In the summer of 1809 English forces were landed on the island of Walcheren off the Netherlands. Their presence on the island served no purpose, and nearly half the force sickened or died of fever. A parliamentary inquiry was begun, but Parliament subsequently dismissed the motion of censure against the Portland administration. See n. 43.

38. Jeffrey to Francis Horner, 26 October 1809, quoted in Cockburn's *Life*, 1:155-56. See also Jeffrey to John Allen, 22 December 1809, *Life*, 2:105.

39. Ibid., 21 December 1809, *Memoirs and Correspondence of Francis Horner*, 1:512.

40. See Jeffrey to John Allen, 4 May 1810, Cockburn's *Life*, 2:105-6.

41. *ER* 15 (January 1810) Art. 15:504-5, 505.

42. Ibid., pp. 511-12, 512.

43. *ER* 15 (January 1810) Art. 15:516, 516-17. In his remarks on ministerial responsibility, Jeffrey may have had in mind the acquittal of Henry Dundas on charges of corruption in 1806. He was clearly referring to the Walcheren Inquiry in the following remarks: "We write this at the present crisis, with a feeling of eager and painful anxiety, in which we believe most of our readers sympathize. The Parliament of England is now occupied with the investigation of the most inglorious and deplorable undertaking that ever disgraced the councils of the country; and the hearts of the whole nation are watching eagerly for their decision, — not, however, to be guided by it in their opinion of the merits of that expedition, but in their opinion of the Parliament itself that is to pronounce that decision."

44. *ER* 15 (January 1810) Art. 15: 520, 520-21.

45. See *ER* 14 (July 1809) Art. 1:278-79.

46. "State of the Nation," 13 June 1810, *Parliamentary Debates (Cobbett's Parliamentary Debates)*.

47. Cockburn, *Life*, 1:195.

48. *ER* 30 (September 1818) Art. 1:276.

49. Jeffrey to Charles Wilkes, 5 August 1818, Cockburn's *Life*, 2:148. See also idem, 15 April 1821 and 27 January 1822, ibid., 2:157-58, 158-59; Jeffrey to Cockburn, 28 August 1835, ibid., 2:214-15; Jeffrey to William Empson, 26 November 1837, ibid., 2:233; Jeffrey to Miss Berry, 24 July 1842, ibid., 2:293-94.

50. Jeffrey, *Contributions*, p. 621 n.

51. Jeffrey became Member for Malton in 1831. On the passing of the First Reform Bill he was returned as Member for Edinburgh, the seat he held until ascending to the Scottish Bench in 1834. While Jeffrey served as Lord Advocate, Cockburn was Solicitor General for Scotland.

52. *Corrected Report of the Speech of the Right Honourable the Lord Advocate of Scotland, upon the Motion of Lord John Russell, in the House of Commons, on the First of March, 1831, for Reform of Parliament* (London: James Ridgway, 1831), p. 19.

53. Jeffrey to Lord Cockburn, 16 August 1833, quoted in Cockburn's *Life*, 1:272.

54. Ibid., 28 March 1833, quoted in Cockburn's *Life*, 1:269.

55. Ibid., 11 April 1833, Cockburn's *Life*, 2:206.

56. H. L. Renwick, *English Literature, 1798-1815*, Oxford History of English Literature, vol. 9 (Oxford: Clarendon Press, 1963): 201 n. 2. In another volume in this series, Ian Jack has given Jeffrey a fuller and more balanced study. See Jack's *English Literature, 1815-1832*, Oxford History of English Literature, vol. 10 (Oxford: Clarendon Press, 1963): 324-29.

57. Jeffrey, *Speech for Reform of Parliament*, pp. 28-29.

58. *ER* 17 (February 1811) Art. 1:281.

59. Jeffrey to William Empson, 26 ---- 1848, Cockburn's *Life*, 2:344.

CHAPTER 6

1. Henry Home, Lord Kames, *Elements of Criticism*, 6th ed. (1785; reprint ed. New York: Garland, 1972), 1:13.

2. Hugh Blair, *Lectures on Rhetoric and Belles Lettres*, ed. Harold F. Harding, Landmarks in Rhetoric and Public Address (1783; reprint ed. Carbondale and Edwardsville, Ill.: Southern Illinois University Press, 1965), 1:36-37.

3. For discussions of this change, see Vincent M. Bevilacqua, "Adam Smith's Lectures on Rhetoric and Belles Lettres," *Studies in Scottish Literature* 3 (July 1965): 41-60; Lothian, *Lectures on Rhetoric and Belles Lettres*, pp. xiii-xxxix.

4. David Hume, "Of the Standard of Taste," *Philosophical Works*, 3:269.

5. Smith, *Lectures on Rhetoric and Belles Lettres*, p. 23.

6. Quoted from a student's compendium of Reid's lectures by Lothian in his Introduction to Smith's *Lectures on Rhetoric and Belles Lettres*, p.xxx.

7. Kames, *Elements of Criticism*, 2:492.

8. Kames hedged on this position. While asserting the existence of a universal standard of taste, he admitted that the taste of the majority of men must be practically ignored (*Elements*, 2:499-500).

9. Blair, *Lectures on Rhetoric and Belles Lettres*, 1:32 n.

10. See Kames, *Elements of Criticism*, 1:9-11, 178-94, 201-2; Adam Smith, *The Theory of Moral Sentiments* (1759; reprint ed. New York; Garland, 1971), pp. 188, 193, 280-81, 283, 284, 290; Blair, *Lectures on Rhetoric and Belles Lettres*, 1:12, 13, 45; Hutcheson, *Inquiry into the Original of Our Ideas of Beauty and Virtue*, pp. 96-107.

11. Kames, *Elements of Criticism*, 2:488.

12. See Hume's "Of the Standard of Taste," *Philosophical Works*, 3:270-80.

13. Hume, "Of the Standard of Taste," *Philosophical Works*, 3:271.

14. See the section of Jeffrey's Oxford essay on "Beauty" quoted in Cockburn's *Life*, 1:39.

15. See *ER* 3 (January 1804) Art. 1:277. Jeffrey probably took his associationism from Hume and Smith rather than from Hartley.

16. For a discussion of Alison's place in eighteenth-century aesthetics, see Samuel H. Monk's *The Sublime: A Study of Critical Theories in XVIII-Century England* (Ann Arbor: University of Michigan Press, 1960), pp. 145-53. Alison's theory had its own teleological side, which Jeffrey politely ignored.

17. See Archibald Alison, *Essays on the Nature and Principles of Taste* (New York: Harper & Brothers, 1844), pp. vii-xvi, 19-113 (Introduction and Essay 1).

18. *ER* 18 (May 1811) Art. 1:3, 13, 25. This review, in revised form, was the article on "Beauty" that Jeffrey contributed, on request, to the Supplement of the 1824 edition of the *Encyclopaedia Britannica*. The article was subsequently published in the 1841 edition of the *Encyclopaedia* and was included in Jeffrey's *Contributions to the Edinburgh Review*. In revising his review, Jeffrey criticized more closely Alison's claim that the free play of associative imagination is the essence of aesthetic response.

19. Jeffrey did attempt a detailed associationist explanation of the appeal of colors in his *Encyclopaedia* version of this review.

20. Alison, *Essays*, p. viii (Introduction).

21. *ER* 18 (May 1811) Art. 1:7.

22. Ibid., pp. 40, 43, 44.

23. Ibid., pp. 44, 9-10; *ER* 18 (August 1811) Art. 1:285; *ER* 28 (August 1817) Art. 9:473.

24. *ER* 18 (May 1811) Art. 1:17, 19-22. See also *ER* 42 (August 1825) Art. 7:409-18; *ER* 21 (February 1813) Art. 1:42-44. Jeffrey had verifiably encountered similar distinctions between universal and accidental associations in Beattie's letters and in Dugald Stewart's essay "On Taste." See *ER* 10 (April 1807) Art. 12:174 and *ER* 17 (November 1810) Art. 9:206-7. Jeffrey, Stewart, and Alison were regular members of the Friday Club, and this distinction may have evolved in conversations on associationist aesthetics.

25. *ER* 18 (May 1811) Art. 1:44-45, 46.

26. *ER* 27 (September 1816) Art. 1:1.

27. The earlier review was that of a new edition of the plays of John Ford, *ER* 18 (August 1811) Art. 1:275-304. See also remarks at the beginning of his review of Thomas Campbell's *Specimens of the British Poets, ER* 31 (March 1819) Art. 11:467. On Coleridge's claim that parts of the 1811 review were something close to plagiarism, see David V. Erdman, "Coleridge and the 'Review Business,'" *The Wordsworth Circle* 6 (Winter 1975): 3-50.

28. A Scot, Thomas Blackwell (1701-57), attempted to explain Homer's greatness in terms of cultural factors in his *Inquiry into the Life and Writings of Homer* (1753). Gerald Chapman believes that in Blackwell's book, "probably for the first time in criticism, poetry and the poet are causally submerged in social history" (*Literary Criticism in England, 1660-1800* [New York: Knopf, 1966], p. 269). Hume, Kames, Smith, and Blair also discussed the characteristics of literature in "rude" and "refined" societies.

29. *ER* 18 (August 1811) Art. 1:284, 278, 276.

30. Ibid., pp. 278, 280, 279; *ER* 27 (September 1816) Art. 1:5.

31. *ER* 27 (September 1816) Art. 1:6, 7; *ER* 18 (August 1811) Art. 1:281.

32. *ER* 27 (September 1816) Art. 1:8.

33. *ER* 23 (April 1814) Art. 9:200, 201.

CHAPTER 7

1. For a study of the reading public in the first quarter of the nineteenth century, see Richard D. Altick's *The English Common Reader* (Chicago: University of Chicago Press, 1957). The high price of new books in this period restricted the size of the book-buying public, but circulating libraries, number-publications, and reprint series served the needs of many who were reluctant or unable to purchase new books.

2. *ER* 31 (March 1819) Art. 11:466-67.

3. See *ER* 16 (August 1810) Art. 1:263-67; *ER* 9 (January 1807) Art. 6:348; *ER* 31 (March 1819) Art. 11:467.

4. Bernard Barton (1784-1849), a Quaker poet, was very popular in the first half of the century. His *Household Verses* (1845), dedicated to Queen Victoria, won him a government pension.

5. Jeffrey also linked Coleridge and Southey with Priestley and other members of the Lunar Society in another attack upon the presumption of "provincial genius," *ER* 9 (October 1806) Art. 9:147.

6. *ER* 1 (October 1802) Art. 8:63. Jeffrey's essays on Wordsworth's poetry have been the focus of most modern studies of Jeffrey's criticism. My own study differs primarily in my emphasis on Jeffrey's practical concern with the taste of the early nineteenth-century reading public. But other studies should be consulted. The following seem to me to be the most important: Joseph M. Beatty, Jr., "Lord Jeffrey and Wordsworth," *PMLA* 38 (June 1923): 221-35; Robert Daniel, "Jeffrey and Wordsworth: The Shape of Persecution," *Sewanee Review* 50 (April-June 1942): 195-213; J. Raymond Derby, "The Paradox of Francis Jeffrey: Reason Versus Sensibility," *Modern Language Quarterly* 7 (December 1946): 489-500; James A. Greig, *Francis Jeffrey of the Edinburgh Review* (Edinburgh and London: Oliver and Boyd, 1948), pp. 173-288; Byron Guyer, "The Philosophy of Francis Jeffrey," *MLQ* 11 (March 1950): 17-26; John O. Hayden, *The Romantic Reviewers, 1802-1824* (Chicago: University of Chicago Press, 1968), pp. 15-22, 78-83; Merritt Y. Hughes, "The Humanism of Francis Jeffrey," *Modern Language Review* 16 (July-October 1921): 243-51; Peter F. Morgan, "Principles and Perspective in Jeffrey's Criticism," *Studies in Scottish Literature* 4 (January-April) 1967): 179-93; Russell Noyes, *Wordsworth and Jeffrey in Controversy*, Indiana University Publications, Humanities Series, no. 5 (Bloomington, Ind., 1941); W. J. B. Owen, "Wordsworth and Jeffrey in Collaboration," *Review of English Studies*, n.s. 15 (May 1964): 161-67; René Wellek, *A History of Modern Criticism, 1750-1950*, vol. 2 (New Haven, Conn.: Yale University Press, 1955): 111-20.

7. *ER* 1 (October 1802) Art. 8:66.

8. Jeffrey to Miss Crockett, 9 March 1792, Cockburn's *Life*, 2:15.

9. *ER* 1 (October 1802) Art. 8:65. For Cowper, see *ER* 2 (April 1803) Art. 5:81; *ER* 18 (August 1811) Art. 1:282-83; *ER* 27 (September 1816) Art. 1:7.

10. *ER* 1 (October 1802) Art. 8:67.

11. See Samuel Taylor Coleridge's *Biographia Literaria*, ed. John Shawcross (London: Oxford University Press, 1907), 2:38-39, 43-44.

12. William Hazlitt, "The Spirit of the Age," *Complete Works*, 11:86.

13. *ER* 1 (October 1802) Art. 8:71-72.

14. *ER* 7 (October 1805) Art. 1:1, 2.

15. Coleridge, *Biographia Literaria*, 2:77.

16. Byron, *Don Juan*, canto 3, lines 889-90.

17. Scott to Miss Seward, 10 April 1806, *Letters*, 1:287.

18. *ER* 11 (October 1807) Art. 14:217.

19. Jeffrey was very sensitive to words with "mean," "low," or "vulgar" associations. His reactions to some words are incomprehensible to a modern reader because the sociolinguistic patterns of the English language have changed greatly since Jeffrey's day. But Jeffrey was a fussy critic, even for his own day. He may have inherited a vestige of the self-conscious correctness of eighteenth-century Scottish men of letters, who were careful to purge their styles of "Scotticisms" or any slang that might incur the ridicule of polite English readers. For Jeffrey's remarks on the unhappy associations of Southey's, Scott's, Hogg's, and Goethe's language, see *ER* 1 (October 1802) Art. 8:78-79; *ER* 7 (October 1805) Art. 1:16;

ER 16 (August 1810) Art. 1:271; *ER* 24 (November 1814) Art. 8:159, 173; *ER* 42 (August 1825) Art. 7, passim.

20. Iona and Peter Opie, eds., *The Oxford Book of Children's Verse* (New York and London: Oxford University Press, 1973), p. vii. For a brief survey of early nineteenth-century reaction to Wordsworth's poetry of childhood, see Barbara Garlitz, "The Baby's Debut," *Boston University Studies in English* 4 (Summer 1960): 85-94. Donald Reiman has edited a valuable collection of contemporary reviews in Part A of *The Romantics Reviewed*, 2 vols. (New York and London: Garland, 1972). But Reiman's introductory remarks on Jeffrey should be read with caution. He portrays Jeffrey throughout as an obtuse critic, and he has attributed the *ER* "Christabel" review to Jeffrey on very shaky grounds.

21. *ER* 11 (October 1807) Art. 14:217-18, 218. Reviewing Horace and James Smith's popular *Rejected Addresses* (1812), Jeffrey described their parody of Wordsworth's style as "by no means a parody, but a very fair, and indeed we think a flattering imitation" of Wordsworth at his most eccentric. But Jeffrey also noted that the parodists had ignored "the higher attributes of Mr. Wordsworth's poetry" (*ER* 20 [November 1812] Art. 10:438).

22. Scott to Miss Seward, 10 April 1806, *Letters*, 1:288. For Coleridge's opinion, see *Biographia Literaria*, 2:129. For Crabb Robinson's account of Coleridge's story, see *Diary, Reminiscences, and Correspondence of Henry Crabb Robinson*, ed. Thomas Sadler, 3d. ed. (London and New York: Macmillan, 1872), 1:159 (entry for 4 November 1810). A later entry in Robinson records William Empson's theory that Jeffrey's attacks upon Wordsworth were "honest — mere uncongeniality of mind," *Diary* (17 August 1837), 2:200, and Jeffrey answered Coleridge's accusations in an editorial note that he affixed to Hazlitt's review of the *Biographia Literaria*, *ER* 28 (August 1817) Art. 10:507-12.

23. See Horner to Francis Jeffrey, 13 August 1804, *Memoirs and Correspondence of Francis Horner*, 1:272-73; Jeffrey to Francis Horner, 3 September 1804, Cockburn's *Life*, 2:78.

24. Jeffrey to Ugo Foscolo, 23 May 1818, *The Letters of Francis Jeffrey to Ugo Foscolo*, ed. J. Purves (Edinburgh and London: Oliver and Boyd, 1934), p. 7.

25. *ER* 18 (May 1811) Art. 1:45, 46.

26. Hazlitt, "The Spirit of the Age," *Complete Works*, 11:94.

27. *ER* 18 (May 1811) Art. 1:24-25; *ER* 11 (October 1807) Art. 14: 215, 228.

28. See *ER* 28 (March 1817) Art. 7:151-74; *ER* 36 (February 1822) Art. 5:445-46; *ER* 37 (November 1822) Art. 8:450; *ER* 62 (October 1835) Art. 11: 131-32.

29. *ER* 24 (November 1814) Art. 1: 1, 4.

30. Wordsworth to Robert Gillies, 14 February 1815, *The Letters of William and Dorothy Wordsworth: The Middle Years*, ed. Ernest De Selincourt (Oxford: Clarendon Press, 1937), 2: 633.

31. *ER* 1 (October 1802) Art. 8: 70; *ER* 24 (November 1814) Art. 1: 10, 3. See also *ER* 25 (October 1815) Art. 4: 355.

32. Coleridge, *Biographia Literaria*, 2: 29.

33. *ER* 1 (October 1802) Art. 8: 67.

34. Crabbe, *The Village*, bk. 1, lines 172-73.

35. *ER* 16 (April 1810) Art. 2: 31, 33.

36. Ibid., p. 32; *ER* 20 (November 1812) Art. 2: 280; *ER* 12 (April 1808) Art. 8: 141. By *fastidious* Jeffrey meant readers who were offended by literary depictions of the lower class. Throughout his reviewing career, he kept a wary eye on the fastidious element among his readers. His associationist aesthetic led him to recognize that the lower orders were legitimate subjects for poetry and prose fiction, and he believed that Crabbe and Scott were fostering social tolerance by their depictions of the lower orders. But, in order that polite readers might be seduced into tolerance, writers must be careful not to *unnecessarily* offend their readers' sensibilities. Thus, Jeffrey praised Burns for having treated humble subjects with "that delicacy, as well as justness of conception, by which alone the fastidiousness of an ordinary reader can be reconciled to such representations" (*ER* 13 (January 1809) Art. 1: 260).

37. *ER* 12 (April 1808) Art. 8: 133. See also Jeffrey's contrast of Wordsworth's characters with Burns's "authentic rustics" in *ER* 13 (January 1809) Art. 1: 276.

38. *ER* 29 (November 1817) Art. 1: 34. See Jeffrey to Francis Horner, 20 July 1810, Cockburn's *Life* 2: 108.

39. This phrase occurs in Jeffrey's review of Campbell's *Gertrude of Wyoming*, *ER* 14 (April 1809) Art. 1: 3.

40. *ER* 12 (April 1808) Art. 8: 139.

41. Horner to Francis Jeffrey, 11 January 1805, *Memoirs and Correspondence of Francis Horner*, 1: 301.

42. *ER* 12 (April 1808) Art. 1: 3.

43. *ER* 6 (April 1805) Art. 1: 19.

44. *ER* 12 (April 1808) Art. 1: 28.

45. Ibid., p. 32.

46. *ER* 16 (August 1810) Art. 1: 293.

47. Edward Copleston, a Fellow of Oriel, wrote *Advice to a Young Reviewer* (1807), the best of many contemporary satires on the *Edinburgh Review*. Scott showed Copleston's pamphlet to Jeffrey, and Jeffrey's first response was to inquire whether Copleston might wish to write for the *Review*. "To be sure," Scott wrote of Jeffrey, "he is the most complete *poco-curante* that I ever knew" (Scott to Miss Seward, 23 November 1807, *Letters*, 1: 398). In time Byron came to admire Jeffrey. In *Don Juan* Byron made public amends for *English Bards*.

48. *ER* 19 (February 1812) Art. 10: 467; *ER* 23 (April 1814) Art. 9: 199; *ER* 36 (February 1822) Art. 5: 420-21, 421.

49. *ER* 29 (November 1817) Art. 1: 1, 4, 6, 5.

50. For a discussion of the publishing slump and its effects, see Jack's *English Literature, 1815-1832*, pp. 421-24.

51. *ER* 24 (November 1814) Art. 11: 208.

52. See *ER* 33 (January 1820) Art. 1: 1-2.

53. For Jeffrey on the poet and the burden of the past, see *ER* 8 (July 1806) Art. 7: 329-30; *ER* 13 (January 1809) Art. 1: 250-52; *ER* 16 (August 1810) Art. 1: 267-69; *ER* 14 (April 1809) Art. 1: 3; *ER* 36 (February 1822) Art. 5: 416-19. Walter Jackson Bate discusses Jeffrey in this context in *The Burden of the Past*

and the English Poet (Cambridge, Mass.: The Belknap Press of Harvard University Press, 1970), pp. 99-103.

54. *ER* 28 (March 1817) Art. 9: 193. Jeffrey did not review many novels, but he praised those which he thought capable of engaging the sympathetic emotions of a large reading public. He preferred *Waverley* to *Ivanhoe*, Galt's *Annals of the Parish* to Lockhart's *Valerius*.

55. *ER* 34 (August 1820) Art. 10: 205-6. See also *ER* 50 (October 1829) Art. 2: 35-37; *ER* 24 (November 1814) Art. 8: 163-64. In the last review, Jeffrey attributed the phrase *pure poetry* to "Wharton." It is found in the Dedication of Joseph Warton's *An Essay on the Genius and Writings of Pope* (1756-82). Jeffrey's judgment of Pope's poetry was apparently influenced by Warton's *Essay*.

56. Jeffrey, *Contributions*, p. 512.

57. Jeffrey to Lord Cockburn, 25 July 1835, quoted in Cockburn's *Life*, 1: 287. Jeffrey did not review any of Shelley's work.

58. Jeffrey to William Hazlitt, 3 May 1818, quoted in *Personal Reminiscences by Constable and Gillies*, ed. Richard Stoddard (New York: Scribner, Armstrong, and Company, 1876), p. 110.

59. Jeffrey to Thomas Moore, 26 May 1816, quoted in Moore's *Memoirs*, 2: 101.

60. *ER* 26 (June 1816) Art. 10: 458.

61. Jeffrey, *Contributions*, p. vi.

62. Kames, *Elements of Criticism*, 1: 6.

63. Beattie, "Essay on Poetry and Music," *Essays*, p. 362.

64. See *ER* 18 (May 1811) Art. 1: 1, 6; *ER* 28 (August 1817) Art. 6: 394.

65. In his review of Paley's *Natural Theology*, Jeffrey commended Paley for having confined his argument to discussions of "the *mechanical* functions and contrivances in organized bodies, as proofs of design" (*ER* 1 [January 1803] Art. 3: 295).

66. *ER* 27 (December 1816) Art. 1: 281, 280; *ER* 36 (February 1822) Art. 5: 438.

67. See *ER* 13 (January 1809) Art. 1: 276.

68. Ibid., p. 253.

69. At least he found Robert Forsyth's argument to that effect "ingenious and important" (*ER* 7 [January 1806] Art. 7: 425). See also *ER* 13 (January 1809) Art. 1: 253.

70. *ER* 13 (January 1809) Art. 1: 254.

71. In *ER* 31 (March 1819) Art. 11: 492-93, Jeffrey modified his 1809 position on the moral character of Burns's writings: "No one who reads all that we have written of Burns, will doubt of the sincerity of our admiration for his genius, or of the depth of our veneration and sympathy for his lofty character and untimely fate. We still think he had a vulgar taste in letter writing, and too frequently patronised the belief of a connexion between licentious indulgences and generosity of character. But, on looking back on what we have said on these subjects, we are sensible that we have expressed ourselves with too much bitterness, and made the words of our censure far more comprehensive than our meaning."

72. Quoted in Boswell's *Life of Johnson,* p. 1140.

73. Anne Grant to Miss C. M. Fanshawe, 6 October 1810, *Memoir and Correspondence of Mrs. Grant of Laggan,* 1: 270.

74. See *ER* 14 (April 1809) Art. 1: 1-2; *ER* 31 (March 1819) Art. 4: 325-32.

75. See Jeffrey to Charles Dickens, 31 January 1845. Cockburn's *Life,* 2: 231. See also the *Life,* 1: 61-62; 2: 216, 258, 231-32, 308-9.

76. *Edinburgh Annual Register for 1809.* "Vol. Second-Part Second" (Edinburgh: James Ballantyne, 1811), p. 572.

77. *ER* 4 (July 1804) Art. 17: 477. On Richardson and Sterne, see *ER* 42 (August 1825) Art. 7: 416; *ER* 5 (October 1804) Art. 2: 23-44.

78. *ER* 1 (October 1802) Art. 8: 64.

79. See *ER* 20 (November 1812) Art. 2: 278-79; *ER* 36 (February 1822) Art. 5: 451-52; *ER* 32 (July 1819) Art. 7: 121-24. Jeffrey also admired the work of Maria Edgeworth and envied her "delightful consciousness of having done more good than any other writer, male or female, of her generation" (*ER* 14 [July 1809] Art. 7: 376).

80. See M. H. Abrams, *The Mirror and the Lamp* (New York: Oxford University Press, 1953), p. 28; John Gross, *The Rise and Fall of the Man of Letters* (Macmillan, 1969), pp. 1-9.

81. *ER* 14 (July 1809) Art. 7: 376. See also *ER* 20 (July 1812) Art. 7: 101.

CONCLUSION

1. Carlyle, *Reminiscences,* 2: 226-27.

2. William Hazlitt, "The Spirit of the Age," *Complete Works,* 11: 130.

3. See John Mill's article on the *Edinburgh Review* in the first number of the *Westminister Review* (January 1824) Art. 11: 206-49. Mill was a contributor to the *Edinburgh Review* earlier in the century.

4. *John Bull,* 3 June 1827, n. p.

5. Coleridge, *Biographia Literaria,* 2: 86.

Works Cited

The Horner Collection. British Library of Political and Economic Science. London School of Economics.

The Jeffrey Correspondence. National Library of Scotland.

Abrams, M. H. *The Mirror and the Lamp: Romantic Theory and the Critical Tradition.* New York: Oxford University Press, 1953.

Alison, Archibald. *Essays on the Nature and Principles of Taste.* New York: Harper and Brothers, 1844.

Altick, Richard. *The English Common Reader: A Social History of the Mass Reading Public, 1800-1900.* Chicago: University of Chicago Press, 1957.

Aspinall, Arthur. "Brougham's 'Life and Times.'" *English Historical Review* 59 (January 1944): 81-112.

——. *Lord Brougham and the Whig Party.* Manchester: The University Press, 1927.

Bate, W. Jackson. *The Burden of the Past and the English Poet.* Cambridge, Mass.: The Belknap Press of Harvard University Press, 1970.

Beattie, James. *Essays: On the Nature and Immutability of Truth; On Poetry and Music; On Laughter and Ludicrous Composition: On the Utility of Classical Learning.* 1776. Reprint ed. New York: Garland, 1971.

Beatty, Joseph M., Jr. "Lord Jeffrey and Wordsworth." *PMLA* 38 (June 1923): 221-35.

Bell, A. S. "An Unpublished Letter on the Edinburgh Review." *Times Literary Supplement,* 9 April 1970, p. 388.

Bentham, Jeremy. *A Fragment on Government and An Introduction to the Principles of Morals and Legislation.* Edited by Wilfrid Harrison. Oxford: Blackwell, 1948.

Berkeley, George. *The Works of George Berkeley, Bishop of Cloyne.* Edited by A. A. Luce and T. E. Jessop. 9 vols. London: Thomas Nelson, 1948-57.

Bevilacqua, Vincent M. "Adam Smith's Lectures on Rhetoric and Belles Lettres." *Studies in Scottish Literature* 3 (July 1965): 41-60.

Blair, Hugh. *Lectures on Rhetoric and Belles Lettres.* Edited by Harold F. Harding. Landmarks in Rhetoric and Public Address. 2 vols.

1783. Reprint ed. Carbondale and Edwardsville, Ill.: Southern Illinois University Press, 1965.

Boswell, James. *Boswell's Life of Johnson.* Oxford Standard Authors ed. New ed. Oxford: Oxford University Press, 1953.

Brightfield, Myron F. *John Wilson Croker.* Berkeley: University of California Press, 1940.

Brougham, Henry Lord. *Brougham and His Early Friends: Letters to James Loch, 1798-1809.* Edited by R. H. M. Buddle Atkinson and G. A. Jackson. London: Darling and Pead, 1908.

———. *The Life and Times of Henry Lord Brougham.* 3 vols. New York: Harper and Brothers, 1871.

Bryson, Gladys. *Man and Society: The Scottish Inquiry of the Eighteenth Century.* Princeton, N.J.: Princeton University Press, 1945.

Carlyle, Alexander. *Autobiography of Dr. Alexander Carlyle of Inveresk, 1722-1805.* Edited by John Hill Burton. London and Edinburgh: Foulis, 1910.

Carlyle, Thomas. *Reminiscences.* Edited by Charles Eliot Norton. 2 vols. London and New York: Macmillan, 1887.

Chapman, Gerald Webster, ed. *Literary Criticism in England, 1660-1800.* New York: Knopf, 1966.

Clive, John. *Scotch Reviewers: The Edinburgh Review, 1802-1815.* Cambridge, Mass.: Harvard University Press, 1957.

Cockburn, Henry Lord. *Life of Lord Jeffrey, with a Selection from His Correspondence.* 2 vols. Philadelphia: Lippincott, Grambo, 1852.

———. *Memorials of His Time.* Edited by Harry A. Cockburn. Edinburgh and London: Foulis, 1910.

Coleridge, Samuel Taylor. *Biographia Literaria.* Edited by John Shawcross. 2 vols. London: Oxford University Press, 1907.

Constable, Archibald, and Gillies, Robert. *Personal Reminiscences of Constable and Gillies.* Edited by Richard Henry Stoddard. New York: Scribner, Armstrong, 1876.

Creevey, Thomas. *Creevey's Life and Times.* Edited by John Gore. London: John Murrary, 1934.

Daniel, Robert. "Jeffrey and Wordsworth: The Shape of Persecution." *Sewanee Review* 50 (April-June 1942): 195-213.

Derby, J. Raymond. "The Paradox of Francis Jeffrey: Reason Versus Sensibility." *Modern Language Quarterly* 7 (December 1946): 489-500.

Dickson, William K. *The History of the Speculative Society, 1764-1904.* Edinburgh: Constable, 1905.

Erdman, David V. "Coleridge and the 'Review Business.'" *The Wordsworth Circle* 6 (Winter 1975): 3-50.

Ferguson, Adam. *An Essay on the History of Civil Society.* 1767. Reprint ed. New York: Garland, 1971.

Garlitz, Barbara. "The Baby's Debut: The Contemporary Reaction to Wordsworth's Poetry of Childhood." *Boston University Studies in English* 4 (Summer 1960): 85-94.

Gay, Peter. *The Enlightenment: An Interpretation: The Rise of Modern Paganism.* New York: Knopf, 1967.

Graham, Henry Gray. *Scottish Men of Letters in the Eighteenth Century.* London: Black, 1901.

———. *The Social Life of Scotland in the Eighteenth Century.* 4th ed. London: Black, 1937.

Grant, Anne. *Memoir and Correspondence of Mrs. Grant of Laggan.* Edited by J. P. Grant. 3 vols. London: Longman, 1844.

Gregory, John. *A Father's Legacy to His Daughters.* Edinburgh: Creech, 1788.

Greig, James A. *Francis Jeffrey of the Edinburgh Review.* Edinburgh and London: Oliver and Boyd, 1948.

Gross, John. *The Rise and Fall of the Man of Letters: A Study of the Idiosyncratic and the Humane in Modern Literature.* London: Macmillan, 1969.

Guyer, Byron. "The Philosophy of Francis Jeffrey." *Modern Language Quarterly* 11 (March 1950): 17-26.

Halévy, Elie. *England in 1815.* Translated by E. I. Watkin and D. A. Barker. 2d ed., rev. 1949. Reprint ed. New York: Barnes and Noble, 1968.

Hayden, John O. *The Romantic Reviewers, 1802-1824.* Chicago: University of Chicago Press, 1968.

Hazlitt, William. *The Complete Works of William Hazlitt.* Edited by P. P. Howe. Centenary ed. 21 vols. London and Toronto: J. M. Dent, 1930-34.

Heseltine, G. C. "Five Letters of Sydney Smith." *London Mercury* 21 (March 1930): 512-17.

Horner, Francis. *Memoirs and Correspondence of Francis Horner, M. P.* Edited by Leonard Horner. 2 vols. Boston: Little, Brown, 1853.

Hughes, Merritt Y. "The Humanism of Francis Jeffrey." *Modern Language Review* 16 (July-October 1921): 243-51.

Hume, David. *A Treatise of Human Nature.* Edited by L. A. Selby-Bigge. 1739-40. Reprint ed. Oxford: Clarendon Press, 1896.

———. *The Letters of David Hume.* Edited by J. Y. T. Greig. 2 vols. Oxford: Clarendon Press, 1932.

———. *The Philosophical Works.* Edited by T. H. Green and T. H. Grose.

4 vols. 1882. Reprint ed. Darmstadt: Scientia Verlag Aalen, 1964.

Hutcheson, Francis. *A Short Introduction to Moral Philosophy.* Glasgow: Foulis, 1747.

——. *An Inquiry into the Original of Our Ideas of Beauty and Virtue.* 2d ed. 1726. Reprint ed. New York: Garland, 1971.

Jack, Ian. *English Literature: 1815-1832.* Oxford History of English Literature, vol. 10. Oxford: Clarendon Press, 1963.

Jardine, George. *Outlines of Philosophical Education.* Glasgow: Anderson and Macdowall, 1818.

Jeffrey, Francis. *Combinations of Workmen: Substance of the Speech of Francis Jeffrey, Esq. upon Introducing the Toast, "Freedom of Labour — But Let the Labourer Recollect, that in Exercising His Own Rights, He Cannot Be Permitted to Violate the Rights of Others" at the Public Dinner Given at Edinburgh to Joseph Hume, Esq. M. P. on Friday the 18th of November 1825.* Edinburgh: Constable, 1825.

——. *Contributions to the Edinburgh Review.* Boston: Phillips, Sampson, 1856.

——. *Corrected Report of the Speech of the Right Honourable the Lord Advocate of Scotland, upon the Motion of Lord John Russell, in the House of Commons, on the First of March, 1831, for Reform of Parliament.* London: James Ridgway, 1831.

——. *The Letters of Francis Jeffrey to Ugo Foscolo.* Edited by J. Purves. Edinburgh and London: Oliver and Boyd, 1934.

Kames, Henry Home [Lord Kames]. *Elements of Criticism.* 6th ed. 2 vols. 1785. Reprint ed. New York: Garland, 1972.

Kerr, Robert. *Memoirs of the Life, Writing & Correspondence of William Smellie.* 2 vols. Edinburgh: Anderson, 1811.

Knutsford, M. J. Holland [Viscountess Knutsford]. *Life and Letters of Zachary Macaulay.* London: Arnold, 1900.

Kyd, James Gray. *Scottish Publication Statistics.* Publications of the Scottish Historical Society, 3d series, no. 44. Edinburgh: Constable, 1952.

Law, Alexander. *Education in Edinburgh in the Eighteenth Century.* London: University of London Press, 1965.

Lehmann, William C. *John Millar of Glasgow.* Publications of the Department of Social and Economic Research, University of Glasgow, no. 4. Cambridge: Cambridge University Press, 1960.

Lockhart, John Gibson. *Memoirs of the Life of Sir Walter Scott.* 10 vols. Boston and New York: Houghton, Mifflin, 1901.

——. *Peter's Letters to His Kinsfolk.* 2d ed. 3 vols. Edinburgh: Blackwood, 1819.

Lovejoy, Arthur O. *Essays in the History of Ideas.* Baltimore, Md.: Johns Hopkins Press, 1948.

Maccoby, Simon. *English Radicalism, 1786-1832.* London: Allen and Unwin, 1955.

Mackenzie, Peter. *The Life of Thomas Muir.* Glasgow: M'Phun, 1831.

McElroy, D. D. "The Literary Clubs and Societies of Eighteenth Century Scotland, and Their Influence on the Literary Productions of the Period from 1700 to 1800." Dissertation, Edinburgh University, 1952.

Meikle, Henry W. *Scotland and the French Revolution.* 1912. Reprt. New York: Augustus M. Kelley, 1969.

"Mentor." *The Dangers of the Edinburgh Review.* London: Rivington, 1808.

Mitchell, Austin. *The Whigs in Opposition, 1815-1830.* Oxford: Clarendon Press, 1967.

Monk, Samuel H. *The Sublime: A Study of Critical Theories in XVIII-Century England.* Ann Arbor: University of Michigan Press, 1960.

Moore, Thomas. *Memoirs, Journal, and Correspondence.* Edited by Lord John Russell. 8 vols. London and Boston: Longman and Little, Brown, 1853.

Morgan, Peter F. "Principles and Perspective in Jeffrey's Criticism." *Studies in Scottish Literature* 4 (January-April 1967): 179-93.

Mossner, Ernest Campbell. *The Life of David Hume.* Austin: University of Texas Press, 1954.

Napier, Macvey. *Selection from the Correspondence of the Late Macvey Napier.* Edited by his son, Macvey Napier. London: Macmillan, 1879.

New, Chester A. *The Life of Henry Brougham to 1830.* Oxford: Clarendon Press, 1961.

Noyes, Russell. *Wordsworth and Jeffrey in Controversy.* Indiana University Publications, Humanities Series, no. 5. Bloomington, 1941.

Opie, Iona and Peter, eds. *The Oxford Book of Children's Verse.* New York and London: Oxford University Press, 1973.

Owen, W. J. B. "Wordsworth and Jeffrey in Collaboration." *Review of English Studies,* n.s. 15 (May 1964): 161-67.

Parliamentary Debates (Cobbett's and Hansard's).

Reid, Thomas. *Essays on the Active Powers of the Human Mind.* 1815. Reprint ed. Cambridge, Mass. and London: The M.I.T. Press, 1969.

—— *Essays on the Intellectual Powers of Man.* 1814. Reprint ed. Cambridge, Mass. and London: The M.I.T. Press, 1969.

—— *The Works of Thomas Reid.* Edited by Sir William Hamilton. 6th ed. 2 vols. Edinburgh: Maclachlan and Stewart, 1863.

Reiman, Donald H., ed. *The Romantics Reviewed: Contemporary Reviews of British Romantic Writers.* Part A. 2 vols. New York and London: Garland, 1972.

Renwick, H. L. *English Literature: 1789-1815.* Oxford History of English Literature, vol. 9. Oxford: Clarendon Press, 1963.

Roberts, Michael. *The Whig Party, 1807-1812.* 1939. Reprint ed. London: Cass, 1965.

Robinson, Henry Crabb. *Diary, Reminiscences, and Correspondence of Henry Crabb Robinson.* Edited by Thomas Sadler. 3d ed. 2 vols. London and New York: Macmillan, 1872.

Saintsbury, George. *Essays in English Literature, 1780-1860.* 3d ed. London: Rivington, 1906.

Schneider, Elisabeth; Griggs, Irwin; and Kern, John D. "Brougham's Early Contributions to the *Edinburgh Review:* A New List." *Modern Philology* 42 (February 1945): 161-73.

Schneider, Louis, ed. *The Scottish Moralists on Human Nature and Society.* Chicago and London: University of Chicago Press, 1967.

Scott, Walter. *The Letters of Sir Walter Scott.* Edited by H. J. C. Grierson. Centenary ed. 12 vols. London: Constable, 1932.

Smith, Adam. *An Inquiry into the Nature and Causes of the Wealth of Nations.* Cannan ed. New York: Modern Library, 1937.

——. *Lectures on Rhetoric and Belles Lettres.* Edited by John M. Lothian. Landmarks in Rhetoric and Public Address. Carbondale and Edwardsville, Ill.: Southern Illinois University Press, 1963.

——. *The Theory of Moral Sentiments.* 1759. Reprint ed. New York: Garland, 1971.

Smith, Sydney. *The Letters of Sydney Smith.* Edited by Nowell C. Smith. 2 vols. Oxford: Clarendon Press, 1953.

——. *The Works of the Rev. Sydney Smith.* London: Longman, 1850.

Somerville, Thomas. *My Own Life and Times, 1741-1814.* Edinburgh: Edmonston and Douglas, 1861.

Stein, Paul. "Law and Society in Eighteenth-Century Scottish Thought." In *Scotland in the Age of Improvement,* edited by N. T. Phillipson and Rosalind Mitchison, pp. 148-68. Edinburgh: Edinburgh University Press, 1970.

Stewart, Dugald. *Works of Dugald Stewart.* 7 vols. Cambridge: Hilliard and Brown, 1829.

Taylor, James. *Lord Jeffrey and Craigcrook.* Edinburgh: David Douglas, 1892.

Topham, Edward. *Letters from Edinburgh in 1774 and 1775.* 1776. Reprint ed. Edinburgh: James Thin, Mercat Press, 1971.

Warton, Joseph. *An Essay on the Genius and Writings of Pope.* 4th ed. 2 vols. 1782. Reprint ed. New York: Garland, 1970.

Watson, J. Steven. *The Reign of George III, 1760-1815.* Oxford History of England, vol. 12. Oxford: Clarendon Press, 1960.

Wellek, René. *A History of Modern Criticism, 1750-1950.* 4 vols. New Haven, Conn.: Yale University Press, 1955-65.

Welsh, David. *Account of the Life and Writings of Thomas Brown.* Edinburgh: Tait, 1825.

Wilson, David Alec. *Carlyle to "The French Revolution," (1827-1837).* London and New York: Kegan Paul, 1924.

Wordsworth, William. *The Letters of William and Dorothy Wordsworth: The Middle Years.* Edited by Ernest de Selincourt. 2 vols. Oxford: Clarendon Press, 1937.

Edinburgh Annual Register
Edinburgh Review
John Bull
Morning Chronicle
New Annual Register
Quarterly Review
Scots Magazine
Westminster Review

Index

Academical Questions (Drummond), 57

Academy of Physics (Edinburgh), 38-39, 55, 178

Account of the Life and Writings of James Beattie, An (Forbes), 61

Account of the Life and Writings of Thomas Reid (Stewart), 64, 67

Adam, Alexander, 25, 26

Addison, Joseph, 22, 23, 28, 31, 38, 145, 148; *Guardian,* 23; *Spectator,* 22, 23, 28, 148; *Tatler,* 23

Advice to a Young Reviewer (Copleston), 201 n. 47

Alison, Archibald, 138-41, 158; *Essays on Taste,* 138-41

Allen, Dr. John, 36, 39, 97, 98, 125

Amiens, Peace of, 101, 102

Anti-Jacobin, 99

Aquinas, St. Thomas, 27

Ariosto, Ludovico, 168

Aristotle, 27

Arnold, Matthew, 171

Arnold, Thomas, 45

Aspinall, Arthur, 123

Austerlitz, battle of, 101

Bacon, Francis, 27, 28, 66, 67, 70, 89; *Novum Organum,* 35, 66

Barton, Bernard, 152

Bayle, Pierre, 45

Beattie, James, 20, 31, 61-63, 137, 172, 187 n. 30; *Essay on Truth,* 61, 62, 187 n. 30

Belles Lettres Society of Edinburgh, 24

Bentham, Jeremy, 55, 77-79, 117; *Traités de législation,* 77

Berkeley, George, 47-48, 51, 60, 61, 64, 65

Black, Joseph, 20

Blackwell, Thomas, 198 n. 28

Blair, Hugh, 20, 135, 137, 174; *Lectures on Rhetoric and Belles Lettres,* 23

Blair, Robert, 98

Boileau, Nicolas, 28

Borough, The (Crabbe), 161, 164

Boswell, James, 49

Brand, Thomas, 130

Braxfield, Robert MacQueen, Lord, 35

Brougham, Henry Peter, Baron Brougham and Vaux, 26, 36, 37, 38, 39, 45, 84, 90, 98, 130; "Don Pedro Cevallos," 104, 121-24, 126

Brown, Dr. Thomas, 38, 39, 184 n. 66

Buchan, David Stewart Erskine, eleventh Earl of, 104

Buffon, Georges Louis Leclerc de, 31

Burdett, Sir Francis, 118, 123, 125, 128, 130

Burke, Edmund, 28, 117, 140, 149, 195 n. 18; *Reflections on the Revolution in France,* 99

Burns, Robert, 26, 173-75, 201 n. 36, 202 n. 71; *Reliques of,* 173

Byron, George Gordon, sixth Baron, 152, 153, 156, 164, 166-67,

172, 173, 201 n. 47; *Cain*, 173; *Childe Harold's Pilgrimage*, 148, 166; *Corsair*, 166; *Don Juan*, 176, 201 n. 47; *English Bards and Scotch Reviewers*, 166; *Giaour*, 166; *Manfred*, 166; *Sardanapalus*, 167; *Two Foscari*, 167

Cain (Byron), 173
Campbell, George, 20, 21; *Dissertation on Miracles*, 21; *Philosophy of Rhetoric*, 23
Campbell, Thomas, 30, 45; *Gertrude of Wyoming*, 175
Carlyle, Alexander ("Jupiter"), 31
Carlyle, Thomas, 45, 55, 82, 84, 87, 93, 177; *Reminiscences*, 177
Cartwright, Major John, 130
Castlereagh, Robert Stewart, Viscount, 107, 125
Cervantes, Miguel de, 35
Charles II, 146
Chaucer, Geoffrey, 168
Childe Harold's Pilgrimage (Byron), 148, 166
Cicero, Marcus Tullius, 28, 46, 86, 145, 176; Middleton's *Life* of, 25
Cintra, Convention of, 103
Clarke, Mrs. M. A., 125
Clive, John, 117
Cobbett, William, 118-20, 121, 123, 124, 125, 126, 130; *Political Register*, 118; *Porcupine*, 118
Cockburn, Henry Thomas, Lord, 24, 26, 37, 39, 84, 86, 95, 96, 131
Coleridge, Samuel Taylor, 153, 154, 156, 158, 159, 161, 179, 198 n. 27; *Christabel*, 200 n. 20; *Lyrical Ballads*, 148, 153, 155, 158, 176
"Committee of Secrecy," 96, 111

Communist Manifesto, The (Marx and Engels), 91
Condorcet, Marquis de, 43, 64
Constable, Archibald, 39, 44, 45, 144
Contributions to the Edinburgh Review (Jeffrey), 171
Convention of Delegates of Reform Societies (Edinburgh, 96
Copleston, Edward, 201 n. 47
Corsair, The (Byron), 166
Courier, 123
Cowper, William, 154, 159
Crabbe, George, 142, 153, 161-64, 175, 201 n. 36; *Borough*, 161, 164; *Poems*, 161; *Tales*, 140, 162-63; *Village*, 161, 164
Cranstoun, George, 30
Creevey, Thomas, 130

Dangers of the Edinburgh Review, The ("Mentor"), 123
Darwin, Erasmus, 165
Das Kapital (Marx and Engels), 93
De la littérature considérée dans ses rapports avec les institutions sociales (de Staël), 80
De l'état de l'Europe (Gentz), 101
De l'influence attribuée aux philosophes . . . sur la révolution de France (Mounier), 39-43
De Rerum Natura (Lucretius), 32
Descartes, René, 61, 70
Dialogues Concerning Natural Religion (Hume), 84, 85
Dickens, Charles, 175; *Dombey and Son*, 175
Dissertation on Miracles, A (Campbell), 21
Dombey and Son (Dickens), 175
Don Juan (Byron), 176
"Don Pedro Cevallos" (Jeffrey and Brougham), 104, 121-24, 126
Douglas (Home), 174
Drummond, William, 57; *Academical Questions*, 57

Dryden, John, 23, 31, 147, 151
Dumont, Etienne, 190 n. 19
Dundas, Henry, Viscount Melville, 95-96, 175, 196 n. 43

Edgeworth, Maria, 169, 203 n. 79
Edinburgh Annual Register, 175
Edinburgh Review (1755-56), 22
Edinburgh Review (1802-1929): beginnings of, 25, 31, 32, 38-46; contributors to, 45; early political neutrality of, 98; early sales of, 44; on government expenditure, 31; on Ireland, 179; on prison reform, 31; on public education, 31; on religion, 84-85, 179, 191 n. 45; on the slave trade, 98, 179; on the war, 99
Edinburgh Society for Encouraging Arts, Sciences, Manufactures, and Agriculture, 22
Edinburgh Society of the Friends of the People, 35, 96
Elements of Criticism (Kames), 22, 23, 135
Encyclopaedia Britannica, 17, 22, 23, 36
Endymion (Keats), 140, 169
Engels, Friedrich, 91; *Communist Manifesto*, 91; *Das Kapital*, 93
English Bards and Scotch Reviewers (Byron), 166
Enquiry Concerning Political Justice (Godwin), 79, 111
Epistles, Odes, and Other Poems (Moore), 82
Erskine, Henry, 36
Essay on Taste, An (Gerard), 23
Essay on the Genius and Writings of Pope, An (Warton), 202 n. 55
Essay on the History of Civil Society, An (Ferguson), 20, 22
Essay on the Nature and Immutability of Truth (Beattie), 61, 62, 187 n. 30

Essay on the Practice of the British Government (Leckie), 112
Essays, Moral and Political (Hume), 117
Essays on the Nature and Principles of Taste (Alison), 138-41
Excursion, The (Wordsworth), 159-61

Fénelon, François de Salignac de la Mothe, 31
Ferguson, Adam, 19, 20, 22, 70, 72; *Essay on the History of Civil Society*, 20 22
Fergusson, Robert, 175
First Book of Discipline (Knox), 18
First Reform Bill, 83, 93, 132, 133, 179
Fletcher, John, 170
Forsyth, Robert, 202 n. 69
Foscolo, Ugo, 158
Fox, Charles James, 99, 100, 101, 109
Franklin, Benjamin, 22; "The Method of Securing Houses from the Effects of Lightning," 22
Friday Club (Edinburgh), 138, 178

Galt, John, 169
Gay, Peter, 46
Gentz, Frédéric, 101; *De l'état de l'Europe*, 101
George III, 61
Gerard, Alexander, 20, 137; *Essay on Taste*, 23
Gertrude of Wyoming (Campbell), 175
Giaour, The (Byron), 166
Gifford, William, 98
Godwin, William, 79, 129; *Enquiry Concerning Political Justice* 79, 111
Goethe, Johann Wolfgang von, 56,

176, 199 n. 19; *Wilhelm Meis-ter's Apprenticeship*, 56
Goldsmith, Oliver, 148
Grant, Mrs. Anne (of Laggan), 34, 175
Grenville, William Wyndham, first Baron, 100, 101, 103, 107, 110
Grey, Charles, second Earl, 100, 101, 103, 107, 109, 130
Guardian (Steele and Addison), 23

Haldane, Robert, 28, 29
Hallam, Henry, 45
Hamilton, Sir William, 188 n. 39
Handel, George Frederick, 139
Hardy, Thomas, 111
Hartley, David, 56, 197 n. 15
Hazlitt, William, 45, 102, 149, 154, 159, 170, 178
Heart of Midlothian, The (Scott), 38
Historical View of the English Government (Millar), 29, 30
History of England, The (Hume), 25, 117, 131, 195 n. 18
History of English Poetry, The (Warton), 148
Hobbes, Thomas, 73
Hogarth, William, 140
Hogg, James, 199 n. 19
Holland, Henry Richard Vassal Fox, third Baron, 101, 103
Holland House, 97, 98, 104, 107, 116, 123, 124
Home, John 174; *Douglas*, 174
Homer, 138, 168; Blackwell's *Inquiry into*, 198 n. 28
Hooker, Richard, 89
Horace (Quintus Horatius Flaccus), 28, 145
Horner, Francis, 36, 37, 38, 39, 45, 55, 67, 82, 84-85, 90, 97, 99, 104, 107, 120, 123, 124, 125, 153, 164, 165
Human Life (Rogers), 175
Hume, David: *Dialogues Concern-*

ing Natural Religion, 84, 85; *Essays, Moral and Political*, 117; *History of England*, 25, 117, 131, 195 n. 18; Jeffrey's reading of, 25, 27, 28, 35; Jeffrey's sympathy with, 46, 56, 57, 62-63, 68, 75, 78, 86, 92, 108, 111-12, 117, 139, 160, 188 n. 38, 189 n. 16; "Of Miracles," 21; "Of the First Principles of Government," 111-12; opinions, 47-51, 53-54, 61, 64, 65, 70, 71, 73, 74, 85, 89, 136, 138, 140, 180; role in the Enlightenment, 17-22, 45, 180; *Treatise of Human Nature*, 47, 50, 51, 70
Hunt, Leigh, 45
Hutcheson, Francis, 19, 28, 70, 71, 73, 137, 171, 172; *Inquiry into the Original of Our Ideas of Beauty and Virtue*, 137

Independent Whig, 101, 125
Inquiry into the Human Mind on the Principles of Common Sense, An (Reid), 20, 51
Inquiry into the Life and Writings of Homer, An (Blackwell), 198 n. 28
Inquiry into the Original of Our Ideas of Beauty and Virtue, An (Hutcheson), 137
Irving, Washington, 192 n. 58

James, William, 64
Jardine, George, 24, 26-29, 31, 33, 36, 45, 57; *Outlines of Philosophical Education*, 26, 27
Jardine, John, 182 n. 25
Jeffrey, Francis, Lord: acquires Craigcrook, 131; becomes editor of *ER*, 45; called to Scottish bar, 34; *Contributions*, 171; duel with Moore,

82-83; family, 25, 33, 45, 82, 83; formal education, 25-31, 33-35, 183 n. 36; membership in clubs and societies, 36-37, 38-39, 138, 178; parliamentary career, 83-84, 132-33, 196 n. 51; retires as editor, 132
John Bull, 178
Johnson, Samuel, 31, 49, 61, 95, 148, 151, 164, 174
Julia de Roubigné (Mackenzie), 174
"Junius" (Sir Philip Francis?), 148

Kames, Henry Home, Lord, 20, 21, 22, 45, 70, 73, 135, 136, 137, 171, 180; *Elements of Criticism*, 22, 23, 135; "Observations upon Shallow Ploughing," 21; "Of Evaporation," 21; "On the Laws of Motion," 21
Kant, Immanuel, 68, 188 n. 39
Keats, John, 170; *Endymion*, 140, 169
Kennedy, Nell, 177
Kinnaird, Charles, 36, 37
Knox, John, 18; *First Book of Discipline*, 18

Lady of the Lake, The (Scott), 166
Lalla Rookh (Moore), 167-68
Lamb, William, Viscount Melbourne, 30, 45
Lay of the Last Minstrel, The (Scott), 165
Leckie, Gould Francis, 112; *Essay on the Practice of the British Government*, 112
Le Clerc, Jean, 45
Lectures on Rhetoric and Belles Lettres (Blair), 23
Letter to Lord Holland (Whitbread), 103, 104

Life of Cicero (Middleton), 25
Literary Society of Glasgow, 20
Locke, John, 27, 28, 31, 47-48, 51, 57, 61, 70
Lockhart, John Gibson, 26, 37, 84
London Corresponding Society, 96, 100, 111
Longfellow, Henry Wadsworth, 168
Longman, Thomas, 44, 45
Lorrain, Claude, 139
Lounger, 22
Lovejoy, Arthur O., 52
Lucretius (Titus Lucretius Carus), 32-33; *De Rerum Natura*, 32
Luddites, 90
Lyrical Ballads (Wordsworth and Coleridge), 148, 153, 155, 158, 159, 176

Macaulay, Thomas Babington, first Baron, 45, 168
Mackenzie, Henry, 26, 138, 175; *Julia de Roubigné*, 174; *Lounger*, 22; *Man of Feeling*, 174; *Man of the World*, 174; *Mirror*, 22
Mackintosh, Sir James, 36, 40; *Vindiciae Gallicae*, 36
Maclaurin, John, 50, 53; *Philosopher's Opera*, 50
Macpherson, James, 175
Madoc (Southey), 155
Malebranche, Nicholas de, 61
Malthus, Thomas, 45, 90, 92
Mandeville, Bernard de, 73, 189 n. 11
Manfred (Byron), 166
Man of Feeling, The (Mackenzie), 174
Man of the World, The (Mackenzie), 174
Marlowe, Christopher, 146
Marmion (Scott), 165
Marx, Karl, 91; *Communist Mani-*

festo, 91; *Das Kapital*, 93
"Method of Securing Houses from the Effects of Lightning, The" (Franklin), 22
Middleton, Conyers, 25; *Life of Cicero*, 25
Mill, James, 45, 203 n. 3
Millar, John, 20, 29-31, 32, 40, 45, 70, 71-72, 78, 89, 92, 96, 183 n. 36, 193 n. 8; *Historical View*, 29, 30; *Observations Concerning the Distinction of Ranks*, 29
Milton, John, 139, 159
"Ministry of All the Talents," 98, 100, 101
Mirror, 22
Monboddo, James Burnett, Lord, 20, 21
Moncreiff, James, 30
Montesquieu, Charles Louis de Secondat de, 31, 40, 43
Moore, Sir John, 81, 103
Moore, Thomas, 45, 82-83, 153, 164, 167-68, 170; *Epistles, Odes, and Other Poems*, 82; *Lalla Rookh*, 167-68
Morehead, Robert, 35, 191 n. 49
Morning Chronicle, 125
Mounier, Jean, 39-43; *De l'influence attribuée aux philosophes*, 39-43
Muir, Thomas, 30, 35, 37, 96

Napoleon Bonaparte, 100, 101, 102, 103, 105, 106, 107
Natural Theology (Paley), 85, 202 n. 65
Nelson, Horatio, Viscount Nelson, 81
New Annual Register, 100
Newspaper Act (1798), 111
Newton, Sir Isaac, 70
Newtonian Society (Edinburgh), 23
Novum Organum (Bacon), 35, 66

Observations Concerning the Distinction of Ranks in Society (Millar), 29
"Observations upon Shallow Ploughing" (Kames), 21
"Of Evaporation" (Kames), 21
"Of Miracles" (Hume), 21
"Of the First Principles of Government" (Hume), 111-12
"On the Laws of Motion" (Kames), 21
"On the Present State of Periodical Criticism" (Scott), 175
Outlines of Philosophical Education (Jardine), 26
Oxford Book of Children's Verse, The (Opie), 157
Oxford History of English Literature, The, 133

Paine, Thomas, 123, 129; *Rights of Man*, 111
Paley, William, 202 n. 65; *Natural Theology*, 85, 202 n. 65
Paris, Treaty of, 107
Petty-Fitzmaurice, Henry, third Marquis of Lansdowne, 36, 37
Philosopher's Opera, The (Maclaurin), 50
Philosophical Essays (Stewart), 64
Philosophical Society of Aberdeen, 20, 61
Philosophical Society of Edinburgh, 20, 21, 24; *Essays and Observations*, 21
Philosophy of Rhetoric, The (Campbell), 23
Poems (Crabbe), 161
Poems in Two Volumes (Wordsworth), 156-58, 159
Political Economy Club (of Glasgow), 22
Political Register (Cobbett), 118
Pope, Alexander, 23, 31, 145, 148
Porcupine (Cobbett), 118
Prelude, The (Wordsworth), 79

Priestley, Joseph, 56, 199 n. 5
Publius (Publilius) Syrus, 39

Quarterly Review, 45, 98, 165
Quintilian (Marcus Fabius Quintilianus), 28

Racine, Jean, 31
Ralegh, Sir Walter, 146
Ramsay, Allan, 174
Rankenian Club (Edinburgh), 23
Reflections on the Revolution in France (Burke), 99
Reid, Thomas, 19, 20, 21, 27, 28, 29, 51-53, 54, 57, 58, 60, 61, 64, 65, 70, 72, 73, 76, 136; *Inquiry into the Human Mind on the Principles of Common Sense*, 20, 51
Rejected Addresses (Smith), 200 n. 21
Reliques of Ancient English Poetry (Percy), 148
Reliques of Robert Burns (Cromeck ed.), 173
Reminiscences (Carlyle), 177
Richardson, Samuel, 175
Rights of Man, The (Paine), 111
Robertson, William, 20, 22, 26
Robespierre, Maximilien de, 40
Robinson, Henry Crabb, 158
Rogers, Samuel, 190 n. 33; *Human Life*, 175
Rousseau, Jean Jacques, 31, 43, 153, 175
Russell, Lord John, 110

Saintsbury, George, 33
Sardanapalus (Byron), 167
Schiller, Johann Christoph Friedrich von, 153
Scots Magazine, 23
Scott, Sir Walter: ed. of Swift's *Works*, 144-45; education, 26; and the *ER*, 44, 98, 104, 124, 175, 199 n. 19, 201 n. 36;

friendship with Jeffrey, 36, 138, 165; *Heart of Midlothian*, 38; *Lady of the Lake*, 166; *Lay of the Last Minstrel*, 165; legal career, 38; *Marmion*, 165; "On the Present State of Periodical Criticism," 175; opinions on other writers, 145, 156, 158, 175; personality, 75, 101, 176; politics, 98, 104, 108; popularity as a writer, 151, 153, 164-66, 168, 169, 172; and the *Quarterly*, 98; *Waverley*, 148, 168, 176
Seditious Meetings Bill (1795), 111
Select Society of Edinburgh, 20
Shaftesbury, Anthony Ashley Cooper, third Earl of, 73, 137, 171
Shakespeare, William, 142, 146, 147, 167, 168, 170, 174
Shelley, Percy Bysshe, 149, 170, 202 n. 57
Sheridan, Thomas, 23
Sidney, Sir Philip, 151
Smellie, William, 23, 36
Smith, Adam: academic career, 19, 27; influence on economic theories of *ER*, 89-90, 92, 94, 192 n. 64; Jeffrey's reading of, 35; opinions, 73, 74, 78, 85, 136, 137, 140; role in Enlightenment, 17, 19, 20, 22, 24, 45, 70, 108, 180; *Theory of Moral Sentiments*, 19; *Wealth of Nations*, 19, 22, 35
Smith, Horace and James, 200 n. 21; *Rejected Addresses*, 200 n. 21
Smith, Sydney, 25, 38, 39, 84, 97, 153, 191 n. 45
Smollett, Tobias George, 23
Southey, Robert, 153, 159, 199 n. 19; *Madoc*, 155; *Thalaba*, 153, 155, 161
Spectator (Addison and Steele), 22, 23, 28, 148

Speculative Society (Edinburgh), 36-37, 45, 55, 57, 178

Staël, Madame de, 80, 131; *De la littérature*, 80

Steele, Sir Richard, 31, 38; *Guardian*, 23; *Spectator*, 22, 23, 28; *Tatler*, 22, 23

Sterne, Laurence, 175

Stevenson, John, 23, 27

Stewart, Dugald, 19, 20, 26, 36, 40, 45, 56, 57, 64-67, 92, 96, 138; *Account of Reid*, 64; Jeffrey studies under, 35; *Philosophical Essays*, 64

Swift, Jonathan, 22, 145; Scott's ed. of *Works*, 144-45

Sybil (Disraeli), 91

Tales (Crabbe), 140, 162-63

Tatler (Steele and Addison), 22

Taylor, Jeremy, 146

Tennyson, Alfred, 168

Thalaba (Southey), 153, 155, 161

Theory of Moral Sentiments, The (Smith), 19

Thomson, James, 148

Thomson, Thomas, 39, 184 n. 68

Tilsit, Treaty of, 101

Tooke, John Horne, 111

Traités de législation (Bentham), 77

Treasonable Practices Bill (1795), 111

Treatise of Human Nature, A (Hume), 47, 50, 51, 70

Turgot, Anne Robert Jacques, 40

Two Foscari, The (Byron), 167

Ulm, surrender at, 101

Vega, Lope de, 35

Village, The (Crabbe), 161, 164

Vindiciae Gallicae (Mackintosh), 36

Virgil (Publius Vergilius Maro), 145

Voltaire (François Marie Arouet), 31

Walcheren, expedition of, 125, 130, 195 n. 37, 196 n. 43

Wardle, Colonel Gwyllym Lloyd, 125

Warton, Joseph, 148, 202 n. 55; *Essay on Pope*, 202 n. 55

Waterloo, battle of, 104, 107, 108

Watt, James, 20

Waverley (Scott), 148, 168, 176

Wealth of Nations, The (Smith), 19

Wellington, Arthur Wellesley, Duke of, 81, 104

Westminster Review, 178

Whitbread, Samuel, 101, 103, 104, 107, 110, 125, 130; *Letter to Lord Holland*, 103, 104

Wilberforce, William, 45, 85

Wilhelm Meister's Apprenticeship (Goethe), 56

Wilkes, Charles, 131

Wordsworth, William, 55, 75, 79, 142, 153-61, 163, 164, 170, 173, 200 n. 21, 201 n. 37; *Excursion*, 159-61; *Lyrical Ballads*, 148, 153, 155, 158, 159, 176; *Poems in Two Volumes*, 156-58, 159; Preface to *Lyrical Ballads*, 55, 153, 155, 156; *Prelude*, 79

Works of Jonathan Swift, The (Scott ed.), 144-45

York, Frederick Augustus, Duke of, 125

Young, Edward, 148